A "Representative"
Supreme Court?

A "Representative" Supreme Court?

THE IMPACT OF RACE, RELIGION, AND GENDER ON APPOINTMENTS

Barbara A. Perry

Foreword by
DAVID M. O'BRIEN

CONTRIBUTIONS IN LEGAL STUDIES, NUMBER 66
Paul L. Murphy, *Series Editor*

GREENWOOD PRESS
New York • Westport, Connecticut • London

Library of Congress Cataloging-in-Publication Data

Perry, Barbara A. (Barbara Ann)
  A representative Supreme Court? : the impact of race, religion,
and gender on appointments / Barbara A. Perry ; Foreword by David M.
O'Brien.
  p. cm.—(Contributions in legal studies, ISSN 0147–1074 ;
no. 66)
  Includes bibliographical references and index.
  ISBN 0-313-27777-X (alk. paper)
  1. United States.   Supreme Court.   2. Judges—United States—
Selection and appointment.   I. Title.   II. Series.
KF8742.P336   1991
347.73'2634—dc20
[347.3073534]   91–14336

British Library Cataloguing in Publication Data is available.

Library of Congress Catalog Card Number: 91–14336
ISBN: 0-313-27777-X
ISSN: 0147–1074

First published in 1991

Greenwood Press, 88 Post Road West, Westport, CT 06881
An imprint of Greenwood Publishing Group, Inc.

Printed in the United States of America

∞™

The paper used in this book complies with the
Permanent Paper Standard issued by the National
Information Standards Organization (Z39.48-1984).

10 9 8 7 6 5 4 3 2 1

Copyright Acknowledgment

The author expresses her gratitude to the publishers for permission to reprint as Chapter
2: Barbara A. Perry, "The Life and Death of the 'Catholic Seat' on the United States
Supreme Court," VI *The Journal of Law and Politics* 1 (Fall 1989).

To My Parents,

Louis and Lillian Perry

Contents

Foreword

Chief Justice Harlan Fiske Stone once likened Supreme Court appointments to a "lottery" drawn from a pool of more or less qualified individuals. Yet, judicial selection is far from random, and it is neither a drawing from a pool open to all who can afford a ticket nor free from political considerations in the final selection of the winning ticket. What Stone had in mind was how a president's personal politics—his political associations and friendships—frequently determine the fate of qualified candidates for the Court. Still, the pool of possible candidates for an appointment also reflects the weight each president and the presidency gives to (1) professional considerations, the legal expertise and reputation of competing potential nominees; and (2) advancing the administration's ideological or policy agenda; as well as (3) rewarding personal and political associates and party-faithful. Moreover, throughout the history of the Supreme Court and U.S. politics, presidents have occasionally included in their calculations demands for "representation" on the Court—that is, appointments aimed at symbolically representing particular geographical regions or the changing composition of the electorate and country in terms of religion, race, and gender.

A "Representative" Supreme Court? is inexorably provocative. That is because it takes to task arguments of both those who consider the idea of "representative" judicial appointments an anathema, a pernicious form of affirmative action that comes at the price of passing over more meritorious potential judicial nominees; and those who stress the importance of political symbolism and diversity on the federal bench for public perceptions of the judiciary's legitimacy. The debate over a "representative"

federal bench has been especially vigorous with respect to appointments
to the lower federal courts. The administration of President Jimmy Carter
appointed an unprecendented number of blacks (37) and women (41) to
the federal bench (out of a total of 265 appointments), while that of President Ronald Reagan named far fewer blacks (5) and women (30) when
filling a greater number of vacancies (382). The debate over a "representative" federal bench, moreover, is certain to continue. For, as Barbara Perry
points out, the growing ethnic and racial diversity of the country is certain
to bring with it increased political demands for the judicial selection of
more Hispanics, Asians, and other minorities.

Perry makes a useful contribution to the debate over a "representative"
federal bench. She does so by eschewing the extremes of the left and
the right, and sensibly arguing for the importance of "representative"
considerations, so long as they do not come at the cost of sacrificing merit
or significantly lower professional standards for those appointed to the
federal bench. Drawing on interviews with members of the Court who
are as divergent in their judicial philosophies as Chief Justice William
H. Rehnquist and Justice William J. Brennan, Jr., and other materials,
Perry underscores that even members of the Supreme Court agree that
diversity on the bench is important and that to bar consideration of potential nominees on the grounds of religion, race, or gender is reprehensible.

Professional qualifications or judicial merit, argues Perry, need not (and
should not) preclude from consideration "representative" appointments
to the federal bench. Moreover, the author makes a compelling case for
politically symbolic "representative" appointments, assuming that they
are drawn from a pool of more or less equally qualified potential candidates. Such appointments are just as defensible as a president's selection
of nominees based on their ideological compatibility with and support of
the president's legal policy goals. In short, the debate over "merit" versus
"representation" in judicial selection is often misleading in suggesting
a simple, stark choice between a "meritorious" or "representative" appointee.

Perry's argument is complex and builds on a series of case studies
exploring and explaining how and why there emerged a Catholic, Jewish,
Black, and Woman's "seat" on the Court. In contrast with the prevailing
expectations for geographical representation on the Court in the nineteenth century, Perry demonstrates that demands and expectations for
religious, racial, and gender representation on the Court emerged only in
the twentieth century with, as the author puts it, "the political coming-of-
age of Catholics, Jews, blacks, and women." Notably, also, Perry meticu-
lously details how the so-called Catholic and Jewish seats were initially
coincidentally secured. They were accidents in the politics of judicial
selection, rather than the result of presidential design. Indeed, the first
Catholics and Jews appointed to the Court faced no uncertain opposition

in the Senate precisely because of their religious affiliations.

More often than not, religion, race, and gender have historically been obstacles to securing the nomination of religious and racial minorites and women. When those factors weighed into a president's final calculations in determining who to nominate to the high bench, they did so only as tertiary considerations, after presidents took into account potential nominees' professional and political "acceptability." Perry finds only two major, late-twentieth-century exceptions—Democratic President Lyndon B. Johnson's 1967 appointment of Justice Thurgood Marshall and Republican President Reagan's 1981 appointment of Justice Sandra Day O'Connor. With both of these appointments, presidents gave explicit and overriding consideration to the political symbolism of representing two groups (blacks and women) who were long excluded from the political process and the federal bench. Significantly, though, both presidents did not discount the professional qualifications of their nominees.

The debate over a "representative" Supreme Court and federal bench is an important one in and for our system of constitutional politics. Barbara Perry has made a notable contribution to that debate. Both sides of the controversy over "representative" appointments to the federal judiciary will benefit from her study of past "representative" appointments to the high bench and her sensibly measured argument for a "representative" Supreme Court.

David M. O'Brien

Preface

This book on the impact of religion, race, and gender on appointments to the United States Supreme Court is the most recent incarnation in which my research has appeared during the past decade. During that time, I have labored to identify the factors that have influenced presidential decisions in Supreme Court nominations and place them in the historical and political contexts in which they were made. In terms of religion, race, and gender considerations, I have ventured into the normative realm of essaying a judgment on whether such "representative" factors *should* play a role in choosing justices to sit on the highest court in the land.

In the midst of my revisions of the manuscript, Associate Justice William J. Brennan, Jr. unexpectedly announced his retirement from the Court, and President George Bush nominated Judge David H. Souter of the United States First Circuit Court of Appeals to fill the position. Although "representative" considerations played no role in the president's selection of Souter, it was clear from Bush's statements, and those of his aides, that he considered matters of race, gender, and even geography (though he ultimately rejected all three) in relation to the Court's makeup and would perhaps do so again in future appointments. Thus, the issue of balancing the Court's membership according to "representative" characteristics is likely to remain a live one in the judicial selection process.

Surely the most pleasant duty in completing such a project is having the opportunity to acknowledge in writing those who have provided scholarly, intellectual, moral, and financial support. I must begin with the first scholar who introduced me to the wonders of constitutional law and that magnificent institution at the pinnacle of our judiciary. The late Mary K. Tachau of the University of Louisville provided the historical foundation for any expertise I may ever achieve in the field of public law. And no graduate student could ever have had a better master craftsman to build on that foundation than Professor Henry J. Abraham of the University of Virginia. As a teacher, adviser, mentor, and now colleague, he has been a constant source of information, inspiration, and motivation.

Many other colleagues generously provided insightful comments and encouragement at various stages of the project: Professors A. E. Dick Howard, Karen O'Connor, David O'Brien, Donald Davison, Kenneth Thompson, Laura Vertz, Donald Kettl, Julie Bunck, and Julia McDonough. A special thanks is reserved for Professor Paul Weber, who first as my undergraduate pre-law adviser spared me the fate of choosing law school over graduate school and then as a colleague introduced me to the publishing world.

I am especially indebted to the following justices of the United States Supreme Court who graciously granted interviews: William J. Brennan, Jr., Sandra Day O'Connor, Lewis F. Powell, Jr., William H. Rehnquist, Antonin Scalia, John Paul Stevens, and Byron R. White.

Fellowships from the University of Virginia's Woodrow Wilson Department of Government and Foreign Affairs, the University of Virginia's Society of Fellows' Forstmann Foundation, and Sweet Briar College's Kenmore Fund lightened my financial burden. A summer at the White Burkett Miller Center for the Study of the Presidency as a Newman Scholar-in-Residence was crucial to the completion of the manuscript.

Mildred Vasan of Greenwood Press exhibited the proper mixture of constructive criticism and friendly support to encourage me to complete the editorial process, especially when my hope of getting the manuscript into its final form began to wane.

Finally, the successful conclusion of this enterprise, like the attainment of all my goals, is due to the unceasing and loving support of my parents, to whom I dedicate my work with deepest affection and gratitude.

Chapter 1

Introduction

President Gerald R. Ford, despite his brief tenure as the nation's chief executive, had the opportunity to make one appointment to the United States Supreme Court. In his presidential memoirs, he observed: "Few appointments a President makes can have as much impact on the future of the country as those to the Supreme Court."[1]

Almost a century and a half earlier, Alexis de Tocqueville, the astute French commentator on the American regime, had articulated the crucial role of the Court in the American Republic, thereby implying the heavy burden of responsibility borne by presidents in choosing its members. In an oft-quoted passage from his celebrated tome, *Democracy in America*, Tocqueville argued that "the peace, prosperity, and very existence of the Union rest continually in the hands of these . . . federal judges. Without them the Constitution would be a dead letter."[2] He qualified his observation, however, with the recognition that the Court's institutional power and legitimacy are rooted in public opinion. The wise Frenchman contended that to nurture and maintain popular support, justices must possess the qualities of good citizenship, education, integrity, and, most important, statesmanship.[3] Indeed, Tocqueville would have readily concurred in former President Ford's analysis of the chief executive's momentous role in the Court-staffing process.

Tocqueville's proffered list of necessary qualities for a Supreme Court justice quadruples the Constitution's offerings, for the U.S. governing document is wholly silent on requisite qualifications for members of the Supreme Court. Nonetheless, an American Enterprise Institute forum, convened to discuss the question of a "representative" judiciary, opened with the observation that "judges, it was conceived, ideally would be appointed on the basis of demonstrated capability, personal and professional integrity, and proven judicial temperament—the merit principle." But to acknowledge the tension between the ideal and the real, the forum noted: "In practice, of course, other factors—political affiliation, religion, race, ethnic background, geography, and personal friendships— have played a role, but always it was supposed, as handmaidens to merit."[4] Such "other factors" as geography, religion, race, and gender have been subsumed under the broader criterion of "representativeness" because presidents have used them to recognize various groups by placing their members on the high court in order to reflect a rough balance in its composition.

Each of the subsequent chapters in this study is devoted to an analysis of one of the three "representative" factors most evident in twentieth-century appointments—namely, religion, race, and gender. The story of the development of each factor reveals a link between such appointments and the political, electoral, social, and demographic contexts in which they were made. As Catholics, Jews, blacks, and women came of political age in this country, presidents tended to recognize each group with at least one seat on the nation's highest court.

Yet, as Chapter 6 concludes, "representativeness," in the form of religious, racial, and gender factors, has played a *primary* role in only two Supreme Court nominations this century. Nevertheless, "representative" considerations are likely to continue to play a part (if only in a tertiary role) in the judicial selection process along with other political factors such as ideological compatibility and friendship. Finally, the concluding chapter argues for a reconciliation between the undeniable demands of politics and symbolic representation in the selection process and the equally compelling need for merit-based judicial appointments.

CONSTITUTIONAL VERITIES

As noted earlier, detailed references in the Constitution to criteria or qualifications for judicial selection are conspicuous by their utter absence from the document. With typical verbal economy, the drafters of Article II, Section 2, Paragraph 2 simply bestowed upon the president the power to "nominate, and by and with the Advice and consent of the Senate, . . . appoint Ambassadors, and other public Ministers and Consuls, Judges of the Supreme Court, and all other Officers of the United States," whose appointments were not otherwise provided for. Article III, which created the federal judiciary, is equally frugal in establishing the Supreme Court and making provisions for congressional ordination of inferior courts without including qualifications for federal judges.

Yet the Philadelphia Convention debates offer some clues (albeit veiled ones) to the drafters' thoughts on the criteria or qualifications for selection.

In the lengthy July 18, 1787, debate over methods of judicial appointment, the delegates evinced an awareness of the role that geographic and regional considerations would eventually play in selecting members of the federal judiciary.[5] Critiquing executive appointment, Gunning Bedford, a delegate from Delaware, argued: "It would put it in his [the executive's] power to gain over the larger States, by gratifying them with a preference of their citizens."[6]

Just two days later, however, James Madison noted a similar inequity that might result from Senate appointment. He recorded in his own journal that to locate the appointment power in the Senate alone would "throw the appointments entirely into the hands of ye Nthern [sic] States, [and therefore] a perpetual ground of jealousy and discontent would be furnished to the Southern States."[7]

A less overt reference to geographic considerations may be found in Roger Sherman's supportive response to Luther Martin's remarks on Senate appointment, which the Maryland delegate advocated on the basis of the upper chamber's representation of all the states. Sherman added that "the judges ought to be *diffused*, which would be more likely to be attended to by the 2d branch, than by the Executive."[8] Sherman's statement, which immediately followed Martin's reference to the equitable representation of the states in the Senate, may have used the word "diffused" to indicate the geographic diversity presumably guaranteed by Senate appointment of federal judges.

The Convention explicitly addressed the possibility of including in the Constitution specific qualifications for judicial, legislative, and executive office holding. The official "Journal" of the debates reported that John Dickinson, another Delaware delegate, "was against any recital of qualifications in the Constitution. It was impossible to make a compleat [sic] one, and a partial one would by implication tie up the hands of the Legislature from supplying the omissions." Dickinson asserted his opposition to making property and solvency explicit prerequisites for holding federal office. The "Journal" recorded his argument—with telling ramifications for current debates over selection: "It seemed improper that any man of *merit* should be subjected to disabilities in a Republic where *merit* was understood to form the great title to public trust, honors, and rewards."[9]

In the *Federalist Papers*, Alexander Hamilton expressed the Founders' hope that vesting of appointing power in the executive would weaken, if not eliminate, the influence of friendship in the choice of government officers.[10] In light of the role that personal friendship has played in influencing presidential appointments to the Supreme Court, Hamilton's faith that the president would "be so much less liable to be misled by the sentiments of friendship and of affection" was misplaced. Yet he was speaking relatively. A single executive would have "fewer personal attachments to gratify, than a body of men who may each be supposed to have an equal number."[11] Nevertheless, the Framers—always with an eye toward less-than-angelic human nature—provided for the Senate check. In Hamilton's words, the Senate "would tend greatly to prevent the appointment of unfit characters from State prejudice, from family connection, from personal attachment, or from a view to popularity."[12]

Hamilton penned several general observations on the importance of merit in the selection process and the necessity of choosing "men who are best qualified"[13] for their respective offices. Yet he was hardly more specific than the document he was expounding in his discussion of requisite qualifications for holding judicial office. Integrity and knowledge of the laws acquired through "long and laborious study"[14] were his only expressed descriptions of merit.

Thus, the historical record indicates that at least several of the Founders were not oblivious to the geographical, political, and interest-group factors, which could influence and indeed have influenced the selection of justices.[15] Hamilton seemingly understood the appointment process as filtering out all such factors beyond the realm of merit. Of course, as with many of the governmental processes established in the Constitution, their ideal, unadulterated operation would fail to become reality—especially after the birth of political parties. In the less than perfect world of judicial selection, what criteria have played the most influential roles?

HISTORY OF SELECTION

Every president from George Washington to Ulysses S. Grant included geographic suitability among his selection criteria. Several motivations— some rather obvious, some more obscure—account for the use of this so-called representative factor. Not surprisingly, strategic political considerations often prompted presidents to reward states or regions with a seat on the high court. For example, President Washington, who inaugurated the concern for geography in Supreme Court appointments, commented about his nomination of James Iredell: "He is of a State [North Carolina] of some importance in the Union that has given no character to a federal office."[16]

As noted above, presidents also attempted to make the Court an inclusive symbol by balancing the Court's membership according to state or region. Again setting an illustrative precedent in his record ten Supreme Court appointments, Washington nominated justices from nine of the thirteen original states. They included New York (John Jay), South Carolina (John Rutledge), Massachusetts (William Cushing), Pennsylvania (James Wilson), Virginia (John Blair), North Carolina (James Iredell), Maryland (Thomas Johnson and Samuel Chase), New Jersey (William Paterson), and Connecticut (Oliver Ellsworth).

Moreover, a mundane reason related to the judicial structure prompted presidential regard for geographic appropriateness when filling Supreme Court vacancies. The landmark Judiciary Act of 1789 created a three-tiered federal judiciary consisting of district and circuit courts and the Supreme Court. Each district had a district tribunal with primarily admiralty jurisdiction, which served as a trial court with a single district judge. Each circuit had a circuit bench with primarily diversity and criminal jurisdiction, which met in each district of the circuit and was composed of the district judge and two Supreme Court justices. Thus, the 1789 act created no separate judgeships for the circuit courts. (This would not occur until the Circuit Court of Appeals Act of 1891 instituted a genuine intermediate appellate court level in the federal judiciary.)

Consequently, two Supreme Court justices were assigned to each circuit to travel to the designated places for convening circuit court, where they would be joined by the district judge. Circuit-riding duties, combined with the fact that the Supreme Court's early caseload was relatively light, meant that the first justices spent most of their time serving as trial judges back in their assigned circuits.[17] Indeed, one of the rationales for instituting circuit riding at the federal level was that it allowed the justices to "mingle in the strife of the jury trials"[18] and, in the process, exposed them to the state laws they would have to interpret on the Supreme Court. Therefore, it only made practical sense for presidents to want each circuit represented on the Supreme Court by an inhabitant of the geographic area covered by the circuit.

In effect, the political, symbolic, and practical motivations for maintaining a geographical balance on the Court took several forms. Throughout the nineteenth century, presidents were concerned to represent individual states, regions, or circuits on the high bench. Always concerned to reward states that had supported ratification of the new Constitution, Washington determined to place a New Yorker, John Jay, in the chief justice's chair. Moreover, Jay's northern ties were decisive for Washington, who believed his administration was already top-heavy with southerners.[19]

After Washington, many nineteenth-century presidents followed the tradition of replacing a justice from one state with a nominee from the same state (see Appendix 1). John Adams replaced North Carolinian James Iredell with Alfred Moore, a resident of the Tar Heel State. President James Madison named Joseph Story of Massachusetts to William Cushing's position; that seat would eventually see a total of six occupants from Massachusetts. When the seat inaugurated by Washington's appointment of Cushing was not filled with a resident of the Bay State, it at least had a New Englander from 1789 to 1932, when Benjamin Cardozo of New York replaced Oliver Wendell Holmes.

Presidents were particularly scrupulous in maintaining a balance among the country's regions prior to the Civil War. For example, in 1860 the Court included three members from the North (Samuel Nelson of New York, Nathan Clifford of Maine, and Robert Grier of Pennsylvania), four members from the South (Peter Daniel of Virginia, James Wayne of Georgia, John Campbell of Alabama, and John Catron of Tennessee), one member from the Midwest (John McClean of Ohio), and one member, the chief justice, from a Mid-Atlantic, border state (Roger Taney of Maryland).

Aside from the dictates of state and regional concerns, presidents also were clearly satisfying circuit-riding needs in their geographic considerations. As the nation expanded and new judicial circuits were created, the chief executives attempted to find residents of those new circuits to fill the appropriate seats. Justice Felix Frankfurter offered an illustration:

Thus, when the western circuit, consisting of Ohio, Kentucky and Tennessee, was established, at a time when litigation dealing with land title and other local property questions was important, the selection of one conversant with those problems was clearly indicated. Therefore, on the recommendation of the representatives in Congress from the interested states, Jefferson named Thomas Todd, the then Chief Justice of the Kentucky Court of Appeals.[20]

Presidents Jackson and Lincoln also had the opportunity to nominate justices for seats created by newly established circuits. Jackson was delighted to name John Catron from his home state of Tennessee, which had just been included in a new western circuit (the Eighth) along with Kentucky and Missouri. The rush to California in the mid-nineteenth century by gold seekers and other fortune hunters spawned a raft of new litigation and inevitably another judicial circuit (the Tenth, which included California and Oregon) and a corresponding seat on the Supreme Court. President Lincoln eagerly filled it with Californian Stephen J. Field, a lawyer knowledgeable in western land and mineral law.[21] Once circuits had been established, presidents before the turn of the twentieth century usually sought to maintain representation for them on the Court by naming a justice from that circuit, if not from the same state as his predecessor.

In the post–Civil War era, even before the advent of the twentieth century, the influence of the geographic factor noticeably waned. Rutherford B. Hayes, Grover Cleveland, and Benjamin Harrison followed its dictates less assiduously than their predecessors. Ushering in a new century, a new administration, and a new protocol in Supreme Court appointments, the brash Theodore Roosevelt denounced the geographic criterion in a letter to Senator Henry Cabot Lodge of Massachusetts: "I have grown to feel, most emphatically, that the Supreme Court is a matter of too great importance to me to pay heed to where a man comes from."[22]

With one or two exceptions, most notably Franklin Roosevelt's insist-ence on appointing Wiley Rutledge because he hailed from west of the Mississippi River, consideration of geography continued to decline in significance during the twentieth century for a number of reasons. At least in theory, the Civil War had abolished the "old order," in which state's rights and regionalism had vied with nationalism for political and constitutional legitimacy. Economic divisions based on sectional differ-ences[23] had also been muted. On a practical level, circuit riding for members of the Supreme Court came to an end in 1891, so there was less impetus to represent circuits with residents from states contained in them. Finally, as this volume will indicate, other more politically relevant "representative" factors pushed geography to the bottom, and eventually off, of the list of selection criteria.

Most recently, however, President Bush recognized that the Supreme Court has been without a member from the South since Justice Lewis F. Powell, Jr. retired in 1987. The president noted that "key members of Congress" had stressed this fact to him as he was considering Justice William J. Brennan, Jr.'s replacement. Nevertheless, the president chose a New Englander, Judge David H. Souter, of New Hampshire. Bush sympathized with feelings of "regionalism" but argued that "in a *national* sense," he had "come up with the best nominee."[24]

Constitutional scholar John P. Frank, in a 1941 three-part article on Supreme Court appointments, noted that considerations of an appointee's age and religion also occasionally entered into the selection process. Moreover, Frank, not surprisingly, found evidence of the importance of a prospective justice's political philosophy and (starting in the late nineteenth century) of his economic views.[25] (President Theodore Roose-velt coined the term "real politics" to describe an individual's true political ideology as opposed to his nominal party affiliation.[26]) A then sitting member of the Court, the erudite Justice Felix Frankfurter, argued keenly in a 1957 address at the University of Pennsylvania Law School, however, that judicial experience, geography, and party affiliation are "irrelevancies" to be excluded from presidential criteria.[27]

Despite Frankfurter's fervent plea, studies in the 1960s and 1970s of federal judicial appointments augmented the growing list of recognized selection criteria. The general criterion of "partisan considerations" was elaborated to include specific factors such as political rewards and recog-nition of party service. Students of the selection process also noted the role of personal friendship in presidential decisions on whom to send to the Supreme Court.[28] Beginning with the Eisenhower administration, case studies of judicial appointments discovered the Founders' criterion of merit to be an oft-stated principle of the process, if not always an achieved goal. For example, the Kennedy administration's "explicit" standards of selection included: (1) unquestioned ability; (2) respected professional skill; (3) incorruptible character; (4) firm judicial temperament; and (5) intellectual capacity to protect and illuminate the Constitution and our historic values.[29]

Professor Henry Abraham has reduced this array of criteria to a logical and manageable quartet: (1) objective merit; (2) personal and political friendship; (3) balancing "representation" on the Court; and (4) "real" political and ideological compatibility.[30]

I have framed my inquiry around the merit versus "representativeness" debate for therein lie the rub and nub of the selection theory controversy. Some observers have made a fervent appeal for "the sole criterion of *merit* as *the* irreducible imperative basic threshold requirement" in Supreme Court appointments.[31] They allow for the reality of "representative" considerations (along the lines of former Justice Lewis F. Powell, Jr.'s "plus" argument in *Bakke*[32]) but only if they remain "wholly dependent upon the demonstrable presence of merit at the threshold."[33]

Others, however, define the merit of the Court's members by their degree of "representativeness" and, therefore, transform the entire tenor of the selection theory dispute. They agree with supporters of the merit principle that the judicial selection process should produce the "best" jurists for our nation's courts, but they argue that "it is difficult to define—much less find—the 'best.' " Nonetheless, they contend that "the 'best' bench may be one composed of persons of all races and both sexes with diverse backgrounds and experiences."[34]

Although it never had the opportunity to place a justice on the Supreme Court, the Carter administration fueled debates in the 1970s over proper judicial selection criteria with its avowed goal of achieving a more "representative" judiciary through affirmative action appointments of women and racial and ethnic minorities to the lower federal benches— a goal it achieved. Thus, the dispute became inextricably bound to the vexatious issues of affirmative action in general. Even some Democratic senators reacted negatively to Carter's judicial selection policy, commenting: "It is not our responsibility to guarantee any fixed percentage of different classes of people. You try to get the best qualified people, not some elusive balance." An aide to a southern conservative Republican senator during the Carter presidency was, not surprisingly, more vehemently opposed to the Georgian's judicial affirmative action plan. The aide explained: "Race or sex has nothing to do with it. Carter has gone too far in trying to impose quotas. . . . We like the principle of merit selection. . . ."[35]

During the Reagan administration, then White House Counsel Fred F. Fielding likewise rejected the use of numerical guidelines in selecting women and minorities for the federal judiciary: "We're mindful of the appearance problem. We would like to identify more candidates for consideration that are women, blacks, and minorities, but we are not going to do it using quotas as a device to accomplish that."[36]

Beyond the ramifications of the two criteria for the qualifications of individual jurists selected lie implications for the judiciary as a whole and its methods of decision making. The classic conceptualization of the judge as interpreter, rather than maker, of the law views judicial decisions as products of "independent," "objective" reasoning, not as results of "representative" thought. Traditionally, representative considerations are assigned to the legislative branch.[37] In debates on the Omnibus Judgeship Act of 1978, Senator Richard Lugar (R.–Ind.) contended that the strength of merit selection was its insurance of an *independent* judiciary even more than its producing a *qualified* judiciary.[38]

Another aspect of the selection theory debate concerns the Court's credibility and legitimacy. On this score, Professor Sheldon Goldman has argued that "if our law is to have legitimacy among every segment of our population, no segment of our population must feel excluded from the law." In advocating the principle of a "representative" judicial branch, he added that "the essential point to keep in mind is that we are dealing with the credibility of our institutions to all the various groups within our society, particularly those who have been discriminated against."[39] Several years earlier, Goldman had expressed his support for the Carter judicial selection process in slightly different, if no less passionate, language: "A pluralistic judiciary . . . is more likely to win the confidence of the diverse groupings in a pluralistic society."[40]

A recently retired member of the Court, and one who was often considered to occupy a "representative" seat in the religion category, Justice Brennan, reemphasized in a 1985 interview his position, first expressed in 1962,[41] that much of the Court's strength lies in its diversity. Justice Brennan commented that we are a diverse nation and that the Court should reflect this heterogeneity.[42]

Nearly thirty years ago, another member of the Court, Justice Felix Frankfurter, made a contrary contention based on merit selection of justices. Like Alexander Hamilton in *The Federalist*, he urged that only the "most qualified" jurists should sit on the nation's highest tribunal. The peroration of his 1957 University of Pennsylvania Law School lecture eloquently summarized his argument that the foundation of the Court's institutional potency is public confidence nurtured through merit-based appointments. Frankfurter argued:

Selection wholly on the basis of functional fitness not only affords the greatest assurance that the Court will best fulfill its functions. It also will, by the quality of such performance, most solidly establish the Court in the confidence of the people, and the confidence of the people is the ultimate reliance of the Court as an institution.[43]

Thus, in part, the debate over how best to select Supreme Court justices centers on how to produce the most "legitimate" tribunal— one whose edicts will be obeyed despite its lack of the power of the purse or sword and one that is the least democratic of the branches because of its very method of selection. This study not only traces the historical use of the "representative" criterion but draws a conclusion on whether its predicted continued use can enhance or diminish the Court's legitimacy.

DEFINING "REPRESENTATION"

The juxtaposition of "representative" and "Supreme Court" initially may seem as oxymoronic as the term "representative bureaucracy."[44] Neither unelected members of the federal judiciary nor appointed bureaucrats in the executive branch would appear to be aptly described as "representative." Indeed, in a recent case to decide whether the federal Voting Rights Act applies to the election of state judges, the Fifth U.S. Circuit Court of Appeals in a split decision reasoned that because judges are not considered "representatives" under the law, they are, therefore, not subject to the act's protection of the rights of minorities "to elect representatives of their choice."[45]

Yet the judiciary and the United States Supreme Court, in particular, have been labeled as "representative" in a variety of contexts. Most pertinent is Professor Walter F. Murphy's observation that, "one can speak of constitutional courts as 'representative' in the sense that their judges are chosen from different sets of important subgroups in the general population."[46]

I have chosen for this study a conceptualization of representation that is predicated on the representative's (in this case, a Supreme Court nominee's) characteristics. This notion of "descriptive representation," as Professor Hanna Pitkin has defined and labeled it, concerns *who* the representative is or *what he or she is like* rather than *what he or she does*. "The representative does not act for others; he 'stands for' them, by virtue of a correspondence or connection between them, a resemblance or reflection."[47] For theorists of this view, "it is the representativeness of each member that makes an assembly truly representative as a whole, that defines representation."[48]

The late Professor Frederick Mosher, an astute student of public administration, applied a similar version of representation to the unelected, appointed bureaucracy and characterized it as "passive representation" (mirroring of societal characteristics). He contrasted it with "active representation" (vigorous pursuit of the interests of the represented). His dichotomy is useful for explaining what "representativeness" means and what it does not mean when applied to the judiciary.[49] Even if one rejects the application of other theories of representation to the judiciary (especially those that stress responsiveness or accountability or "active representation"), descriptive representation has demonstrably played a role in the selection process and the institutional identity of the Court.

Pitkin actually criticized the narrowness of the descriptive view: "It has no room for any kind of representing as acting for, or on behalf of, others; which means that in the political realm it has no room for the creative activities of a representative legislature, the forging of consensus, the formulating of policy." She concluded that in the descriptive formulation, "representing . . . can at most mean being typical or resembling."[50] Chapter 6 argues that in this narrow sense of the term, the Court *should* be "representative."

NARROWING THE LIST OF "REPRESENTATIVE" FACTORS

Undoubtedly, factors such as political persuasion, age, and judicial experience have played varyingly important roles in Supreme Court appointments, but they fall into different classifications from the three "representative" factors of religion, race, and gender that I have chosen to emphasize. For example, while a potential nominee's political persuasion is almost always a prime element in a president's decision, his intention in considering it is an endemic facet of party-in-power raison d'être rather than "representativeness," as I utilize the term in this study. When presidents have appointed jurists from the political opposition, they have almost always done so as a gesture to the "out party" (rather than to mirror a societal characteristic) *and*, be it noted, only after having ascertained the acceptability of the candidate's "real politics." President William Howard Taft's selection of three nominally Democratic appointees—Horace H. Lurton, Edward D. White, and Joseph R. Lamar—is illustrative of that fact of political life, as is President Warren G. Harding's tapping of a conservative Democrat, Pierce Butler, whose nomination Taft recommended from his position as chief justice.[51] (Selection of members of the opposition party has accounted for 15 percent of presidential appointments to the Supreme Court. In most instances, other factors such as friendship, geography, experience, merit, and certainly ideological compatibility outweighed nominal party affiliation.[52])

The age factor may be viewed as an historical element in the selection process, but it is in effect a "nonrepresentative" one, recognized by bar, bench, and the public as an objective consideration of whether a candidate is too elderly or too youthful to serve effectively. Several presidents in this century have preferred candidates for the Supreme Court to be in their mid-fifties in the hope that they would have benefited from several decades of experience in the legal profession or public life and yet remain sufficiently vigorous to meet the rigors of life on the nation's highest bench.

President Richard M. Nixon, for example, sought potential nominees who were about fifty-five years of age.[53] Stanley Reed, Franklin D. Roosevelt's second appointment, was considered at fifty-three to be at an optimum age for ascending the Court.[54] President Dwight D. Eisenhower established sixty-two as the upper age limit for his Supreme Court nominees unless they had otherwise outstanding qualifications.[55] Ironically, Ike was sixty-two himself when he entered the White House to commence what would be his eight-year stay there.

Earlier in this century, President Taft made a commitment to replace "senile," elderly members of the Court with more youthful appointees; but he reneged on his promise in his successful nomination of Horace Lurton, who was sixty-five at the time of his appointment. Yet Taft had found Lurton to be an ideological and political soul mate, despite the latter's nominal Democratic party affiliation. And Taft's promotion of the sixty-six-year-old Associate Justice Edward White to the chief justice's seat may have been ulteriorly motivated by the rotund president's own desire to serve in that position upon departing the White House.[56]

Although Taft may have secretly hoped that his nominee for chief justice would not match the longevity of many of his predecessors on the bench,[57] President Reagan certainly had the opposite motivation in his avowed goal of appointing young conservatives to the lower benches. His well-recognized motivation was to offset, and with long years of service overtake, Carter's 258 judicial appointments from the opposite end of the ideological spectrum.[58] Reagan's judicial appointees averaged approximately fifty years of age, which was slightly younger than his predecessor's average age for appointments.[59] Reagan's appointments to the nation's highest court also demonstrated the same strategy of finding relatively young ideological kin, who may shape the direction of the Court well into the next century. Sandra Day O'Connor was fifty-one at the time of her appointment in 1981; Justice Rehnquist was sixty-one when Reagan promoted him to chief justice; and Antonin Scalia and Anthony Kennedy were fifty and fifty-one years of age, respectively, when they were nominated in 1986 and 1987. President Bush seems to be following in his predecessor's footsteps by nominating fifty-year-old David Souter to fill the seat vacated by Justice Brennan. Thus, the age of judicial appointees has surfaced as an issue in the selection process, but presidents have never sought to represent any particular age group in American society. Rather, the sole apparent consideration has usually been how the appointee's age would affect his or her performance or length of service on the bench.

Likewise, judicial experience has been a somewhat objective, "nonrepresentative" concern primarily because it, too, does not reflect a societal characteristic. Discussions of whether a candidate for the high bench should have prior judicial experience center on questions of evaluating attributes considered necessary for a successful jurist or predicting his philosophical predilections. Sheldon Goldman has identified eight qualities that are generally considered the necessary attributes of an "ideal" judge. Among them, he contended that neutrality, fair-mindedness, cognitive and verbal skills, and judicial temperament may best be measured if the candidate has had previous judicial experience.[60] President Eisenhower, thoroughly disappointed with the jurisprudential tack taken by Earl Warren once on the Court, added previous judicial tenure to his list of selection criteria as a means of determining the candidate's judicial philosophy.[61] President Reagan took his Republican predecessor's lesson to heart in nominating Rehnquist, Scalia, Bork, and Kennedy—jurists with demonstrated judicial track records. (Ironically, Bork's "paper trail" of judicial opinions and academic writing proved to be his downfall). Although a judicial service record may be a useful, although admittedly imprecise, guide to a Supreme Court nominee's fitness for the position or his jurisprudence, presidents have not attempted to "represent" judges as an occupational group.

The three "representative" factors that I chose to examine have been used, primarily by twentieth-century presidents, to shape the Court as a reflection or mirror of elements in American society. (In addition to being primarily a nineteenth-century phenomenon in Court appointments, geography differs somewhat from the other three societal and sociological factors in that it lacks the personal quality of religion and the immutability of race and gender, but presidents have employed it similarly as a "balancing" factor in making Supreme Court nominations. Still, geography entailed a different presumption of representation, dating back to its first use as a consideration by President Washington. Although he used geography to balance the Court and reward states of strategic political importance, as future presidents would reward religious, racial, and gender groups, Washington and his successors presumed that justices would *actively* represent the concerns of each section of the country. This latter point also distinguishes geography from the "passive representation" expected of religion, race, and gender groups.)

After geography, the next "representative" factor to play a key role in presidential appointments to the nation's highest court was religion, with the establishment of the so-called "Catholic seat" and, later, the "Jewish seat." Chief Justice Roger B. Taney became the first Roman Catholic member of the Court in 1836. Those who identify a "Catholic seat," however, often trace its establishment to Edward White's 1894 appointment for two reasons. First, Taney's Catholicism was not a factor in his selection by President Andrew Jackson. Second, White's appointment clearly initiated a trend with four Catholics following him on the high bench. The only interruption came from 1949 to 1956, when President Harry Truman did not replace Frank Murphy with an appointee of the latter's faith. In 1956, Eisenhower reverted to the trend by selecting William J. Brennan, Jr. The additions of Antonin Scalia and Anthony Kennedy in 1986 and 1988, respectively, meant that an unprecedented trio of Roman Catholics served on the high court until Justice Brennan's resignation in July 1990.

The "Jewish seat" dates to President Woodrow Wilson's 1916 selection of Louis Brandeis as the first Supreme Court justice of that religious persuasion. After Brandeis's appointment, at least one Jewish member remained on the high tribunal until Justice Abe Fortas's forced resignation in 1969.

The last several decades have witnessed the addition of race and gender categories to the list of "representative" factors with the appointments of Thurgood Marshall and Sandra Day O'Connor to the Court in 1967 and 1981, respectively. At the very least, the placement of a black and a woman on the Supreme Court fits into the larger historical picture of the changing importance of "representative" factors in appointments. Yet only the nature of future nominations will signal whether a "black seat" or a "woman's seat" is firmly established on the Court.

NOTES

1. In late 1975, President Ford named John Paul Stevens to succeed the retired Associate Justice William O. Douglas. Gerald R. Ford, *A Time to Heal* (New York: Harper & Row and Readers Digest Association, 1979), p. 334. See Laurence H. Tribe, *God Save This Honorable Court: How the Choice of Supreme Court Justices Shapes Our History* (New York: Random House, 1985), for basic historical proof of the accuracy of Ford's statement.

2. Alexis de Tocqueville, *Democracy in America*, trans. George Lawrence, ed. J. P. Mayer (Garden City, N.Y.: Doubleday, 1969), p. 150.

3. Ibid.

4. John Charles Daly, "Whom Do Judges Represent?" (Washington, D.C.: American Enterprise Institute, 1981), p. 1. Unfortunately, the Forum's participants wandered into the tangentially related minefield of the judicial activism/restraint debate and never emerged to clarify the more salient issue of "representativeness" in judicial appointments. An appropriate definition of "representativeness" would have undoubtedly made the debate's focus sharper and its outcome more fruitful.

5. Max Farrand, *Records of the Federal Convention of 1787*, 3 vols. (New Haven, Conn.: Yale University Press, 1911–1937), vol. 1, pp. 41–44.

6. Ibid., p. 43.

7. Ibid., pp. 80–81.

8. Ibid., p. 41. (emphasis added).

9. Ibid., vol. 2, pp. 121–25. (emphasis added).

10. Alexander Hamilton in *The Federalist Papers* (New York: Mentor Books, 1961), No. 76, pp. 454–59. Introduction by Clinton Rossiter.

11. Quoted by Elliot E. Slotnik in "Reforms in Judicial Selection: Will They Affect the Senate's Role?" 64 *Judicature* 2 (August 1980): 62.

12. Hamilton, *The Federalist Papers*, p. 457.

13. Ibid., No. 66, p. 405; No. 77, pp. 456, 458; No. 78, p. 462.

14. Ibid., No. 78, p. 471.

15. John R. Schmidhauser, *Judges and Justices: The Federal Appellate Judiciary* (Boston: Little, Brown and Co., 1979), p. 15.

16. As quoted by Fred L. Israel, "James Iredell," in Leon Friedman and Fred L. Israel, eds., *The Justices of the United States Supreme Court, 1789–1969*, 5 vols. (New York: Chelsea House, 1969), vol. 1, p. 128.

17. See the Supreme Court Historical Society, *The Documentary History of the Supreme Court of the United States, 1789–1800*. The third volume in the eventual eight-volume series, *The Justices on Circuit: 1795–1800* (New York: Columbia University Press, 1990), offers a vivid and poignant portrayal through primary sources of the hardships of riding circuit.

18. As quoted in Russell R. Wheeler and Cynthia Harrison, *Creating the Federal Judicial System* (Washington, D.C.: Federal Judicial Center, 1989), p. 9. This brief study provides a fascinating account of the history and development of the federal judicial structure.

19. Henry J. Abraham, *Justices and Presidents: A Political History of Appointments to the Supreme Court*, 2d ed. (New York: Oxford University Press, 1985), p. 79.

20. Felix Frankfurter, "The Supreme Court in the Mirror of the Justices," 105 *University of Pennsylvania Law Review* (1957): 791.

21. Ibid.

22. Quoted by Abraham in *Justices and Presidents*, p. 155.

23. John P. Frank, "The Appointments of Supreme Court Justices: Prestige, Principles, and Politics," 16 *Wisconsin Law Review* (1941): 175.

24. *Washington Post*, July 24, 1990, p. 12. (emphasis added).

25. Frank, "The Appointments of Supreme Court Justices," pp. 345, 470, 480.

26. Daniel S. McHargue, "Appointments to the Supreme Court of the United States: The Factors That Have Affected Appointments, 1789–1932" (Unpublished Ph.D. dissertation, University of California, Los Angeles, 1949). Quoted by Glendon A. Schubert, *Constitutional Politics* (New York: Holt, Rinehart and Winston, 1960), pp. 39–40.

27. Frankfurter, "The Supreme Court," pp. 781–96.

28. Joel B. Grossman, *Lawyers and Judges: The ABA and the Politics of Judicial Selection* (New York: John Wiley, 1965), p. 28; Samuel Krislov, *The Supreme Court in the Political Process* (New York: Macmillan, 1965), p. 5.

29. Quoted in Harold W. Chase, *Federal Judges: The Appointing Process* (Minneapolis: University of Minnesota Press, 1972), p. 67.

30. Henry J. Abraham, *The Judicial Process: An Introductory Analysis of the Courts of the United States, England, and France*, 5th ed. (New York: Oxford University Press, 1986), pp. 64–78.

31. Henry J. Abraham, " 'A Bench Happily Filled': Some Historical Reflections on the Supreme Court Appointment Process," 66 *Judicature* 7 (February 1983): 286.

32. *Regents of the University of California v. Bakke*, 438 U.S. 265 (1978).

33. Abraham, " 'A Bench Happily Filled,' " p. 286.

34. Sheldon Goldman, "Should There Be Affirmative Action for the Judiciary?" 62 *Judicature* 10 (May 1979): 488–94.

35. Both quotations appear in Elliott E. Slotnik's "Reforms in Judicial Selection: Will They Affect the Senate's Role?" Part II, 64 *Judicature* 3 (September 1980): 117.

36. Quoted in the *Washington Post*, March 31, 1985, p. 4.

37. Grossman noted this difference between "independent," "objective" thought and "representative" thought in referring to the judicial process, *Lawyers and Judges*, p. 9.

38. Quoted by Slotnik, "Reforms in Judicial Selection," Part II: p. 119.

39. Daly, "Whom Do Judges Represent?" pp. 15, 26.

40. Quoted by Robert J. Lipshutz and Douglas B. Huron, "Achieving a More Representative Federal Judiciary," 62 *Judicature* 10 (May 1979): 484.

41. See "A Visit with Justice Brennan," produced by Fletcher Knebel in *Look*, December 18, 1962, pp. 127–37.

42. Personal interview, Justice William J. Brennan, Jr., Washington, D.C., April 1, 1985.

43. Frankfurter, "The Supreme Court," p. 796.

44. Samuel Krislov, *Representative Bureaucracy* (Englewood Cliffs, N.J.: Prentice-Hall, 1974), p. 130.

45. Reported in the *Washington Post*, January 19, 1991, p. 2.

46. Walter F. Murphy, Joseph Tanenhous, and Daniel L. Kastner, *Public Evaluations of Constitutional Courts: Alternative Explanations* (Beverly Hills, Calif.: Sage Publications, 1973), p. 7.

47. Hanna Pitkin, *The Concept of Representation* (Berkeley: University of California Press, 1967), p. 61.

48. Ibid., p. 75.

49. Frederick C. Mosher, *Democracy and the Public Service*, 2d ed. (New York: Oxford University Press, 1982), pp. 12–17.

50. Pitkin, *The Concept of Representation*, p. 90.

51. See David J. Danelski's case study of the Butler nomination for numerous references to the Harding administration's attempt to place a "safe" Democrat on the bench. *A Supreme Court Justice Is Appointed* (New York: Random House, 1964).

52. Abraham, *The Judicial Process*, pp. 68–74.

53. Ibid., p. 73.

54. Abraham, *Justices and Presidents*, p. 216.

55. Ibid., p. 251.

56. Ibid., pp. 164–72.

57. Professor Henry Abraham is fond of observing that, as an identifiable occupational group, only symphony orchestra conductors have exceeded the life expectancy of Supreme Court justices. " 'A Bench Happily Filled,' " p. 282.

58. Reagan surpassed Carter's previous record of 258 judicial appointments

with 346. Sheldon Goldman, "Reagan's Judicial Legacy: Completing the Puzzle and Summing Up," 72 *Judicature* 6 (April–May 1989): 319.

59. Ibid., pp. 322, 325.

60. Sheldon Goldman, "Judicial Selection and the Qualities That Make a 'Good' Judge," 462 *Annals of the American Academy of Social and Political Science* (July 1982): 113–17.

61. Abraham, *Justices and Presidents*, p. 251.

Chapter 2 _____

Religion: A "Catholic Seat"?

Before taking for granted the establishment of a "Catholic seat" and a "Jewish seat"[1] on the Supreme Court, it is useful to determine to what extent, if any, the religious affiliation of the eight Roman Catholic and five Jewish justices was a factor in their individual appointments to the Supreme Court. Further, if religion played a role in a given appointment, can it be isolated as a "representative" factor? In other words, does evidence exist to determine whether the appointing president made a deliberate effort to nominate a justice to "represent" (in the descriptive sense) either Catholics or Jews in the population?

A closely related, and perhaps inseparable, aspect of the religion factor is whether presidents who nominated members of the Catholic or Jewish faith were more concerned with the electoral ramifications of their appointments. As Catholics and Jews emerged as potentially significant voting blocs, did presidents attempt to woo their votes through Supreme Court appointments? Of course, presidential electoral and "representative" motivations may be indistinguishable. What better way to attract or "pay off" Catholic and Jewish ballots than by offering "representation" on the Supreme Court to those minority religious groups? Placing these appointments in their broader context of demographic, sociological, geographic, and electoral aspects of the respective histories of Catholics and Jews in the United States illuminates the relationship between the religion factor and Supreme Court appointments.

ANTI-CATHOLICISM IN AMERICA

While Catholics gradually gained political parity with the Protestant majority, anti-Romanist suspicions lurked just beneath the surface of

American politics and society. During the first century and a half of U.S. history, there emerged a cyclical pattern of antiforeign nativism that bubbled to the surface in episodes of virulent, and sometimes violent, displays of anti-Catholicism. Between incidents, the nativist outbreaks would subside and anti-Romanism would fester under the surface of politics only to erupt when next provoked. In the nineteenth century, provocations came often as relentless waves of immigrants carved out enclaves and remade the American political landscape.

Between 1790 and 1850, for example, 1,071,000 Catholic immigrants arrived on the shores of the United States, outstripping the native Catholic population by quantum leaps and giving the church a decidedly foreign flavor. The latter especially provided grist for the nativists' mill. Traditional anti-Catholicism combined with new and worrisome economic conditions to produce a fresh campaign of nativism in 1830. That year witnessed the inauguration of an explicitly anti-Catholic weekly newspaper, *The Protestant*, founded by a group of Protestant clergymen. Over the next several decades the case against the foreign-born, particularly Catholics, was spread throughout the land by numerous local nativist societies.[2]

The indictment against Catholics charged that they could never be proper Americans for they owed their allegiance to a foreign prelate—the Prince of Rome. Moreover, the nativists argued that the hierarchical church structure produced an antidemocratic ethos among Romanists that was incompatible with the American regime. Further, in these "huddled masses," xenophobic Americans saw a threat to American societal and economic well-being as the dregs of European societies flooded the labor market and turned sections of U.S. cities into teeming, vice-ridden ghettoes. At their most extreme, nativists foresaw the introduction of the Inquisition to American soil.[3]

ROGER B. TANEY

Given an environment seething with nativist hostility, the success of Maryland Catholic Roger B. Taney in achieving high executive offices and *the* highest judicial position in the land is all the more remarkable. How did Taney overcome the handicap of belonging to a persecuted religious minority? What role, if any, did religion play in Taney's professional career?

The American Revolution swept away official restrictions on Catholic education in Maryland, and its 1776 constitution granted religious equality to all *Christians*. Thus, Roger Brooke Taney, born in the year following the start of the Revolution, did not have to seek a European education as his father had. Instead, he attended rural schools near his family's home.[4] When it came time to continue young Taney's schooling, his father chose Dickinson College, a Presbyterian institution in Pennsylvania, because the nascent Catholic colleges in the United States were deemed inadequate.[5]

Although Taney was the product of secular educational institutions, he remained a devout Catholic throughout his life. Memoirs and biographies are replete with stories of his piety as a young man, his turning to prayer before Supreme Court sessions, and his comfort gained from Catholicism in his final years of physical infirmity and personal grief. Taney, however, married an Episcopalian; and tradition has it that he and his wife made a prenuptial agreement to raise male offspring Catholic and female children Episcopalian. The mixed marriage resulted in an unusual amount of religious toleration in the Taney household.[6] (Sadly, Taney and his wife, whom he adored, were not united in death. According to prevailing custom, Mrs. Taney was interred in her family's Protestant burial plot, while the chief justice was laid to rest in a Catholic cemetery.)

Taney's religion was an integral part of his personal life; yet it did not disrupt his professional success. No doubt, Taney's membership in two established and prominent Maryland families (Catholic though they were) provided him with educational opportunities that might well have been barred to his less-well-off coreligionists, particularly recent immigrants. As Professor John Schmidhauser's social background analysis of the justices demonstrates,[7] Taney shares his prominent social status and educational background with the majority of Supreme Court justices throughout history.

These social and educational opportunities allowed Taney to move in political and professional circles in which his talents ultimately could be recognized and rewarded. In forming his cabinet, President Andrew Jackson searched for Democratic party loyalists who would zealously support his administration. A mutual friend of Jackson's and Taney's recommended the Marylander for the position of attorney general.[8] Although Jackson was not yet well-acquainted personally with Taney, the president told Francis Scott Key (Taney's brother-in-law) that he knew his choice for attorney general practiced sound constitutional thinking.[9] Jackson was not disappointed in Taney's performance, and the attorney general eventually became the president's "most trusted and most confidential adviser." Later, because Jackson knew he could rely on Taney's loyalty and political skill in the bitter dispute over the Bank of the United States, he named Taney to be secretary of the treasury in a recess appointment. The Senate, however, rejected the nomination in an act of opposition to the administration's handling of the bank controversy.[10]

Jackson then determined to reward Taney's efforts on behalf of the administration with a Supreme Court appointment. His first opportunity arrived just six months after the Senate rejected Taney's nomination to head the Treasury Department. Associate Justice Gabriel Duval, another Marylander, had resigned his seat on the Court in January 1835, and Jackson immediately nominated Taney to replace him. Again, the anti-Jackson forces in the Senate buried the nomination—this time by postponing the vote.[11]

Several months later, when the eminent Chief Justice John Marshall died, Jackson had still not filled the Duval vacancy. A recent Jackson biographer observed that the president probably never doubted that Taney would be his nominee for the Court's center chair. "Taney was his choice. No one else. And Taney he meant to have."[12] In a brilliant strategy, Old Hickory precluded any Senate opposition based on the customary geographic balance on the Court by pairing Taney's nomination with that of Virginian Philip Barbour for associate justice. Thus, although the seats were reversed, Jackson offered representation to Maryland and Virginia— the home states of former Justices Duval and Marshall, respectively. As in all of Jackson's Court appointments, geography, politics, and friendship constituted the president's criteria for selection.[13] Taney's legal acumen and professional ability, however, were well-known to supporters and opponents alike.

There is no evidence that Taney's religious affiliation played any part in Jackson's decisions to appoint him either to the cabinet or the Court. Still, "Taney was widely criticized on the ground that he was a Catholic, and therefore subservient to a 'foreign potentate.' "[14] Such criticism was not a product of the media. In fact, the press reported Taney's religion but almost as an afterthought. The *New York Herald* edition that announced Taney's confirmation as chief justice first criticized his brief stint as secretary of the treasury but praised his legal skills. The item concluded:

One fact ought not to be omitted—Mr. Taney is a Catholic in his religion, and on that ground may offend a certain sect of religionists. But the selection of such a man for Chief Justice, is a signal example of practical religious liberty in the actions of the government of the United States.[15]

Although these closing sentiments were admirable, the *Herald*'s top headline of the same day read "Movements of Maria Monk," followed by some of the most blatant anti-Catholic propaganda of the 1830s nativist movement. In 1836, a young woman named Maria Monk had published a sensational tome provocatively entitled *Awful Disclosures of the Hotel Dieu Nunnery of Montreal*. Among other revelations, she claimed that young nuns in this Montreal convent were ordered by their mother superior to submit to intimate relations with priests. Monk alleged that the offspring from these sinful unions were immediately baptized and strangled. Maria Monk's mother explained that her daughter's fantastic tales were the product of brain damage incurred when in infancy Maria "had run a slate pencil into her head."[16] The product of mental illness or not, the Maria Monk story played directly into the hands of the nativists, who wanted to believe the worst about Roman Catholics.

Given such a hostile and extreme anti-Catholic climate, Taney's rise to the highest judicial position in the land proves the strength of other factors (namely, merit, politics, friendship, and geography) in his overcoming a potentially ruinous religious handicap. Taney's tenure as chief justice and the Court's first Roman Catholic lasted until his death in 1864. There was not to be another Catholic on the high court for the next three decades.

During these decades, waves of Catholic immigrants arrived in the United States from Ireland, Germany, France, Italy, Spain, Austria, and the nations of Eastern Europe. Their ethnic clannishness in religious affairs carried over to the political world. Irish Catholics were especially adept at forming and operating political machines. In the final third of the nineteenth century, they also formed a crucial element in the Democratic party coalition—a role they would continue to play in the twentieth century.

Republican candidates, including such presidential hopefuls as Rutherford B. Hayes and James A. Garfield, predictably campaigned against the old bugaboo of Romanist influence in the opposing party. By the 1884 presidential election, Irish Catholics constituted a half-million votes for the lucky candidate who could woo their support. Republican James G. Blaine very likely lost the support of New York Catholics and ultimately the 1884 presidential election when a Protestant minister declared publicly at a meeting of fellow clergymen that they would not vote for Blaine's Democratic opponent, Grover Cleveland, because he represented the party of "rum, Romanism, and rebellion."[17]

EDWARD D. WHITE'S FIRST APPOINTMENT

In the midst of a revival of anti-Catholicism, spearheaded by the American Protective Association (APA), founded in 1887, President Grover Cleveland appointed the second Roman Catholic, Edward D. White, Jr., to sit on the Supreme Court. Although his father had married into a Maryland Catholic family,[18] White was born in Thibodaux, Louisiana, a small but religious town with a Catholic convent, school, and church, where young White was baptized.

Unlike Chief Justice Taney who was educated in Protestant institutions, White began his education at a Jesuit preparatory school in New Orleans. After nine years, his family sent him to Mount Saint Mary's in Emmitsburg, Maryland, where he studied one year before enrolling at Georgetown University. When the Civil War forced White to return to the South, he continued his studies with the Jesuits in New Orleans at a college that was eventually incorporated into Loyola of the South.[19] Thus, like his twentieth-century successor, Justice Scalia, White was educated predominantly in Jesuit institutions.

Speculation on Cleveland's motivations for appointing White to the Supreme Court in 1894 has unearthed a variety of possible explanations, most of which are related to the machinations of executive and legislative politics of the day.[20] One theory explains White's selection as an effort to find a candidate who could survive the confirmation process. In filling the seat left open by the death of Justice Samuel Blatchford of New York, Cleveland offered the seat to three candidates before he approached White. The first two—William B. Hornblower and Wheeler H. Peckham— met the geographic criterion as both were New Yorkers. Hornblower and Peckham, however, had run afoul of a Tammany Hall political feud. Consequently, New York Senator David B. Hill, a major participant in the feud, and an opponent of the president, scuttled both appointments. Cleveland's third nominee, Frederic Coudert, declined the nomination, allegedly due to prior commitments to his legal clients. Finally, Cleveland selected White, a U.S. senator from Louisiana, who received immediate confirmation from his Senate colleagues on February 19, 1984. The "common interpretation" in Washington was that if Cleveland could not place an anti-Hill man on the bench, he would go as far away as possible to find a man neither pro- nor anti-Tammany.[21]

White's southern heritage may have been meaningful for Cleveland for reasons other than avoiding the Tammany Hall problem. The *New York Times* speculated that Cleveland had chosen White to offer the South "a representative on the Court who could be expected to be closely in touch with the legal controversies of the fourteen states on the Southern border."[22]

Other putative factors relate to White's record as a legislator. Allen Nevins, Cleveland's authorized biographer, wrote that White had earned the president's praise and gratitude for supporting him in the repeal of the Sherman Silver Purchase Act in 1893.[23] White also was considered an advocate of the income tax.[24] On the other hand, White had stubbornly advocated the interests of his sugar-growing constituents in Louisiana and opposed Cleveland's tariff reduction bill. One theory holds that Cleveland, by "kicking White upstairs," removed a formidable tariff opponent from the Senate.[25]

In addition to the political and geographic considerations related above, merit probably was another criterion. The *New York Times* reported on the day after White's confirmation that Cleveland, in his first presidential term (1885–89), had considered White for a Supreme Court vacancy that eventually went to Mississippi's Lucius Q. C. Lamar. Yet Cleveland "had learned of Mr. White's great legal ability, and, as he had judicial experience, he seemed to be peculiarly fitted for the high office."[26]

The religion factor is rarely mentioned by historians as playing a significant role in the White appointment, with one exception. Most sources relate the rather charming anecdote of how Cleveland overheard White's question (as they both departed a Saturday evening party) of where he might attend an early mass the next morning. According to educator Bliss Perry, Cleveland was so impressed by White's piety and morality that he decided to put him on the Court.[27]

Regardless of whether religion was a consideration for President Cleveland, the contemporary press took note of White's Catholicism. The *New York Times* reported that Cleveland's critics had attacked his second choice to fill the Blatchford vacancy, Wheeler Peckham, because of his bigotry in his opposition to Roman Catholic participation in politics. The *Times* noted further that these critics of the president were "apt to be confused by the nomination of Senator White, who is a Roman Catholic." The article concluded: "That fact, however need not cause any alarm among reasonable people. The bench has been occupied by a Roman Catholic Judge before, and his religious belief does not appear to have affected his judgment or his reputation."[28] The Catholic press celebrated the fact that "in these days of religious revival of Know-Nothingism . . . Mr. White's religious belief was no bar to his advancement to the exalted office to which he has just been appointed."[29]

Historian Robert Cross explained that religion was a positive factor in White's appointment rather than a handicap. Cross wrote:

Either from gratitude for Catholic principles [Taft had called Catholicism "one of the bulwarks against socialism and anarchy in this country"] or from fear of the increasing Catholic voting power, politicians began to extend governmental aid to the Church. . . . Both major parties gave Catholics greater recognition than ever before. In 1892, both had Catholics as national campaign chairman. President Cleveland named the first Catholic to the Supreme Court since Roger Taney, and McKinley made Joseph McKenna the first Catholic cabinet officer since the Civil War; later McKenna was named to the Supreme Court.[30]

While the history of the Catholic Church and its growth in electoral influence in the latter half of the nineteenth century lent some credence to Cross's thesis, no concrete evidence supports a *direct* relationship between Catholic voting strength and Cleveland's appointment of the Court's second Roman Catholic. As such, the White appointment resembles Taney's in that political factors other than religion or its electoral ramifications determined each man's selection. Moreover, White's personal background—his birth into a prominent Catholic family in a state with a strong Catholic heritage—may have allowed him, like Taney, to overcome the extant anti-Catholic bias. Nevertheless, whereas Taney's religion seemed unrelated to Jackson's choice, White's appointment suggests that religion might have become a positive criterion in the presidential selection process for Supreme Court members.

In the last two decades before the dawn of the twentieth century, the Catholic population in the United States nearly doubled from 6,259,000 in 1880 to 12,041,000 in 1900.[31] Catholic immigration and natural increase were each over 1 million per decade. Irish Catholics continued their dominance of Democratic party machines in the northeastern cities of New York and Boston and added Albany, Jersey City, and Hoboken to their column. Their influence spread to the Middle West as Chicago and Kansas City developed their own Irish-Catholic political machines devoted to the Democratic party.[32]

On the national scene, Catholics initially had another reason to shun the Republican party in the 1890s. The APA was influential in GOP politics in some sections of the country—as Democrats dutifully pointed out to Roman Catholic voters. The Republican convention's presidential nominee in 1896, William McKinley, never a boatrocker, eschewed all opportunities to distance himself from the APA, whose sole *raison d'être* was Catholic-baiting. Likewise, the convention, as a whole, refused to criticize explicitly the bigoted APA. Nevertheless, Archbishop John Ireland of St. Paul, one of the esteemed spokesmen of the church at that time, had successfully persuaded the GOP platform committee to exclude an APA-supported plank opposing the use of public money for sectarian purposes; and the prelate spoke in the party's behalf to his fellow Catholics.[33] Robert Cross has argued that in the 1896 election large numbers of Catholics had deserted the radicalism of William Jennings Bryan and helped to decide the election in McKinley's favor. As Cross elaborated:

Furthermore, having helped decide the election, they [Catholics] could rightly expect to have considerable influence on the new administration. [Archbishop] Ireland, in fact, was gratified to discover that recommendations to McKinley were more favorably received than those he made to Harrison. Joseph McKenna, a prominent Catholic, was appointed Attorney General, and later elevated to the Supreme Court.[34]

JOSEPH MCKENNA

Joseph McKenna's life was rooted in the development of immigrant, as opposed to old-Maryland, Catholicism in the United States. The future justice's mother and father emigrated from England and Ireland, respectively, to Philadelphia, where their son Joseph was born in 1843—just one year before the infamous nativist-Catholic riots in that city.[35]

At the age of eight, young McKenna was sent to St. Joseph's College, a newly founded Jesuit primary school in Philadelphia, where he studied for four years. He completed his education in the public schools of California, when his family moved there in 1855, apparently in an attempt to escape nativist bigotry. Although McKenna never returned to Catholic education, his family attended a local parish and young Joseph received religious instruction. In 1879 he married a German-Catholic immigrant who was a prominent supporter of the church's eleemosynary programs.[36]

Unlike Justices Taney and White, religion often became an issue in McKenna's public life. For example, after McKenna lost his first bid to win a congressional seat in 1876, he blamed his Roman Catholicism. In fact, many of his coreligionists may have abandoned his candidacy simply because he was of the "wrong" party (Republican) or, more likely, because he had sponsored measures supporting public schools when he was a state legislator. McKenna also suffered more traditional prejudice as he approached the beginning of his judicial career. Given the potential for opposition from the anti-Catholic APA, President Benjamin Harrison closely consulted various advisers on the wisdom of appointing McKenna to the Ninth Circuit Court of Appeals.[37] In spite of the opposition, Harrison made the appointment.

William McKinley was also concerned with potential nativist reaction to a McKenna nomination. McKinley had previously struggled with the APA while governor of Ohio, when they demanded that he fire two guards at the state penitentiary because they were Catholic. McKinley had consulted with his confidante H. H. Kohlsaat for advice in responding to the demand.[38] Kohlsaat replied, "I would tell them to go to hell." Insulting the APA was not a politically viable option. The fear of losing 63,000 APA votes, 90 percent of which were Republican, in his upcoming reelection bid was too overwhelming. Governor McKinley did not accept Kohlsaat's advice, but he did vow to tell the APA that "under our Constitution a man is guaranteed his religious liberty, and until these men do something that will warrant their discharge, they will hold their places."

McKinley related the incident to his assistant, political boss Mark Hanna, who immediately engineered a counterstrategy to prevent the loss of Catholic votes from McKinley's column. The governor won reelection by 81,995 votes, more than 60,000 votes above his 1891 victory margin. In so doing, he enhanced his chances for the 1896 presidential nomination.

Kohlsaat's memoirs also record how the Catholic issue again arose when McKinley considered elevating his former congressional colleague, McKenna, from his seat on the Ninth Circuit Court of Appeals to the cabinet. President-elect McKinley had expressed interest in McKenna as secretary of the interior. By the time McKinley summoned McKenna to Canton, Ohio, for a tête-à-tête, the Californian had heard the rumors about a position for him at the Interior Department. He frankly warned McKinley: "I don't believe you realize what you are doing. I am a Roman Catholic, and the Protestants will never permit a Catholic to have charge of the Indian Missions."[39] As Margaret Leech, McKinley's biographer, observed: "Visions of the APA must have rushed with the speed of light through McKinley's mind."[40]

The president-elect was undeterred. McKinley later told Kohlsaat: "Without taking my eyes from his I said: 'The place I want you for, judge, has nothing to do with the Indian Missions. I want you for Attorney General.' " McKenna replied that he had been misinformed and accepted McKinley's offer with alacrity. McKinley "laughingly" reported to Kohlsaat: "I don't believe the judge suspected that I switched him! We were in Congress together several years, and it never occurred to me that he was a Catholic!"[41] As such, the theory that McKinley knowingly appointed McKenna to be attorney general in order to repay Catholic voters seems unfounded.[42] Yet if Kohlsaat's account refutes this notion of McKenna's appointment as repayment, it also reveals that McKinley was well aware of McKenna's religious affiliation when he named him to the Supreme Court two years later.

The December 1897 nomination to the Court certainly was not unexpected. Since the previous July, the press had been predicting that McKenna would "undoubtedly" replace the failing Associate Justice Stephen J. Field upon his death or retirement. The *New York Times* reported that McKenna's elevation to the Court had been one of the conditions of his accepting the position of attorney general.[43] The geographic factor was also duly noted; McKenna would be the logical replacement for Field, who was also a Californian.[44] Equally obvious factors in the appointment were the friendship between McKenna and McKinley and the former's support of, and loyalty to, the administration.

A more tenuous explanation of the appointment is that McKinley intended to use his choice of McKenna to prove his nonalliance with the APA.[45] Given McKinley's well-documented ambivalence toward the APA during his political career, the theory seems weak. Indeed, McKinley's past electoral successes clearly demonstrate his skill, or that of Mark Hanna's, at juggling one of the political hot potatoes of the day: the polarization between Catholics and nativists. Still, it is possible that as McKenna's biographer, Matthew McDevitt, has argued, McKinley perceived the APA and its power to be on the wane. With nativist influence weakening, "there was a general belief that any such intolerant opposition might be advantageous to McKinley when it came to a senatorial vote."[46]

If McKinley can be credited with such a strategy, it apparently paid off. True to form, the APA protested McKenna's nomination and argued that government departments were being "Romanized."[47] The *New York Times* reported that the APA opposition would, if anything, help McKenna in the Senate.[48] In general, however, senators were unenthusiastic about the nomination, which one member, speaking anonymously, called the weakest "in many years."[49] A few senators reportedly opposed McKenna because of the Catholic issue (that is, the widespread nativist complaint that Catholic officeholders could not act without consulting the pope or other high church officials) but abandoned their cause for fear that any legitimate opposition would be undermined by a prolonged religious controversy.[50] The Senate Judiciary Committee also received a letter from "members of the Pacific Coast bar" charging that McKenna lacked "the legal training and judicial experience to fit him for the position."[51]

After McKenna's nomination was reported out of committee favorably, Senate Judiciary Committee Chairman George F. Hoar introduced the nomination on the Senate floor, and argued that the APA opposition was, "entirely un-American and unpatriotic and should not for a moment receive the consideration of fair-minded men."[52] Senator Allen, a Populist from Nebraska, sought and obtained a delay in the vote on the nomination, partly to consider, "the charge . . . that large corporations had been instrumental in securing Mr. McKenna's nomination,"[53] but the nomination was confirmed overwhelmingly by voice vote a week later despite continued opposition from Allen based on McKenna's legal qualifications.[54]

Although McKinley's motivations in choosing McKenna remain uncertain, the role of religion in the appointment had arguably become more significant than in the nominations of Taney (in 1835) or White (in 1894). With Taney, religious affiliation was purely coincidental to the appointment; with White's appointment, Roman Catholicism was, at most, a peripheral issue. In the McKenna nomination, traditional factors such as geography, friendship, and political compatibility may have preceded religion as considerations in McKinley's decision. Nevertheless, religious elements in the form of the APA movement were significant in McKinley's previous campaign, and he was cognizant of them in McKenna's appointment—particularly after McKenna had emphasized his Roman Catholicism in his 1896 Canton summit with McKinley. Of course, because Justice White was already on the Court, McKinley's concern may have been more with attracting Catholic electoral support for the 1900 election than providing "representation" for Catholics. Yet, regardless of McKinley's reasoning, the appointment of McKenna moved religion into the position of an "over-the-top" factor. That is, given favorable considerations of geography, friendship, and political loyalty, McKenna's religion and the possibility of attracting his fellow Catholics to the McKinley fold may have put McKenna over the top in his selection as Justice Field's replacement.

EDWARD D. WHITE'S PROMOTION TO CHIEF JUSTICE

The Catholicism factor surfaced again in 1910 when President William Howard Taft decided to promote Associate Justice Edward White to the chief justiceship. The nomination of White caught the outside world by surprise because Associate Justice Charles Evans Hughes had been considered the front runner for promotion to the center chair.[55] Taft's biographer, Alpheus T. Mason, and others have offered various explanations for Taft's unexpected action.[56] White was a logical choice because of his ideological agreement with Taft on political and economic issues, his acceptance by the progressive faction in the Republican party, and his friendship with Taft.[57]

Taft reportedly told a group of senators that he declined to select Justice Hughes because of his judicial inexperience and because he believed that former President Theodore Roosevelt, Taft's political mentor, might be annoyed by a Hughes appointment.[58] Merle Pusey, Hughes's biographer, and others, however, suggested an ulterior motive on Taft's part. They believed that the president coveted the chief justiceship. An appointment of the forty-eight-year old Hughes would probably have precluded a future president from appointing Taft as chief justice.[59]

Fourteen years after the decision, Taft noted the following factors in White's favor: "his great ability and learning, his long experience on the Bench, and his high character."[60] In this same explanation of White's appointment, Taft took exception to suggestions that as a Freemason, he should have overlooked White because of his Catholicism. He argued that allowing White's religion to exclude him from the appointment would have constituted a violation of the presidential oath of office.[61]

The promotion of White to chief justice may have cost Taft some political support. Anti-Catholicism in the United States hardly had disappeared with the demise of the APA.[62] Yet, Taft was convinced that his past and future electoral success depended on the support of Catholics, whose population had increased to 16,363,000 by 1910.[63] Taft's naval aide Archie Butt, in a revealing letter written to his sister-in-law in 1911, expressed concern over the president's attempts to garner Catholic votes. Butt wrote that Taft was "very strong with the Catholics, and in nearly every city we visit he manages to show some special mark of respect for them and to have a few minutes conference with some of their leaders." Butt continued:

He says he will get the solid Catholic vote—and I think he will, but he might pay very dearly, for there is another side to the picture which he does not see. The great Protestant denominations are beginning to see the way he panders to Catholics and are becoming resentful. It is with the greatest difficulty that we can get him to stand up to receive greetings of thousands of school children banked on the sidewalk in front of a school, but he will stop the whole procession to get out and shake hands with two nuns and a handful of children. But he knows what he is about. He says the Catholics elected him last time, and he thinks they can do it again. I hope so, for I think sometimes he encourages them to separate themselves from the rest of Americans, who gather to pay him homage.[64]

As with the McKenna appointment, White's Catholicism seems to have "put him over the top," given his other qualifications (at least in Taft's eyes) of judicial experience, meritorious legal skills, strong moral character, and age. Butt's letter, with its references to Taft's views, is significant, however, for it offers the first explicit statement by a president that he linked his election victories with perceived Catholic support. Therefore, Taft evidently had the motive to consider White's religion when selecting him for chief justice.

Catholic immigration to the United States in the first ten years of the twentieth century soared to nearly 2.5 million. In this century's second decade, however, the number of Catholic immigrants dropped to 1,202,000.[65] Still, Catholics constituted one-sixth of the U.S.'s population as World War I drew to a close.[66] Pressure increased on Congress to implement a quota system on immigration, particularly from Southern and Eastern Europe, which accounted for three-quarters of the total flood of new arrivals in 1914. Demands for restrictive legislation were tinged with religious bigotry. One church historian, Martin Marty, has noted that "moderates throughout the nation were no less disturbed than [Ku Klux] Klansmen about the threat that America would go Catholic by immigration."[67] The calls for quotas succeeded with the passage of the Reed-Johnson Act in 1924.

PIERCE BUTLER

Nonetheless, in 1922, another Catholic was sent to the Supreme Court. Like Justice McKenna, Pierce Butler was a first-generation Irish Catholic. Minnesota, where Butler spent his childhood, lacked Catholic schools. Instead, Butler attended a one-room common school and ultimately received a degree from Carleton College, a Congregationalist institution. Despite the lack of formal Catholic training, Butler's devout parents instilled in him a devotion to, and an appreciation for, the tenets of his Roman Catholic faith. As an adult his friends included several influential Catholic prelates.[68]

As in the promotion of Edward White to the chief justiceship, Butler's appointment bore the stamp of William Howard Taft. This time, however, he advised the president from the chief justice's chair, to which Harding had appointed him in 1921. Certainly guilty of understatement, Taft, in a letter to Walter L. Church regarding Butler's successful appointment, commented: "I recommended him as well as I could to the President, and I think perhaps that had some influence." George Wickersham, who had served in Taft's cabinet as attorney general, was more candid and accurate in a letter to the chief justice: "I congratulate *you* on the President's selection of Pierce Butler for the existing vacancy in your Court."[69]

According to Alpheus Mason, Taft's first concern in recommending nominees for Harding's consideration was ideological orientation. Taft was well-acquainted with Butler and his views. The latter's many years of experience as a railroad lawyer suggested to Taft that Butler would be a logical and reliable counter to Justice Louis Brandeis's perceived radicalism. Moreover, Butler's nominal Democratic party affiliation appealed to Taft, who thought the Court was top-heavy with seven Republicans.[70]

Despite Taft's exhortations to treat religion as an irrelevancy, other participants and observers in the selection process inevitably raised the issue. Charles D. Hilles, a close friend of Taft, advocated the selection of a Roman Catholic. With Chief Justice White's death in 1921, and the anticipated demise of McKenna, the Court was to be left with one "Hebrew" and no Catholic. Hilles predicted that there would be a "demand" for another Roman Catholic on the Court. Taft balked at Hilles's suggestion for the same reason that he had raised in describing his decision to name White chief justice—namely, that an individual should not ascend the Court either despite, or because of, his religion.

Taft's colleague on the bench, Justice Willis Van Devanter, disagreed. He believed that Democrats, Catholics, and Southerners would insist upon an appointment from their respective groups because each had "recently lost representation on the Court." Similarly, Taft's brother Harry supported Butler, whose religion and party affiliation he found "peculiarly appropriate" at the time.[71] Thus there was a deliberate effort to find Catholics with otherwise acceptable credentials.

In the end, ideological considerations triumphed over religious affiliation and geographic appropriateness as a primary concern. Indeed, Taft's first choice was John W. Davis, a non-Catholic Democrat with "sound views." When Davis declined the nomination, Taft focused on securing the appointment for his second choice, Pierce Butler. The chief justice continued to proclaim his view that merit should be the primary criterion of any jurist's appointment, and he sincerely believed that Butler was meritorious. Yet Taft was well-aware of the importance of Butler's religion as an ancillary factor in his nomination. Hence, both Taft and Justice Van Devanter worked behind the scenes to attract support for Butler from the Catholic hierarchy. Taft counted on Catholic support for Butler to offset any Progressive opposition in the Senate to the railroad lawyer's corporate ties.[72]

The Senate confirmed Butler by a sixty-one to eight margin less than one month after his nomination.[73] As Taft had anticipated, the Progressives did not consent to the nomination.[74] Several Democrats also voted "nay."[75] A *New York Times* editorial presumed that these five negative votes were a result of anti-Catholic pressure from the Klan.[76] The Catholic newspaper of the Boston archdiocese commended Harding for justly recognizing the faithful service of Catholics to the nation during the

"World War" and for overcoming the revitalized anti-Catholic movement in appointing Butler.[77]

More than any of the other previous appointments of Catholics to the Supreme Court, Butler's selection evinces numerous aspects of religion as a "representative" factor. Schmidhauser has argued that "representation" of Catholics was not an issue in the Butler nomination because McKenna was still on the Court.[78] It is apparent from Hilles's advice to Taft, however, that they were looking to the near future when the ailing McKenna would no longer be on the high bench. Butler's merit, ideology, and party affiliation may have been among the first considerations for Taft in making his recommendation to Harding, but religion was also on the list of important factors weighing in Butler's favor. Indeed, with Butler's selection, religion moved beyond its previous status as an "over-the-top" factor: it had now become one of the primary considerations in choosing a Supreme Court justice.

In 1928, American Catholics rejoiced that one of their number had received the Democratic party's highest honor—a presidential nomination. Catholic pride in Alfred E. Smith's candidacy turned to disillusionment, however, when his campaign revived latent anti-Catholicism. Old nativist propaganda was dusted off and reissued. Even the Maria Monk story made the rounds again.[79] On more sophisticated but no less bigoted levels, Smith's beliefs on church and state were severely questioned. When challenged about an encyclical issued by the pope, Smith reportedly threw up his hands in frustration and exclaimed: "Will someone please tell me what the hell a papal encyclical is?"[80] Smith did not deny his devout devotion to his Roman Catholic faith; but, like the more successful John F. Kennedy thirty-two years later, Smith asserted his belief in complete separation of church and state and the primacy of the Constitution in his public life.[81]

Franklin D. Roosevelt, who would appoint the next Catholic to the Court, had recognized the importance of Catholic electoral influence early in his career when he dealt with the Tammany Hall faction of New York politics. By 1932, he was well-aware of the significance of Catholic support, especially if he hoped to carry the eastern states in a national election. Indeed, a good portion of F.D.R.'s 12 million-plus victory margin over President Herbert Hoover undoubtedly came from Roosevelt's strong showing in the country's twelve largest urban areas, which contained significant Catholic populations.[82]

As George Q. Flynn described in his book on the relationship between American Catholics and Franklin Roosevelt, "It was F.D.R. who maintained the allegiance of American Catholics toward the [Democratic] party by the recognition he extended them and the finesse with which he treated them."[83] F.D.R. nurtured Catholic support, in part, by appointing Roman Catholics to office in unprecedented numbers. In the entire history of the country prior to 1932, fewer than a handful of Catholics had ever served in presidential cabinets. Roosevelt, in his first term alone, appointed two Roman Catholics to his cabinet: James A. Farley as postmaster general and Thomas J. Walsh as attorney general. In judicial appointments, F.D.R. surpassed the Republican record in the 1920s of one Catholic nominee for every twenty-five at the lower federal court level. During Roosevelt's twelve-year tenure in office, he averaged one Catholic for every *four* judicial appointments.[84] No wonder a Gallup poll in October 1936 revealed that 78 percent of Catholics surveyed intended to vote for F.D.R. in the upcoming election.[85] As in 1932, F.D.R. racked up overwhelming majorities in urban areas, where most of the Catholic votes were concentrated.[86]

FRANK MURPHY

Another victor in the 1936 elections was one of Roosevelt's earliest and staunchest supporters, Frank Murphy, who became the first Roman Catholic governor of Michigan. Murphy was to be the subject of key personnel decisions during Roosevelt's second term—first being named attorney general in 1938 and then associate justice of the Supreme Court two years later.

Like three of the four Catholics who preceded him on the Court, Frank Murphy was of Irish ancestry. His devoutly Catholic mother instilled in him a deep devotion to his faith. Because there was no Catholic school in Murphy's hometown of Sandbeach, Michigan, he received all of his education in public schools. Nevertheless, he followed the traditions of his faith by becoming an altar boy at the age of seven and receiving the sacrament of confirmation five years later. Arthur Krock, a non-Catholic, once attended mass with Joseph Kennedy and Murphy. Krock later joked with Kennedy that he found Murphy the better model to follow in order to keep up with the service's rituals that called for kneeling, standing, or sitting at the proper times. Kennedy, referring to Murphy's prowess in the formalities of the Catholic mass, replied: "That character . . . ought to have been a priest."[87]

Nonetheless, although Murphy's calling was political rather than clerical, he was more than willing to allow his religion to enhance his electoral fortunes. In 1923, when young Murphy ran for Detroit's Recorder's Court, a priest wrote to him promising to distribute a Murphy campaign card to every parishioner at Easter Sunday services. Murphy became the youngest candidate ever elected to the court and was hailed by Catholic congregations. The adulation of his coreligionists prompted Murphy to write to his family that the Catholics of Detroit "seem very proud of me."[88] Likewise, as mayor of Detroit several years later, Murphy re-ceived high marks from Catholic constituents who labeled him "a model Catholic layman, truly good and devout and thoroughly Catholic."[89]

Murphy was an early supporter of Roosevelt. While this can be partially attributed to his unwavering ideological kinship with New Deal policies, Murphy also may have sensed the potential for political bonuses in exchange for his early backing of F.D.R. With an eye toward his political future, the then mayor of Detroit perhaps theorized that Roosevelt would turn to an urban Catholic as a running mate in order to balance his support from rural areas and the South.[90] Murphy surely could swing a significant number of Catholic votes to the Democratic ticket, not only from the mayor's own personal following but from the even larger group of Catholic adherents to Murphy's friend Father Charles E. Coughlin, the so-called radio priest, whose parish was located in Detroit. Taking no chances while on Murphy and Coughlin turf, Roosevelt quoted Pope Pious XI in a Detroit campaign speech in October 1932. A month later, on election day, F.D.R. received 62.4 percent of Detroit's vote and carried the state of Michigan by 130,000 votes—an impressive victory in a traditionally Republican state. Many observers credited Murphy's tireless efforts on behalf of the Democratic ticket for F.D.R.'s success in the mayor's city and home state.[91]

Sydney Fine, a biographer of Murphy, has noted that "Roosevelt was anxious to provide suitable recognition of the substantial Catholic element in the Democratic party, and a major appointment for Frank Murphy nicely served this objective."[92] Murphy's first preference was for attorney general, but he had to settle for his second choice, governor-general of the Philippines, when the former position went to another Catholic, Senator Thomas Walsh.[93] In his Philippine post, Murphy found a natural environment for the expression of his Catholicism. The Roman Catholic Filipinos welcomed their fellow coreligionist with open arms, and the governor-general, in turn, embraced every opportunity to display his piety.[94]

As the 1936 reelection campaign approached, the Roosevelt administration expressed fears of Catholic defections from the Roosevelt coalition. Roosevelt successfully prevailed upon Murphy to return to Michigan in order to run for governor and, F.D.R. hoped, unite the Democratic party in Murphy's home state and prevent a Catholic exodus from the Roosevelt column. F.D.R.'s ultimate victory margin proved that his earlier fears were unwarranted. Ironically, the president's coattails carried Murphy to victory and helped him to overcome an anti-Catholic bias in the state of Michigan at large.[95] Roosevelt, however, could not save Murphy in his off-year reelection bid two years later when the governor lost to his Republican opponent by nearly 100,000 votes.[96]

Murphy, a staunch New Dealer and defender of F.D.R.'s ill-conceived and ultimately unsuccessful "Court-packing" plan, had been rumored to be in the running for each of the Supreme Court vacancies that had occurred while he was governor. He was reportedly considered for the vacancy created by Justice George Sutherland's retirement in 1938. Some observers speculated that the president, in hopes of making up for the embarrassment of Justice Hugo Black's Ku Klux Klan connections, planned a sensational nomination of a second Catholic or the first woman—rumored to be Florence Allen of Ohio—to the Court. In the end, Stanley F. Reed became F.D.R.'s second appointment.[97]

Unemployed as a result of his defeat in 1938, Murphy was considered a front-runner to fill the Supreme Court seat, which had been vacated by the untimely death of Benjamin Cardozo.[98] In July 1938, Harold Ickes, Roosevelt's secretary of interior, asked "brain truster" Thomas Corcoran who he thought would replace Cardozo. Corcoran promptly answered "Governor Murphy of Michigan or Judge [John P.] Devaney of Minnesota," both of whom were Catholic. Ickes recorded in his diary: "It seems the Catholics are after this appointment. They are not entitled to it, but the Roman church is after all it can get. It is asserting claims out of proportion to its numerical strength and influence in this country." The "Old Curmudgeon" elaborated later in his journal "that the Catholic minority of this country, because it was well organized, active, and aggressive, was able to protect people of that religion and get more recognition for them than numerically they were entitled to."[99] It appears that Ickes was suggesting that two seats for Catholics on the Court were clearly unacceptable in terms of proportional representation but that one "Catholic seat" was numerically defensible, given the fact that Catholics were approaching nearly 20 percent of the population at that time. Whatever Ickes's argument in discussing the "representation" of Catholics on the Court, he was well aware of the political realities that made Murphy's odds nearly even for replacing the aging Pierce Butler, who, like Murphy, was a Catholic midwesterner.

Cardozo's "Jewish seat" went to another faithful New Dealer, Harvard Law School Professor Felix Frankfurter. Several days before Frankfurter's nomination, Roosevelt appointed Murphy to the position he had coveted at F.D.R.'s initial election—attorney general.[100] Political observers had expected F.D.R. to find a position for Murphy in the administration because of the well-known personal and political ties between the two men.[101]

Murphy had served as attorney general for less than a year when Associate Justice Pierce Butler died on November 16, 1939. President Roosevelt wasted no time in making his decision on Butler's replacement. According to Fine, F.D.R. buttonholed Murphy to tell him the news of his nomination after a Cabinet meeting on the very day of Butler's death.

After having been considered for each of the preceding Court vacancies during F.D.R.'s tenure, the factors that finally made Murphy "the right person in the right spot at the right time" (to anticipate Sandra Day

O'Connor's own description of her historic appointment more than forty years later) are clear. Ever true to his Catholicism, Murphy credited "some good guardian angel." At the same time, he noted that it was not merit. While he may have been exhibiting false modesty, the statement itself was all too true.[102]

Several factors are evident in the Murphy appointment, including the decade-old personal and political friendship between F.D.R. and Murphy. Newspaper accounts of the nomination stress the criteria of political and ideological compatibility and "representativeness." A *New York Times* article that appeared the day following Butler's demise reported that Murphy's name had come "to the fore, inasmuch as he is a Catholic like Mr. Butler" and also a midwesterner. Moreover, the *Times* described the attorney general as "a liberal and vigorous supporter of President Roosevelt" and observed that Butler's death gave F.D.R. his fifth appointment to the Court. His long-awaited opportunity to fashion a majority sympathetic to his political, social, and economic ideas— something Roosevelt had impatiently and unsuccessfully attempted to do in his 1937 "Court-packing" scheme—had finally arrived.[103]

Scholars, such as Sydney Fine and the meticulous J. Woodford Howard, Jr., have stressed Roosevelt's logic in selecting the Catholic, midwestern, progressive Murphy to replace Butler. In fact, Howard has argued convincingly that Murphy "was the first Roman Catholic Justice to have been appointed from *explicitly* religious criteria."[104]

Another factor prominently mentioned by Murphy biographers concerns his position and performance as attorney general immediately prior to his Supreme Court nomination. Howard, for example, has asserted that Murphy's "elevation to the bench made it possible for the President to relieve a nagging personnel log-jam." Ickes's copious notes on F.D.R.'s desire to promote the eminently well-qualified Solicitor General Robert H. Jackson to attorney general and move Murphy to the office of secretary of war (a job Murphy desired) support Howard's theory. The "log-jam" had occurred due to Harry H. Woodring's (the incumbent secretary of war's) reluctance to vacate his position. Thus, moving Murphy to the Supreme Court allowed the president to promote Jackson to attorney general.[105]

More controversial, yet perhaps most crucial to Murphy's ultimate nomination to the Court, are the various versions of the "kicked upstairs" theory. Robert Jackson's own view was that Murphy's incompetence and unpredictability prompted the president to remove him from the Department of Justice. A second explanation of the "kicked upstairs" theory suggests that F.D.R. was concerned about Murphy's plan to prosecute Edward Kelly and Frank Hague, two Democratic political bosses, whose support the president was courting in his 1940 bid for an unprecedented third presidential term. Fine has maintained that Murphy came to accept this second explanation of his removal from the Justice Department.[106] Another biographer, Richard D. Lunt, provocatively has suggested that Murphy himself may have leaked the second version to detract from Jackson's reports of the attorney general's incompetence.[107]

Undoubtedly, all of the above factors were involved in Murphy's appointment, and it is impossible to prioritize them in the exact order that Roosevelt had in mind. Yet, for the questions raised in this study, the implications of Murphy's appointment for the issue of religion as a "representative" factor are significant. Murphy's Catholicism may not have been the primary element in his nomination, but it must be considered one of the leading two or three factors in making Murphy *the* choice to fill Butler's "Catholic seat." As if to emphasize the role of Murphy's Catholicism in the new justice's life as well as his appointment, Homer Cummings pointedly remarked that with Murphy on the Court F.D.R. would achieve his goal of increasing the number of seats on the high bench because Murphy would "bring with him as colleagues Father, Son, and Holy Ghost."[108]

Indeed, Murphy's selection to fill the "Catholic seat" that had evolved on the Court over the first half of the twentieth century was the pinnacle of Catholic "representation" on the high bench. Upon Justice Murphy's death in 1949, President Harry S Truman nominated a Protestant, Tom C. Clark, and stated defiantly: "I do not believe religions have anything to do with the Supreme Bench. If an individual has the qualifications, I do not care if he is a Protestant, Catholic, or Jew."[109] Nevertheless, a 1953 article in the Catholic magazine *The Commonweal* noted the absence of Catholics on the United States Supreme Court:

Just as there is, *traditionally at least,* one Catholic in the Cabinet, so there usually has been one Catholic on the Court. Since Frank Murphy's death that has not been true. The President is under no obligation to appoint a Catholic to any position, but in recognition of the fact that Catholics constitute about one fifth of the total population, it has been deemed equitable and perhaps politically expedient to allocate a certain number of top appointive positions to members of the Roman Catholic Church. In the cities and state governments, the Catholics are in government positions pretty much in the same ratio as that of the Catholic population to the total population in the city or state.[110]

Catholic "representation" had become an important issue in American politics. The continued concentration of America's largest single religious denomination (20 percent of the total population) in urban areas gave Catholics an important role in the presidential electoral college system. "More than 80 percent of the Catholic voters lived in fewer than a dozen key industrial states including those with the largest electoral college vote."[111] In recognition of this situation, approaching the presidential nominating convention in the summer of 1956, Democratic politicians debated the wisdom of putting a Catholic vice-presidential candidate on the ticket.[112] In fact, Senator John F. Kennedy of Massachusetts nearly captured that honor, but lost a bitter convention struggle with Senator Estes Kefauver of Tennessee, the eventual vice-presidential nominee on the hapless Democratic ticket headed by Adlai E. Stevenson, Jr.

WILLIAM J. BRENNAN, JR.

Just two months before Republican President Dwight D. Eisenhower overwhelmed the Stevenson/Kefauver ticket with his landslide reelection victory in November 1956, he was faced with a vacancy on the Supreme Court. Sherman Minton, a Truman appointee, announced his retirement in early September. The press speculated that Attorney General Herbert Brownell, United States Ninth Circuit Court of Appeals Judge Stanley N. Barnes, Secretary of State John Foster Dulles, and former New York Governor Thomas E. Dewey were on Eisenhower's short list of possible replacements. At a news conference several days after Minton's announced retirement, Eisenhower listed the following selection criteria: "reasonable age" (generally considered fifty-five or younger); legal and judicial experience; recognition by the community and the legal profession, especially the American Bar Association; and "unimpeachable character and accomplishment." On September 30, the *New York Times*'s front-page headline proclaimed, "President Names Jersey Democrat to Supreme Court," "Selection is Surprise."[113] To the public and the nominee (William J. Brennan, Jr.) alike, Eisenhower's choice was indeed surprising.

Brennan's humble origins provided no clue that he would eventually sit on the nation's highest tribunal. He was born in 1906 to Irish immigrant parents in Newark, New Jersey. Brennan's family of ten was poor in economic terms but rich in Irish-Catholic tradition. Recently, he movingly described how "very Catholic" his parents were and how they maintained an abiding faith in God and His willingness to provide aid and comfort, especially during times of crisis.[114] As Brennan's father struggled to make ends meet at his job in a Newark brewery, and rose through the ranks to become the leader of his union, young Brennan received the first eight years of education in a parochial school. In better economic times, the future justice would have attended a Catholic high school, but his parents could not afford the annual $20 tuition fee for him and his seven siblings.[115] Thus, Brennan distinguished himself academically at a public high school. He had an equally successful undergraduate career at the University of Pennsylvania, from which he was graduated magna cum laude. He received a scholarship to Harvard Law School; and in 1931 he was graduated in the top 10 percent of his law school class.[116]

At the time of his nomination, Brennan met several of Eisenhower's expressed criteria for selection: he had been an outstanding trial lawyer;

he was an experienced judge, whose reputation and achievement were applauded by the bar; and he was only fifty years old. Eisenhower plucked Brennan from his seat on the New Jersey Supreme Court, whose distinguished Chief Judge Arthur T. Vanderbilt had written a "laudatory letter" to the president in Brennan's behalf.[117] Justice Brennan believed at the time of his appointment—and still maintains—that his substitution for the indisposed Judge Vanderbilt at a Washington judicial conference in the summer of 1956 was crucial to his selection. Not only did Brennan deliver a major address to the conference in place of Vanderbilt, who had suffered a stroke, but he also met daily with members of the administration's Department of Justice "team," which included Attorney General Brownell and Deputy Attorney General William P. Rogers, both of whom would be instrumental in selecting Minton's successor later that year.[118]

When interviewed at the time of his nomination, Judge Brennan dismissed the importance of party affiliation in his selection. Although a lifelong Democrat, Brennan noted that he had not been politically active. In fact, he had been appointed to each of his previous judicial positions by members of New Jersey's Republican party.[119] Of course, he may have inadvertently stated his very appeal to Eisenhower, particularly in an election year. The president probably thought Brennan to be a "safe" Democrat, who had gained the respect of other Republican officeholders.

One analysis of the Brennan appointment reported that Eisenhower may have promised Francis Cardinal Spellman that he would restore the "Catholic seat" on the Court, which had been vacant since Justice Murphy's death in 1949.[120] In a 1985 discussion of the role played by Catholicism in his own appointment, Justice Brennan voluntarily launched into a description of Spellman's possible influence on Eisenhower. Spellman may have been a lifelong Democrat, but he was also Ike's good friend from his days as "Military Vicar" during World War II. Justice Brennan stressed, however, that at the time of his appointment he was unaware of Spellman's involvement (if any) in Eisenhower's decision.

After his appointment to the Court, Justice Brennan's pastor at Sacred Heart parish in Fairhaven, New Jersey, where the new justice had long worshipped, informed Brennan that one Monsignor Shanley (brother of Bernard Shanley, Eisenhower's White House appointments secretary and a friend of Brennan) had made inquiries "to see if Brennan was a good Catholic." Recently, Justice Brennan related the anecdote that when Eisenhower's press secretary, James B. Haggerty, learned that the virtually unknown Brennan was Ike's choice for the Minton vacancy, the only descriptive credentials that came to Haggerty's mind for a press release were that Brennan was "a judge on the New Jersey Supreme Court and a good member of the Holy Name Society."[121] Clearly, the administration had considered Brennan's religious affiliation.

Justice Brennan has offered another possible motivation for Eisenhower's selection of an *Irish* Catholic for the Supreme Court in the months preceding the election. Senator Kennedy's near-victory at the 1956 Democratic convention in the race for his party's vice-presidential nomination may have prompted Ike to recognize the Irish Catholic constituency.[122] Some 3 million of the Catholics who voted in the 1952 presidential election had cast their ballots for General Eisenhower.[123] At a minimum, Ike must have been anxious at least to maintain that Catholic support in the upcoming 1956 election, especially in the traditionally Democratic Northeast, with its abundance of electoral votes.

Arthur Krock, the veteran *New York Times* editorialist, may have best explicated and ranked Eisenhower's criteria in Brennan's selection. After noting Judge Brennan's legal merit, judicial experience, impeccable professional reputation, and optimum age, Krock concluded his editorial: "And the appointment to the Supreme Court of a Catholic to succeed retiring Justice Minton was not only service to a fine American tradition: it was obviously good politics as well."[124] The religion criterion played a less important role in Justice Brennan's appointment than in Justice Murphy's selection, in which the nominee's Catholicism was one of the major factors guiding President Roosevelt's decision. In Justice Brennan's case, experience, merit, age, party affiliation, and geography all may have preceded his Catholicism as factors favoring his selection. Nevertheless, his religion arguably gave him the crucial edge because of Eisenhower's desire to "represent" Catholics on the Court in return for past, and anticipated, electoral support.[125]

The impact of John F. Kennedy's landmark victory in 1960 on the Supreme Court's "Catholic seat" may have been indirect but it was, nevertheless, profound. It symbolized the removal of a stigma that had prevented Roman Catholics from reaching the highest elected office in the land and punctuated their long assimilation process into American society and politics.[126] As Lawrence H. Fuchs's book-length study on Kennedy and American Catholicism argues, J.F.K.'s electoral success invigorated the forces for modernization within the American Catholic Church because Kennedy represented "the antithesis of the stereotyped, separationist, parochial, anti-intellectual, superstitious, tribalistic, and fatalistic Catholic of Protestant literature and conversation."[127]

Ironically, Catholic movement to the center stage of American politics and society may have eliminated the raison d'être of the Court's "Catholic seat." That is, the assimilation of Catholics into American politics to the point of capturing the Oval Office in 1960 arguably removed the "equitability" justification, and perhaps even the electoral motivation, for offering "representation" on the Court to Catholics as a group. "J.F.K.'s election lessened the psychological defensiveness that had historically marked the Catholic American."[128] Presidents would not have to compensate for Catholic feelings of inferiority or inequity by reserving one seat on the high court for Roman Catholics.

ANTONIN SCALIA

Justice Brennan remained the Court's sole Catholic member until fellow Roman Catholic Antonin Scalia joined him in September 1986. Although Brennan's and Scalia's presence on the nine-person Court reflected the approximate percentage (25 percent or 52 million) of Catholics in the U.S. population in 1986, it is unlikely that President Reagan or his advisers were guided by such a consideration. It is similarly improbable that the White House gave more than passing notice (if that) to the fact that the inevitable departure from the Court of the then eighty-year-old Justice Brennan would vacate the "Catholic seat."

Indeed, if the Reagan administration was concerned with any "representative" consideration, it was more likely ethnic rather than religious. Virtually every press account of Scalia's nomination cited the fact that he would be the first Italian-American to serve on the nation's highest bench.[129] For example, *Time* magazine implied that Scalia's ethnic heritage weighed in his favor and reported that "Scalia offered Reagan the chance to place the first Italian American on the high court."[130] Not surprisingly, politicians of Italian descent responded warmly and enthusiastically to Scalia's nomination. Republican Senator Pete V. Domenici of New Mexico hailed Reagan's decision to name Scalia as a "magnificent tribute" to Italian-Americans. Congressman Mario Biaggi, a Democratic Representative from the Bronx, added his praise: "Of course, there is a special pride I feel as an Italian American. Our community has always asked for consideration based on merit."[131]

Even ideological foes were hard-pressed to challenge Scalia's demonstrably meritorious credentials. By all accounts, devotion to his religious faith and academic pursuits had guided the future justice's youth. A product of New York public schools at the primary level,[132] Scalia was graduated from Xavier High School, a Jesuit institution in Manhattan. A former classmate offered the following description of the young Scalia: "This kid was a conservative when he was 17 years old. An archconservative Catholic. He could have been a member of the Curia. He was the top student in his class. He was brilliant, way above everybody else."[133]

Scalia continued his pattern of academic excellence at Georgetown University, from which he was graduated as valedictorian and summa cum laude. He earned his law degree at Harvard, where he served as an editor of the law review and a postgraduate fellow. "His [Harvard] classmates remember . . . Scalia as being heavily influenced by his Roman Catholic education."[134] Upon leaving Harvard, Scalia began a six-year stint as an associate at a Cleveland law firm. He left the firm to join the law faculty at the University of Virginia and never returned to private practice. Instead, he alternated between government positions (1971–72, general counsel, White House Office of Telecommunications Policy; 1974–77, assistant attorney general) and academic appointments at the Georgetown Law Center, the American Enterprise Institute, Stanford Law School, and the University of Chicago Law School. He had been a Chicago law professor for five years when in 1982 President Reagan nominated him for a seat on the United States Court of Appeals for the District of Columbia.[135]

Unlike Brennan's appointment in 1956, Scalia's nomination thirty years later came as no surprise to Court observers. One year before Reagan's announcement of Scalia as his choice to fill the seat of the promoted Justice William Rehnquist, *The New Republic* had written: "A Scalia nomination makes political sense." The prognostication continued with a quotation from an unnamed "White House official," who had exclaimed about Scalia, "What a political symbol. Nino would be the first Italian-Catholic on the Court. He's got nine kids. He's warm and friendly. Everybody likes him. He's a brilliant conservative. What more could you want?" Moreover, the fifty-year-old Scalia was ten years younger than Judge Robert Bork, who also was rumored to be on Reagan's list of potential Supreme Court appointees[136]—as indeed he had been on the occasion of every vacancy since the late 1960s. In light of the firestorm over Bork's ideology when he was nominated in 1987, it is indeed ironic that *Time* magazine reported in the summer of 1986 that Bork had lost out to Scalia because the latter "was a more energetic true believer" in the conservative cause.[137]

Attorney General Edwin Meese, a member of the three-man panel that made recommendations to Reagan on Court appointments, listed three basic criteria followed by the president in his decision to promote Associate Justice Rehnquist and name Scalia as his replacement. The criteria included: intellectual and lawyerly capability, "integrity," and "a commitment to the interpretation of the law rather than making it from the bench."[138] The president's announcement of his intention to nominate Scalia cited his "great personal energy, the force of his intellect and the depth of his understanding of our constitutional jurisprudence [which] uniquely qualify him for elevation to our highest court."[139]

Scalia's impeccable professional and personal attributes, his well-articulated conservative ideology, and his demonstrable restraintist jurisprudence provided a perfect fit with the Meese committee's and Reagan's expressed selection criteria. Moreover, Scalia's age (the same as Brennan's at his nomination) assured that, barring ill-health or ideological conversion, he could carry the tenets of Reagan jurisprudence well into the twenty-first century. Finally, the Reagan administration was assuredly not blind to ethnic realities and the potential political capital generated by naming the first Italian-American to the Court.

Scalia's Catholicism constituted at most an additional positive factor on the administration's lengthy list of other, more pertinent, considerations such as ideology, jurisprudence, merit, age, and nationality. The "Catholic seat" tradition clearly was not a prime motivating factor for the Reagan administration. Yet it is possible that a final point in Scalia's favor may have been his ability to occupy and maintain a Catholic seat on the bench when Justice Brennan would eventually leave the Court. Regardless of Reagan's intentions, the National Catholic News Service reported to its Catholic readers across the country that with the Senate's September 1986 confirmation of his nomination "Scalia became the second Catholic on the current U.S. Supreme Court," joining his coreligionist, Justice Brennan.[140]

ANTHONY M. KENNEDY

No one could have predicted that a little over a year after Scalia's appointment, President Reagan would nominate another Roman Catholic to the Supreme Court; but Anthony M. Kennedy would become the third Catholic to sit on the 1988 Court. Still, although Kennedy was prominent in Catholic circles in his home state of California, there is no evidence indicating that his religious affiliation played any part in Reagan's decision to nominate him. In fact, the considerations for placing him on the Supreme Court can only be understood within the context of the failed Bork nomination.

Judge Bork's perceived ideology was the key factor leading to his devastating fifty-eight to forty-two rejection at the hands of the Senate.[141] Senator Edward M. Kennedy, in his harangue on the floor of the upper chamber, fired the opening salvo in the battle against Bork's record on abortion and civil and criminal rights. In a fit of exaggeration, Senator Kennedy declared: "Robert Bork's America is a land in which women would be forced into back alley abortion, blacks would sit at segregated lunch counters, and rogue policemen could break down citizens' doors in midnight raids."[142] Despite the distorted nature of Kennedy's prediction, his words became a rallying point for liberal interest groups, like "People for the American Way," in their opposition to Bork. Surprisingly, given his superb background and credentials, Bork was not able to convince a majority of the Senate, the Senate Judiciary Committee, or the American public that his views were part of mainstream conservatism. As the hearing and publicity surrounding them took on an unprecedented vitriolic character, Judge Bork and his nomination sank inextricably into the mire of partisan and ideological politics.

Soon thereafter, in an unprecedented turn of events, President Reagan withdrew his second nomination for Powell's seat, that of Judge Douglas

H. Ginsburg, at the nominee's request, amid controversy over his past use of marijuana and other issues.[143] The president wasted no time in announcing his third nominee, Judge Anthony M. Kennedy of the Ninth Circuit Court of Appeals. After a seven-month ordeal to fill the Court's ninth seat, the Senate voted unanimously (97–0) on February 3, 1988, to confirm the Kennedy nomination. At the age of fifty-one, Kennedy became the Court's youngest member.

With the Bork and Ginsburg debacles still fresh in the country's collective memory, Kennedy proved to be the perfect nominee. Born in Sacramento, California, on July 23, 1936, the future justice reportedly had a remarkably trouble-free youth that included regular service as an altar boy at his Roman Catholic parish church. A Phi Beta Kappa graduate of Stanford University, Kennedy attended the London School of Economics before enrolling in Harvard Law School, from which he was graduated cum laude in 1961.

He returned to California to practice law with a San Francisco firm, but he left after two years to take over his father's practice in Sacramento. Described by associates as "intellectual," Kennedy apparently disliked the flesh-pressing required of lobbying work in the state capital. Nevertheless, he was involved in California politics behind the scenes. Notably, he drafted Governor Ronald Reagan's tax-limitation initiative known as Proposition 1. Kennedy's expertise prompted Reagan to recommend him to President Gerald Ford, who appointed Kennedy to the U.S. Court of Appeals for the Ninth Circuit in 1975.[144]

Significantly for the ideological fallout over the abortive Bork nomination, Kennedy was described as a moderate conservative cast in the Gerald Ford, rather than Barry Goldwater, mold. Liberals were quick to label Kennedy "open-minded" in contrast to the "reactionary" Bork.[145] Yet the more accurate picture of Kennedy's ideology in contrast to Bork's was not that it was less conservative but that it was less readily identifiable. The 430 opinions that Kennedy had drafted in his tenure on the Ninth Circuit did not reveal a clear jurisprudential posture on such controversial issues as civil rights, women's rights, and the issue that was Bork's downfall, the right to privacy. This absence of political identity prompted one observer to write soon after Kennedy's confirmation: "Kennedy's has been a low-profile career marked by few forays into the marketplace of ideas."[146] Unlike Bork's academic penchant for writing and speaking, Kennedy had left "no paper trail of law review articles and speeches."[147]

Thus, Kennedy's personal integrity, his judicial experience, and his less identifiable ideology made him the perfect candidate to fill Justice Powell's "swing" seat on the Court after the controversy surrounding the Bork and Ginsburg nominations. Although Kennedy's religious affiliation played no apparent role in his selection, the Catholic press took note of the current status of his religion. His pastor described Kennedy's faith as "strong" and "deep" and the key to his maintaining his equilibrium when his father died suddenly in 1963, and later, when his only brother, his only sister, and his mother died in quick succession in 1980 and 1981.[148]

Despite the Catholic press's understandable preoccupation with Kennedy's religious credentials, the secular media paid little, if any, attention to the new and unprecedented trio of Roman Catholics on the Court. For purposes of tracing the rise and fall of the Supreme Court's "Catholic seat," that fact is significant. In effect, it signaled the demise of the "Catholic seat" as a relevant consideration in presidential decisions to select Supreme Court nominees.[149]

SUMMING UP THE "CATHOLIC SEAT"

Of course, in none of the eight Catholic appointments (nine counting White's promotion to chief justice) was religion the *overriding* factor in the president's selection. Nevertheless, the above discussion of considerations involved in the nomination of Catholics to the Supreme Court demonstrates the evolution of Catholicism from a coincidental factor or actual handicap to be overcome (Taney and White's first appointment), to what I label an "over-the-top" consideration (McKenna and White's promotion), to an explicit concern of advisers to the president (Butler), to its high point as one of the president's top two or three concerns (Murphy). The gap between Murphy's and Brennan's tenures on the Court, and the lessening emphasis on the latter's religion, weakened the tradition of the "Catholic seat." More recently, Scalia's Catholicism was arguably not an unwelcome characteristic for President Reagan and his advisers to consider, but it is apparent that his ideology, jurisprudence, age, and even ethnic ties were all more decisive factors in his selection. Finally, Kennedy's appointment has brought Catholic religious affiliation full circle to its previous status as a purely coincidental factor in nominations to the Supreme Court.

The "Catholic seat," even at its zenith, when it was occupied by Justice Murphy, has never been "representative" beyond the descriptive sense.[150] In fact, Catholics on the Court have exhibited an exaggerated degree of religious impartiality[151] (as did President Kennedy in the White House)—perhaps, in part, as a defense mechanism against the charges of nativists and anti-Catholic bigots. Moreover, Catholic religious affiliation has provided virtually no reliable clue to a future justice's jurisprudence. Catholics on the Court have ranged from the doctrinaire member of the conservative "Four Horsemen," Pierce Butler, to the equally doctrinaire New Dealer and civil libertarian, Frank Murphy. Similarly, the three Catholics who served together on the Court from 1988 until Justice Brennan's retirement in the summer of 1990 occupied divergent positions on the ideological/jurisprudential spectrum, with Justice Brennan leading the dwindling liberal wing and Justices Scalia and Kennedy settling into the increasingly influential conservative faction. The range of ideologies portrayed by Catholic justices may reflect what Professor Martin Marty, of the University of Chicago, has referred to as the dualithic, and perhaps multilithic, character of American Roman Catholicism.[152] Despite the lack of predictive value of Catholic affiliation for *judicial* behavior, this retrospective on Catholic appointments to the Supreme Court has provided insight into *presidential* behavior in selecting Supreme Court justices, and it has identified and elucidated the demonstrable link between considerations of Catholicism as a selection factor and American Catholic historical and political development. The pattern observed in a close examination of the "Catholic seat" serves as a framework for the study of other "representative" factors in judicial selection.

NOTES

1. See Appendix 2 for a list of all Roman Catholic and Jewish justices who have served on the Supreme Court. James F. Byrnes, who was appointed to the Court in 1941 by Franklin Roosevelt and who served for just one year, was born and raised a Roman Catholic and attended parochial schools in Charleston, South Carolina. As a young man however, Byrnes converted to Episcopalianism. Some have suggested he did so to enhance his political career in the South, which often was less than supportive of Roman Catholic candidates. See Walter F. Murphy, "James Byrnes," in Leon Friedman and Fred L. Israel, eds., *The Justices of the United States Supreme Court, 1789–1969*, 5 vols. (New York: Chelsea House, 1969), Vol. 4, pp. 2517–40. Whatever Byrnes's motivation, his conversion leaves the number of Catholic justices who have served on the Court at eight and places Byrnes in the most often "represented" religion on the Court—Episcopalianism. To date twenty-eight Episcopalian justices have served on the nation's highest bench. See Henry J. Abraham, *Justices and Presidents: A Political History of Appointments to the Supreme Court*, 2d. ed. (New York: Oxford University Press, 1985), p. 63, for a statistical breakdown of the religious affiliations of the justices at the time of their respective appointments.

2. New economic developments included the decline of the shipping trade, the tariff of abominations in 1838, and the increased competition for jobs. John Tracy Ellis, *American Catholicism*, 2d ed. (Chicago: The University of Chicago Press, 1969), p. 63.

3. Theodore Maynard, *The Story of American Catholicism* (New York: Macmillan, 1942), p. 282.

4. Samuel Tyler, *Memoir of Roger Brooke Taney: Chief Justice of the Supreme Court of the United States* (Baltimore: John Murphy, 1872), Ch. 1.

5. Carl B. Swisher, *Roger B. Taney* (New York: Macmillan, 1935), p. 8.

6. Ibid., pp. 50–51.

7. John Schmidhauser, "The Justices of the Supreme Court: A Collective Portrait," 3 *Midwest Journal of Political Science* (February 1959): 1–57; *The Supreme Court: Its Politics, Personalities, and Procedures* (New York: Holt, Rinehart and Winston, 1960), pp. 30–62; *Judges and Justices: The Federal Appellate Judiciary* (Boston: Little, Brown, 1979), pp. 41–101.

8. Tyler, *Memoir of Roger Brooke Taney*, p. 167.

9. Swisher, *Roger B. Taney*, p. 140.

10. Tyler, *Memoir of Roger Brooke Taney*, pp. 190–91, 221, 233.

11. Ibid, pp. 239–40.

12. Robert V. Remini, *Andrew Jackson and the Course of American Democracy, 1833–1845*, Vol. 3 (New York: Harper & Row, 1984), p. 267.

13. Ibid, p. 628.

14. Swisher, *Roger B. Taney*, p. 317.

15. *New York Herald*, March 18, 1836, p. 1.

16. For a complete account of this and other bizarre anti-Catholic literature see Ray Allen Billington, *The Protestant Crusade, 1800–1860: A Study of the Origins of American Nativism* (New York: Rinehart, 1938), Ch. 4.

17. Lawrence Fuchs, *John F. Kennedy and American Catholicism* (New York: Meredith Press, 1967), pp. 58–59.

18. Robert B. Highsaw, *Edward Douglass White: Defender of the Conservative Faith* (Baton Rouge: Louisiana State University Press, 1981,) pp. 13, 16.

19. Sister Marie Carolyn Klinkhamer, O.P., *Edward Douglas White, Chief Justice of the United States* (Washington, D.C.: The Catholic University of America Press, 1943), p. 11.

20. See Highsaw, *Edward Douglass White*, pp. 51–55.

21. *New York Herald*, February 20, 1894, p. 5.

22. *New York Times*, February 20, 1894, p. 5.

23. Allan Nevins, *Grover Cleveland: A Study in Courage* (New York: Dodd, Mead, 1933), p. 547.

24. Klinkhamer, *Edward Douglas White*, p. 37.

25. Highsaw, *Edward Douglass White*, pp. 53–54.

26. *New York Times*, February 20, 1894, p. 5.

27. Bliss Perry, *And Gladly Teach* (Boston: Houghton Mifflin, 1935), pp. 146–47.

28. *New York Times*, February 20, 1894, p. 5.

29. *Catholic Review*, as quoted by Highsaw, *Edward Douglass White*, p. 56.

30. Robert D. Cross, *The Emergence of Liberal Catholicism in America* (Cambridge, Mass.: Harvard University Press, 1958), p. 35.

31. Gerald Shaughnessy, S.M., *Has the Immigrant Kept the Faith?* (New York: Macmillan, 1925), pp. 166, 172. Shaughnessy has provided the most reliable statistics on Catholic population and immigration between 1820 and 1920.

32. Fuchs, *John F. Kennedy and American Catholicism*, pp. 116–17.

33. Cross, *The Emergence of Liberal Catholicism*, p. 104. Donald L. Kinzer, in *An Episode in Anti-Catholicism: The American Protective Association* (Seattle: University of Washington Press, 1964), told a detailed story of the APA and its intraassociational squabbles over which candidates to endorse. And Margaret Leech, in her book, *In the Days of McKinley* (New York: Harper & Brothers, 1959), explained that McKinley's passivity prevailed even when some sections of the

APA turned on him with anti-Catholic propaganda—despite the fact that he was a devout Methodist.

34. Cross, *The Emergence of Liberal Catholicism*, p. 105.

35. Brother Matthew McDevitt, *Joseph McKenna: Associate Justice of the United States* (Washington, D.C.: The Catholic University of America Press, 1946), pp. 1–4.

36. Ibid, pp. 4–13, 20–21.

37. Ibid, pp. 41, 60, 78.

38. For a recapitulation of this episode, including the quotations contained in the following paragraph, see H. H. Kohlsaat, *From McKinley to Harding: Personal Recollections of Our Presidents* (New York: Charles Scribner's Sons, 1923), pp. 18–20.

39. Ibid., pp. 59–61.

40. Leech, *In the Days of McKinley*, p. 106.

41. Kohlsaat, *From McKinley to Harding*, pp. 59–61.

42. See, for example, Cross, *The Emergence of Liberal Catholicism*, p. 105.

43. *New York Times*, July 25, 1897, p. 8.

44. *New York Times*, October, 14, 1897, p. 1.

45. Abraham, *Justices and Presidents*, p. 153.

46. McDevitt, *Joseph McKenna*, p. 104.

47. *New York Times*, December 7, 1897, p. 7.

48. *New York Times*, December 17, 1897, p. 3.

49. Ibid.

50. Ibid.

51. *New York Times*, January 12, 1898, p. 3.

52. *New York Times*, January 15, 1898, p. 4.

53. Ibid.

54. *New York Times*, January 22, 1898, p. 4. For the record of the voice vote on confirmation, see 31 *Congressional Record* 824 (1898).

55. Supreme Court insiders had also not anticipated the action. Justice Holmes had written: "As to the Chief Justice . . . he will appoint Hughes . . . I think White the ablest man likely to be thought of. I don't know whether his being a Catholic will interfere . . . I am too old. . . I am afraid White has as little chance as I." Quoted in Highsaw, *Edward Douglass White*, p. 58.

56. For one of the more interesting explanations, see Highsaw, *Edward Douglass White*, p. 58, concluding that Taft may have been influenced by the fact that both were "huge men of considerable girth who looked like they ought to be judges even if one of them was not."

57. Ibid, p. 57.

58. Judith Icke Anderson, *William Howard Taft: An Intimate History* (New York: W. W. Norton, 1981), p. 192.

59. Ibid.

60. Letter from Taft to Walter Lenoir Church, July 10, 1924, as quoted by Alpheus T. Mason in *William Howard Taft: Chief Justice* (New York: Simon and Schuster, 1965), p. 40.

61. Anderson, *William Howard Taft*, p. 192.

62. See Klinkhamer, *Edward Douglas White*, p. 55, for suggestions that Taft actually lost votes in the 1912 Pennsylvania primary in part because of his "concessions" to the Catholic Church.

63. Shaughnessy, *Has the Immigrant Kept the Faith?*, p. 190.

64. Archie Butt, *Taft and Roosevelt: The Intimate Letters of Archie Butt, Military Aide*, Vol. 2 (Garden City, N.Y.: Doubleday, Doran, 1930), p. 757.

65. Shaughnessy, *Has the Immigrant Kept the Faith?*, p. 190.

66. Ellis, *American Catholicism*, p. 139.

67. As quoted by James Hennesey, S.J., in *American Catholics: A History of the Roman Catholic Community in the United States* (New York: Oxford University Press, 1981), p. 237.

68. Noteworthy among these friends were Archbishop John Ireland of St. Paul, Bishop John P. Carroll of Helena, and Bishop William Turner of Buffalo. David J. Danelski, *A Supreme Court Justice Is Appointed* (New York: Random House, 1964), Ch. 1.

69. Taft and Wickersham were quoted by Mason, *William Howard Taft*, p. 169.

70. Ibid., pp. 163–68.

71. Danelski, *A Supreme Court Justice Is Appointed*, pp. 43–52.

72. Ibid., pp. 53–89.

73. *New York Times*, December 22, 1922, p. 11.

74. Progressive Republicans voting against the Butler nomination included Senators Robert M. LaFollete (Wis.), George W. Norris (Neb.), and Peter Worbok (S.D.). *New York Times*, December 22, 1922, p. 11.

75. The Democrats who voted against Butler were Senators William Harris (Ga.), James Hefflin (Ala.), Morris Sheppard (Tex.), Park Trammel (Fla.), and Walter George (Ga.). *New York Times*, December 22, 1922, p. 11.

76. *New York Times*, December 23, 1922, p. 12.

77. Danelski, *A Supreme Court Justice Is Appointed*, p. 91.

78. Schmidhauser, *The Supreme Court*, p. 40.

79. John Cogley, *Catholic America* (New York: The Dial Press, 1973), pp. 89–91.

80. As quoted by Fuchs, *John F. Kennedy and American Catholicism*, p. 140.

81. Hennesey, *American Catholics*, pp. 252–53.

82. George Q. Flynn, *American Catholics and the Roosevelt Presidency, 1932–1936* (Lexington: University of Kentucky Press, 1968), Ch. 1.

83. Ibid., p. ix.

84. Flynn, *American Catholics and the Roosevelt Presidency*, pp. 50–51.

85. Leo V. Kanawada, Jr., *Franklin D. Roosevelt's Diplomacy and American Catholics, Italians, and Jews* (Ann Arbor, Mich.: UMI Research Press, 1982), p. 47.

86. Flynn, *American Catholics and the Roosevelt Presidency*, p. 233.

87. Sydney Fine, *Frank Murphy: The Detroit Years*, Vol. 1 (Ann Arbor: The University of Michigan Press, 1975), pp. 4–12; Quotation at p. 286 of *Frank Murphy: The New Deal Years*, Vol. 2 (Chicago: The University of Chicago Press, 1979).

88. Fine, *Frank Murphy*, Vol. 1, pp. 110, 117.

89. Ibid, p. 454.

90. Ibid, p. 442.

91. Ibid., pp. 446–50.

92. Ibid., p. 450.

93. Walsh died en route to the inauguration and Roosevelt turned to Homer Cummings to fill the vacancy. Ibid., pp. 450–51.

94. Fine, *Frank Murphy*, Vol 2, p. 31.

95. Ibid., pp. 225–28, 250–53.

96. Ibid., pp. 509–10.

97. Ibid., p. 527.

98. Ibid.

99. Harold L. Ickes, *The Secret Diary of Harold L. Ickes*, Vol. 2 (New York: Simon and Schuster, 1954), pp. 423, 505, 510.

100. Ickes's diary gave a blow-by-blow account of the complex personnel maneuvers in the Roosevelt administration in which F.D.R. was trying to juggle positions so that Murphy would ultimately become secretary of war and Robert Jackson would be named attorney general.

101. *New York Times*, January 2, 1939, p. 17.

102. Sidney Fine, *Frank Murphy: The Washington Years*, Vol. 3 (Ann Arbor: The University of Michigan Press, 1984), p. 130.

103. *New York Times*, November 17, 1939, p. 1.

104. J. Woodford Howard, Jr., *Mr. Justice Murphy: A Political Biography* (Princeton, N.J.: Princeton University Press, 1968), p. 444 (emphasis added).

105. Ibid., p. 215. See also Ickes, *Diary*, Vols. 2 and 3.

106. Fine, *Frank Murphy*, Vol. 3, p. 131.

107. Richard D. Lunt, *The High Ministry of Government: The Political Career of Frank Murphy* (Detroit: Wayne State University Press, 1965), p. 216.

108. Fine, *Frank Murphy*, Vol. 3, p. 138.

109. Quoted in Abraham, *Justices and Presidents*, p. 64.

110. Daniel F. Cleary, "Catholics and Politics," in *Catholicism in America* (New York: Harcourt, Brace, 1953), pp. 101–02 (emphasis added).

111. Fuchs, *John F. Kennedy and American Catholicism*, p. 151.

112. Ibid.

113. *New York Times*, September 8, 1956, p. 1; September 9, 1956, p. 56; September 12, 1956, p. 23; September 30, 1956, p. 1.

114. Personal interview with Justice William J. Brennan, Jr., Washington, D.C., April 1, 1985.

115. Ibid.

116. Donna Haupt, "Justice William J. Brennan, Jr." *Constitution* (Winter 1989): 53.

117. *New York Times*, September 30, 1956, p. 76; October 1, 1956, p. 19.

118. Brennan interview.

119. *New York Times*, October 1, 1956, p. 19.

120. Donald M. Morrison, "Apostle of Justice," *Pennsylvania Gazette*, October 1977, p. 18.

121. Brennan interview.

122. Ibid.

123. Cleary, "Catholics and Politics," p. 97.

124. *New York Times*, October 2, 1956, p. 2.

125. Brennan has noted that he has not *actively* represented American Roman Catholics and acknowledges, "I have been a disappointment to some Roman Catholics. Father Andrew Greeley wrote a piece in which he said that if the Roman Catholics who played a role in the Brennan selection had any idea he would turn out the way he did, he would never have been appointed." Jeffrey T. Leeds, "A Life on the Court," *New York Times Magazine*, October 5, 1986, p. 79.

126. For such an interpretation, see generally Ellis, *American Catholicism*; Hennesey, *American Catholics*; Cogley, *Catholic America*; and Fuchs, *John F. Kennedy and American Catholicism*. Professor Martin Marty of the University of Chicago has argued that Kennedy's 1960 victory was a symbol of complete transition for Catholics but that their "mainstreaming" into the general population began with their use of the G.I. Bill after World War II. The concomitant increase in the levels of education and movement to the suburbs made them full participants in American society and politics. Martin Marty, Lecture at Rollins College, Winter Park, Florida, September 22, 1988. Recent survey data support Marty's thesis. See George Gallup, Jr. and Jim Castelli, *The American Catholic People: Their Beliefs, Practices, and Values* (Garden City, N.Y.: Doubleday, 1987). For the most textured treatment of the issue of assimilation of Catholics, both on an individual and group level, see Philip Gleason, *Keeping the Faith: American Catholicism Past and Present* (Notre Dame, Ind.: University of Notre Dame Press, 1987).

127. Fuchs, *John F. Kennedy and American Catholicism*, p. 229.

128. Hennesey, *American Catholics*, pp. 308–9.

129. See *New York Times*, June 18, 1986, p. 31; *Washington Post*, June 18, 1986, p. 15; *Chicago Tribune*, June 18, 1986, p. 1; *Time*, June 30, 1986, p. 24.

130. *Time*, June 30, 1986, p. 26.

131. *New York Times*, June 18, 1986, p. 32.

132. Interview with Justice Antonin Scalia, Washington, D.C., March 18, 1987.

133. *New York Times*, June 18, 1986, p. 31.

134. *Time*, June 30, 1986, p. 30.

135. Ibid.

136. *The New Republic*, June 10, 1985, p. 26. Academic observers had commented similarly about Scalia's positive attributes. See Jeffrey Segal and Harold Spaeth, "If A Supreme Court Vacancy Occurs, Will the Senate Confirm a Reagan Nominee?" 69 *Judicature* 4 (1986): 186–90.

137. *Time*, June 30, 1986, p. 28.

138. *New York Times*, June 18, 1986, p. 32.

139. Ibid., p. 30.

140. *The Florida Catholic*, September 26, 1986, p. 1.

141. See Ethan Bronner's *Battle for Justice: How the Bork Nomination Shook America* (New York: Norton, 1989), for an intriguing and balanced account of this judicial selection drama.

142. As quoted in ibid., p. 98.

143. See Chapter 3.

144. *1988 Current Biography Yearbook*, p. 290.

145. David P. Bryden, "How to Select a Supreme Court Justice: The Case of the Bork Nomination," *American Scholar* (1988): 216.

146. Charles F. Williams, "The Opinions of Anthony Kennedy: No Time for Ideology," *American Bar Association Journal* (March 1988): 61.

147. Ibid.

148. *The Louisville Record*, November 19, 1987, p. 6.

149. The clear irrelevancy of Roman Catholic church affiliation for the appointment of the third Catholic to the Court should be contrasted to President Lyndon Johnson's refusal to consider his friend William Campbell, the senior federal

district court judge for Chicago, for a seat on the Supreme Court in the 1960s. When Senator Everett Dirksen (R.–Ill.) suggested Campbell's name to the president, L.B.J. initially responded, "Great idea." Then on second thought, he observed, referring to Justice Brennan, "Of course Bill's Catholic." Johnson concluded, "I don't think I'd like to disturb the religious balance on the Court, and I'm afraid I couldn't take him [Campbell]." See Bruce Allen Murphy, *Fortas: The Rise and Ruin of a Supreme Court Justice* (New York: William Morrow, 1988), p. 282. Judge Campbell, who was the youngest federal judge ever to be appointed when Franklin Roosevelt named him to the district court in 1940, was interviewed about the Johnson anecdote in 1986. At age 80, he was still sitting on the district court (in West Palm Beach, Florida) and had become the longest-serving federal judge in the nation. Johnson's response to a possible Supreme Court nomination for Campbell, as related to the judge by Dirksen, was more bigoted in tone. Dirksen reported that L.B.J. had argued, "I've got one of them [a Catholic]. That's enough." *Miami Herald*, March 17, 1986, p. 3C.

150. See Chapter 1.

151. For an analysis of Catholic justices' votes on church-state cases up to 1960, see Harold Chase et al., "Catholics on the Court," *The New Republic*, September 26, 1960, p. 13. The article concluded that "the ideas of the Catholic Justices as a group are not distinguishable from the ideas of non-Catholics." The study's findings confirmed Senator John F. Kennedy's assertion during the 1960 presidential campaign that no Catholic justice "was ever challenged on the fairness of his rulings on sensitive church-state relations." Ibid.

152. Marty, Rollins College lecture.

Chapter 3 _____

Religion: A "Jewish Seat"?

This chapter examines the five appointments of Jewish justices to the United States Supreme Court in light of the questions raised in Chapter 2 regarding religious "representation."[1] A definitional query that does not arise in discussions of Catholicism, however, must be explored at the outset—namely, what is the proper anthropological or sociological label for Judaism? The question is particularly pertinent to the initial appointments of Jews to the Court when references to Judaism as a "race" were prevalent. In a book on Jewish political behavior in America, Stephen D. Isaacs observed and delineated the varied perceptions of Judaism: "Some people consider Jewry strictly as a religion. Some consider it a race. Others view Jews as members of an ethnic group. Still others consider Jewry a 'religious civilization.' " Isaacs concluded that "America's Jews . . . [are] a unique blend of Jewish religion and Jewish and American history and tradition; in short, . . . an ethnoreligious culture." Most important for my study of presidential overtures and responses to American Jews as a group, Isaacs accepted as a "fact that those in politics—Jews and non-Jews—. . . treat them as a bloc in their planning of strategy, campaign literature, speeches, pleas for contributions, polls, and judgments."[2]

AMERICAN JEWISH HISTORY

Like American Catholic history, the story of American Jewry is inextricably tied to the history of Jewish immigration to the United States, which is divisible into three distinct waves: the Sephardic immigration during the colonial period, the influx of German Jews in the nineteenth century, and the wave of Russian and East European Jewry, which immigrated to the United States in the late nineteenth and early twentieth centuries.

Once in the New World, immigrant Jews faced the same types of discrimination directed at Catholics and some Protestant sectarians.[3] Like anti-Catholic prejudices, anti-Jewish attitudes were transplanted from "the old country" but in a particularly virulent variety, which combined centuries-old religious biases against Jews with seventeenth- and eighteenth-century hatreds that stemmed from European "economic and social pressures of urbanization and the growth of the national states."[4]

The first two decades of the new American nation saw the Jewish population increase from less than 2,000 to just under 3,000. During the next thirty years, from 1820 to 1850, the Jewish population swelled to nearly 50,000—a seventeenfold increase. The general population had multiplied two and one-half times during that same period. Because of marriage outside the Jewish faith, attrition was high; immigration alone maintained the astronomical growth rate. Jewish immigrants, particularly from Bavaria, added to the population of their coreligionists in the United States.[5]

The growing Jewish population managed to avoid the severest forms of persecution that it had experienced in other parts of the world. Yet while religious freedom was the law of the land, anti-Jewish "folkways" often intruded into everyday social and political relationships between Jews and Gentiles. Jews were no more immune than Catholics from nineteenth-century nativist charges directed against all "foreign" elements. Still, the legally and constitutionally guaranteed separation of church and state and free exercise of religion provided a basis for Jews to counter *overt* bigotry.[6]

Jewish political allegiance in the early years of the republic tended toward the Jeffersonians and then the Republican-Democrats rather than the Hamiltonians or the Federalists for two reasons: (1) the Jeffersonian support for low tariffs, international trade, and states' rights appealed to Jewish export and maritime interests; and (2) the transformation of the Jewish community from Iberian to German predominance, which, in turn, reflected the social and political liberalism or radicalism of the German immigrants.[7]

In the four decades preceding the Civil War, Jews in the North tended to affiliate with the Democratic party. The flourishing Jewish community in New York City, for example, manifested its influence in local politics by its powerful representation in the Tammany Hall machine. On the national level, the administration of President Martin Van Buren provides an early illustration of an American president possibly responding to Jewish support through policy initiatives. In return for Jewish backing,[8] "or perhaps as a matter of principle," Van Buren responded to vehement Jewish protests against the so-called Damascus ritual murder incident in 1840. The infamous case involved authorities in Damascus falsely accusing seven Jews of kidnapping two Christians allegedly for purposes of consuming the murdered captives' blood as part of the Passover ritual. Ottoman officials arrested several rabbis and sixty-four children, several of whom died under torture. Others of those falsely arrested converted to the Muslim faith under threats and many of the rest were sentenced to death. Van Buren's Secretary of State John Forsyth issued a forceful order to the American minister to the Ottoman Empire to prevail upon the sultan to cease the injustices perpetrated against the Jews in his empire.[9]

Prior to the Civil War, two Jewish politicians rose to prominence in electoral politics. David Levy Yulee became the first Jewish member of the United States Senate, when Florida entered the Union in 1845 and chose him to represent it.[10] The second member of the Jewish faith to be elected to the United States Senate was a much more colorful and politically successful figure—Judah Philip Benjamin.[11] Descended from Sephardic Jews, who had been expelled from Spain, Benjamin's father was a lowly fishmonger in England before immigrating to South America. Like his senatorial predecessor, Judah Benjamin was born in the West Indies and made his way to the United States. He attended Yale and there displayed his keen intellect, but he was expelled without a degree and under a cloud of suspicion. He eventually migrated to New Orleans, where he married into a prominent Creole Catholic family and established a thriving legal practice and sugar plantation. In 1852 Benjamin was elected to the United States Senate from Louisiana and served in that office until the war began and his adopted state seceded from the Union. Subsequently, he held several positions in the Confederate cabinet—the first Jew to serve in an executive cabinet in this country.[12]

Scholars have commented that both Benjamin and Yulee had disassociated themselves from the Jewish community before embarking on their respective political careers[13] (although no historian has implied a causal connection between the two actions). Nonetheless, Benjamin's religious affiliation was well known and often the subject of comments and taunts in the political world. "An Israelite with Egyptian principles," "that Jew from Louisiana," and "Judas Iscariot" were some of the anti-Semitic epithets hurled at Benjamin by his political enemies.[14]

Several sources refer to an alleged offer of a Supreme Court nomination that Benjamin may have received from President Millard Fillmore in 1852;[15] but Benjamin, a future Confederate, reportedly declined, perhaps preferring the activity of the partisan political arena, where he could advocate the South's proslavery interests. A. L. Todd's definitive and award-winning work on the appointment of Louis D. Brandeis to the

Court concluded, however: "My own research [which was extensive] . . . has led me to believe there is no primary evidence to document this story." Todd thought the veracity of the report was only important for determining historical firsts—that is, whether to consider Benjamin or Brandeis the first Jew to be picked for a seat on the nation's highest court.[16] Yet the question may reach beyond the realm of Supreme Court trivia. If the Benjamin nomination story is true, it might indicate a presidential awareness of Jewish interests in making Supreme Court appointments a full sixty-four years before the successful appointment of the first Jew to the Court in 1916. Unfortunately, Benjamin himself offered no clues: he burned his personal papers, some before he fled from the advancing Union Army in 1865 and the rest before his death in 1884.[17]

The second wave of Jewish immigration to this country (primarily from Germany) increased the Jewish population in the United States a hundredfold between 1800 and 1880. An 1877 Jewish population survey conducted by the Board of Delegates of American Israelites placed the number of American Jews at 230,257. Germans of all faiths constituted the single largest immigrant group in the United States in the nineteenth century, which made assimilation for the German Jew easier in this country. The postwar economic boom in the United States raised the standard of living for American Jewry and brought with it a concomitant increase in the influence of the Jewish community.[18]

While the total U.S. population more than doubled between 1880 and 1925 (from 50 million to 115 million), the population of Jews in the United States witnessed a sixteenfold increase owing to the emigration of an astounding one-third of East European Jewry from "the old country" to the United States. In 1880, American Jews numbered 250,000. By the turn of the century, that figure had increased to 1 million and then quadrupled to 4 million by 1925. American Jewry had become the largest Jewish population in the world.[19]

The geographic and demographic concentration of Jews in the United States corresponded directly with the amount of coherence and influence displayed by the Jewish community. By the end of the first quarter of the twentieth century, over 40 percent of America's Jews had congregated in the greater New York area and more than 80 percent were living in just six states: New York, Pennsylvania, Illinois, Massachusetts, New Jersey, and Ohio. "Such concentration made possible the rapid establishment of Jewish institutions, the proliferation of organizations and some degree of political presence, if not power."[20]

The dawn of the twentieth century coincided with some instances of early recognition of a "Jewish vote." For example, in late October 1899, Yiddish handbills signed by "Jewish Members of the Republican State Committee" were distributed throughout New York City's Lower East Side and urged Jews to vote for Theodore Roosevelt for governor of New

York. Historian Abraham J. Karp perceptively analyzed the symbolic importance of this seemingly incidental political action:

To the immigrant Jew, the campaign handbill said many things. In this country, each male Jewish citizen had something of great value, *his vote. Those in power valued and wanted it.* Not only the neighborhood Tammany lackey sought it, but so, too did the patrician Republican State Committee.

This appeal for his vote suggested to him that it was legitimate to vote one's own ethnic self-interests. The citizen in America had the right to determine not only for whom to cast his ballot, but also for what reasons. If Jewish pride was important to him, it was proper to permit it to determine his choice. The immigrant community might well conclude that its integration into the American social and cultural fabric would be permitted in accordance with its own perceptions of America and in response to its own particular needs.[21]

Several Jews rose to political prominence on the national scene at this time. One of them, Oscar Solomon Straus, was appointed by President Grover Cleveland in 1887 to be envoy extraordinary and minister plenipotentiary to Turkey. Straus's religion was apparently a key consideration, for Cleveland intended his appointment of Straus to be an indirect reaction to Austria-Hungary's refusal to accept as minister an American appointee whose wife happened to be Jewish. In 1906, President Theodore Roosevelt named Straus to be his secretary of commerce and labor. Straus thus had the distinction of being the first Jew to serve in a U.S. president's cabinet. Again, Straus's religious affiliation was not lost on the appointing president. T.R. supposedly told his new secretary of commerce and labor: "I want to show Russia and some other countries what we think of the Jews in this country." Straus set several precedents for his coreligionists. Two other Jews, Henry Morgenthau, Sr., and Abram I. Elkus, eventually served as ambassadors to Turkey; and Morgenthau's son, Henry Jr., served as President Franklin D. Roosevelt's secretary of the treasury. These governmental posts were not the nation's most powerful, but enough anti-Semitism existed in this country to bar many of the most influential offices to all but members of the WASP (White Anglo-Saxon Protestant) establishment.[22]

THE RISE OF AMERICAN ANTI-SEMITISM

Like the rise of anti-Catholic movements during periods of intense immigration of Catholics to the United States, the overwhelming numbers of East European Jews who made their pilgrimage to this country provoked a new wave and new variety of anti-Jewish bias in their new home. Jews in colonial America had faced a primarily *political* form of prejudice directed at their rights to vote and hold public office. In the last third of the nineteenth century, however, anti-Semitism was manifested in the *social* ostracism of American Jews.[23]

One of the most famous incidents marking the transition to the new variety of anti-Semitism occurred in 1877, when Joseph Seligman, prominent businessman, public servant, and leading layman in the Jewish community, was refused accommodations by the Grand Union Hotel in Saratoga, New York. In refusing Seligman's registration, the hotel manager informed him that "no Israelite shall be permitted in the future to stop in the hotel."[24]

The decade after Seligman's humiliation witnessed the exclusion of Jewish students from New York City's private schools, and advertisements for summer camps and hotels announced that Jewish patrons were not welcome.[25] In some cases, this religious segregation persisted until the post–World War II era.[26] Significantly, the ostracism of Jews from some educational institutions, particularly in the East, did not stifle Jewish immigrants' desires for education. The Immigration Commission conducted a survey in 1908 of 77 institutions of higher learning and discovered that 8.5 percent of the students were first- or second-generation American Jews and that 18 percent of pharmacy students and 13 percent of law students were Jewish. At the time, Jews comprised approximately 2 percent of the American population.[27] Unfortunately, such statistics resulted in the imposition of quotas after World War I on Jewish students and faculty members at some of this country's most prestigious universities.

An even more horrific incident of anti-Jewish activity occurred in the years preceding the U.S.'s entry into World War I. The Leo Frank case[28] conjures up scenes from Charles McArthur's play *The Front Page*—without the humorous results. From all reports, Leo Frank was a mild-mannered young man of German-Jewish heritage, who had received an engineering degree from Cornell and then moved to Atlanta to become manager of the National Pencil Company factory. He married a local Jewish woman and was elected president of the Atlanta chapter of B'nai B'rith, in recognition of his intellectualism, his university education, his Germanic roots, and his cosmopolitan background. All of these characteristics gave him a distinct edge over the majority of southern Jews, who tended to be provincial, lower-middle-class merchants, salesmen, brokers, and manufacturers.

On May 26, 1913, Leo Frank's rather charmed life was changed irreparably by the murder of a teen-aged female employee of the pencil factory, whose body was discovered in the factory's cellar. A Georgia jury convicted Frank and sentenced him to hang on the basis of circumstantial evidence and false testimony from a black ex-convict.

Frank took his appeal to the United States Supreme Court, but his cause was denied. Justice Oliver Wendell Holmes wrote a courageous dissent, in which he was joined by Justice Charles Evans Hughes. Holmes eloquently pleaded: "Mob law does not become due process of law by securing the assent of a terrorized jury. We are not speaking of mere disorder, or mere irregularities in procedure, but of a case where the processes of justice are actually subverted."[29]

The governor of Georgia, John M. Slaton, was persuaded and commuted Frank's sentence to life in prison on June 21, 1915. But two months later, mob rule prevailed when a group of vigilantes stormed the prison facility, where Frank was serving his sentence, and kidnapped him. The mob drove him to a remote area and lynched him. Several years later, the black ex-convict, who had testified against Frank, confessed to the murder of the young factory worker.[30]

LOUIS D. BRANDEIS

Like the appointment of the first Roman Catholic to sit on the United States Supreme Court, which occurred in the midst of a vehement anti-Catholic campaign (marked by the Maria Monk propaganda[31]), the nomination of the first Jew to ascend the nation's highest tribunal came just four months after the tragic denouement of the Leo Frank case. Unlike in Roger B. Taney's appointment, however, Louis D. Brandeis's religious affiliation was an issue from start to finish in the bitter fight to place him on the Court.

Ironically, Brandeis's Judaism was a more salient feature of his public life than of his private affairs. Brandeis's parents were part of the great wave of German-Jewish immigrants who made their way to the United States in the middle of the nineteenth century. The elder Brandeises first settled in Cincinnati and then migrated a hundred miles down the Ohio River to establish their residence in Louisville, which, like the Queen City, had a thriving Jewish community in the decades prior to the Civil War. The future justice was born in Louisville in 1856 and distinguished himself academically in the public schools there. He left his native city as a teenager, when his family returned temporarily to Germany, and eventually settled in Boston after attending Harvard Law School.

Unlike the parents of many of the Catholic justices, who instilled in their children a strong religious faith, the Brandeises avoided religious indoctrination in raising their four children. As a commentator on Jewish political thought in America, David S. Berlin, has written:

The Brandeis home was devoid of formal religion or self-conscious ethnicity. In fact, references in Brandeis's letters indicate that the German heritage was apparently as important as the Jewish in his early years. . . . Neither a practicing Jew nor a man with strong ties to his ethnic brethren, Brandeis came to Jewish identification late in life, mainly through Zionism. In spite of his leadership in the Zionist movement, the source of his interest seemed to originate outside the world of Jews and Judaism. In the controversy surrounding his appointment to the Court, his religion and background did become a public issue. Yet the fundamentals of his Jewish identification remained confused, or concealed. In these respects, Brandeis is certainly not an atypical Jewish-American, nor an atypical American. It is precisely his *representativeness* which makes him interesting.[32]

It also makes his appointment to the Supreme Court interesting. The death of Justice Joseph Lamar of Georgia on the second day of the new year, 1916, raised speculation that President Woodrow Wilson would have to fill the Court's "southern seat"—"as if the Court were somehow required to reflect an unchanging geographic balance."[33] But President Wilson's primary criterion for Court selection was the "progressive" credentials of the potential nominee. He had chosen his first nominee, James C. McReynolds, on the mistaken premise that the latter's prosecution of the tobacco trust while attorney general guaranteed his "progressive" bent.[34] Much to Wilson's chagrin, McReynold's became one of the most reactionary justices in the Court's history.

Louis D. Brandeis's progressive political views, however, were far more solid and trustworthy. By Wilson's first election to the White House in 1912, Brandeis had earned a national reputation for fighting legal battles on behalf of the common man (and woman, through his famous "Brandeis Brief" in the 1908 case of *Muller v. Oregon*) and had garnered the sobriquet "the People's Lawyer" for his crusading efforts. Wilson had occasionally consulted with Brandeis before his election to the presidency and had been so impressed with the Boston attorney's brilliance, legal acumen, and progressive ideology that he considered him for a cabinet post in his first administration. Speculation on a position for Brandeis in Wilson's first cabinet centered on the posts of attorney general and secretary of commerce or labor. Massachusetts Democratic party leaders apparently balked at the naming of Brandeis, a nominal Republican, to any of these positions; and Wilson tabled the idea.[35]

When Associate Justice Lamar's seat became vacant, several advisers to Wilson, including Attorney General Thomas W. Gregory, urged Brandeis's nomination. The president needed little prodding; although he had been unsuccessful at placing him in the cabinet, he had turned to Brandeis for advice on domestic legislation regarding the Federal Reserve bill and antitrust laws. Ignoring the precedent and tradition of senatorial courtesy, Wilson sent Louis Brandeis's name to the Senate for its advice and consent on his appointment to the Supreme Court in January 1916, without consulting Massachusetts's two senators.[36]

News of Brandeis's selection landed in the staid United States Senate like a bomb—to borrow the description of the United Press at the time.[37] In his memoirs on the Wilson administration, in which he served as secretary of the navy from 1913 to 1921, Josephus Daniels aptly described the reasons for the incendiary nature of the Brandeis nomination:

[His] appointment was a blow full in the face for the forces of privilege. He was not a conformist. He had fought and defeated the privileged classes and drawn blood. He was a Jew. He was a radical. It would never do for such a man to go on the conservative Supreme Court. The nomination aroused class and purse and racial antagonism of the most bitter character.[38]

The acrimonious controversy surrounding the nomination necessitated a keen strategy from Brandeis and his supporters. During the nearly five-month-long battle to confirm Brandeis, he adhered to his pledge to remain on the sidelines, content to let his trusted law partner, Edward G. McClennen, engineer the nomination proceedings in his behalf. Yet Brandeis was never far removed from the fray. As his nomination became mired in unending charges from opponents, Progressive Senator Robert M. LaFollette, Jr., of Wisconsin, asked Brandeis to draft an anonymous brief countering the objections to his appointment. In *this* "Brandeis Brief" the future justice succinctly summarized the charges to be addressed: "The dominant reasons for the opposition to the confirmation of Mr. Brandeis are that he is considered a radical and is a Jew."[39]

Massachusetts Senator Henry Cabot Lodge, caught between the proverbial rock and hard place in the Brandeis nomination, delineated *three* arguments against Brandeis: his religion, his fitness for service on the Court (the judicial impartiality argument), and election-year politics.[40] Wilson countered such charges in a strategic letter "requested" by Senator Charles A. Culberson, chairman of the Senate Judiciary Committee, after the confirmation hearing had stretched into months of wrangling over Brandeis's fitness. The appointing president waxed eloquent on his nominee's outstanding and meritorious record, calling Brandeis "qualified by learning, by gifts, and by character for the position." Wilson continued:

I cannot speak too highly of his impartial, impersonal, orderly, and constructive mind, his rare analytical powers, his deep human sympathy, his profound acquaintance with the historical roots of our institutions and insight into their spirit, or of the many evidences he has given of being imbued, to the very heart, with our American ideals of justice and equality of opportunity; of his knowledge of modern economic conditions and of the way they bear upon the masses of the people, or of his genius in getting persons to unite in common and harmonious action and look with frank and kindly eyes into each other's minds, who had before been hated antagonists.[41]

Reservations raised about Brandeis's impartiality were undoubtedly thinly disguised objections to his "real politics." Questions regarding

Wilson's election-year politicking were more legitimate, and they have been related to the role of Brandeis's religious affiliation in his appointment. Lodge had been explicit on this point: "For the first time in history a man has been nominated to the Supreme Court with a view to attracting to the President a group of voters on racial grounds."[42]

Virtually all press accounts of Brandeis's selection referred to the fact that he was the first member of his religion to be chosen for the Supreme Court. A small headline on the front page of the *New York Times* read, "First Jew Named for Supreme Court."[43] Another New York paper, the *Sun* (an arch-Republican daily), proclaimed: "He's First Jew Ever Picked for Bench." Unlike the more restrained *Times*, the *Sun* made numerous references to Brandeis's faith. It remarked on Wilson's possible electoral motives in choosing the first Jew to serve on the Court: "The circumstances [Brandeis's religion] would have a decided effect upon the attitude of the hundreds of thousands of Jewish voters in the United States toward President Wilson. This vote in New York is very large and without that state President Wilson would fail of reelection."[44] Ultimately, Wilson's Republican opponent, former Associate Justice Charles Evans Hughes, carried New York (his home state) in the 1916 election; nevertheless, Wilson was victorious in his bid for reelection.[45]

Determining the actual impact of Brandeis's religion on Wilson's popular vote tally is problematic. As illustrated by the 1960 presidential race, a highly visible religious issue in an election can lose, as well as gain, votes for a candidate. Statistics from the 1916 election indicate that Wilson captured 55 percent of the Jewish vote as compared to 45 percent for his opponent, Hughes.[46]

In addition to potential electoral benefits to be gained from Brandeis's religious affiliation, the *New York Sun* theorized that Wilson deliberately chose a Jew because senators would be reluctant to vote against the nomination for fear of being labeled anti-Semitic.[47] Undoubtedly, President Wilson was well-aware of Brandeis's religious faith. At the time Wilson considered the Boston attorney for a cabinet position, objections were raised because "Brandeis was a Jew." The president-elect reportedly responded: "And a fine one!"[48] Another account of Wilson's familiarity with, and appreciation for, Brandeis's religious affiliation reports that Wilson used to refer to the Boston attorney as "Isaiah" because of his obsession with justice. A friend of Wilson allegedly asked the president: "Isn't it a pity that a man as great as Brandeis should be a Jew?" Wilson supposedly replied: "But he would not be Mr. Brandeis if he were not a Jew."[49]

Wilson was also familiar with the religious composition of the Court, which Brandeis would join if confirmed. The Woodrow Wilson papers contain a memo, requested by the president, listing two Catholics (White and McKenna), two Methodists (Day and Van Devanter), one Unitarian

(Holmes), one Baptist (Hughes), one Episcopalian (Pitney), and one member of the Christian Church (McReynolds) on the Court.[50]

Former President William Howard Taft, who, as I have noted, decried the use of religious affiliation as a criterion in Supreme Court appointments,[51] was apoplectic over the role (as he perceived it) of Brandeis's Jewishness in the selection process. In a letter to his close friend, Gus J. Karger, of Cincinnati, Taft described himself as wounded by the Brandeis nomination because, like many other of Brandeis's opponents, Taft believed "the People's Lawyer" totally unsuited by background and temperament to sit on his beloved Supreme Court. Taft believed Wilson's selection was a skilled but devious political move to attract Jewish support to the president's camp. But Taft's most splenetic attack was reserved for the nature of Brandeis's religious conviction. He accused the future justice of deliberately using his Jewishness to win a presidential appointment, after missing his chance for a cabinet post in 1913. According to Taft, Brandeis then willfully determined to become a "representative Jew" by embracing Zionism.[52] The former president wrote: "Brandeis . . . favors the new Jerusalem, and has metaphorically been recircumcised."[53]

For whatever purposes President Wilson intended to recognize American Jewry through his appointment of Brandeis to the high court, the fact is that Jews and Gentiles alike viewed the historic nomination as such a recognition. The *Boston Traveler*, in an editorial published immediately after Brandeis's nomination, wrote: "Mr. Wilson has recognized the Jews of the country."[54] The *Boston Globe* quoted David Lourie, president of the Boston Home for Jewish Children: "The Jews of America will feel highly complimented because one of their race has been chosen for one of the highest offices in the land." And prominent Boston attorney David Stoneman commented for the *Globe*: "He [Brandeis] is a credit to the Jewish people and his appointment is a recognition of them." Even the epitome of the Irish-Catholic pol, former Boston Mayor John F. Fitzgerald, grandfather of John F. Kennedy, told the *Boston Herald*: "Such recognition of the Jewish race, coming, as it does, immediately after the nation had responded so splendidly yesterday to the call for funds to relieve suffering among the Jews abroad is very timely." Some Jews had to overcome their initially lukewarm support for Brandeis based on the perception that he was not a devout Jew or on the fear that his religion would provoke yet another wave of anti-Semitism. Considerations of the potential stature and legitimacy that a successful Brandeis appointment would bestow on the Jewish community eventually outweighed the early reservations.[55]

Finally, on June 1, 1916, more than four months after President Wilson's announcement, the Senate voted to confirm the Brandeis nomination by a vote of 47 to 22. He received the votes of all the Democratic senators except Nevada's Francis G. Newland. Republicans cast the twenty-one other negative votes. George W. Norris of Nebraska, Robert M. LaFollette of Wisconsin, and Miles Poindexter of Washington—all Progressive Republicans—were the only GOP senators to vote in Brandeis's favor. Wilson's gamble had paid off. Brandeis's overwhelmingly meritorious credentials and his progressive, prolabor political stands, all of which had attracted Wilson's attention at least several years earlier, undoubtedly led the president to his historic decision. Yet, Wilson most likely gave careful consideration to the potential benefits and liabilities of Brandeis's Judaism in nominating him to be the first Jewish Supreme Court justice.

The role of religious representation in Brandeis's appointment to the Court might be summarized with a reference to the concept of the "court Jew." Developed in the Middle Ages, the concept referred to "the wealthy notable who [had] special privilege and influence with men of power." It was thought that the court Jew's "individual influence, used discreetly and wisely might protect the interests of the broad mass of Jews."[56] With allowances for modernity and the judicial role, it might be said that Louis Brandeis moved from "court Jew" to "Court Jew" and, thereby, established a "Jewish seat" on the United States Supreme Court.

Justice Brandeis began his distinguished service on the Court in the midst of World War I, which offered new opportunities and challenges to American Jewry. Like their Catholic countrymen, Jews welcomed the chance to prove their patriotism through service to the nation in time of war. The American Jewish community united to aid their European coreligionists, who were direct victims of the conflict across the Atlantic. When the war ended, a majority of American Jewry praised the Balfour Declaration as the first step toward establishing a Jewish homeland in Palestine.

Nevertheless, the newfound hope of American Jews was dashed by yet another wave of anti-Semitism that developed in the United States between the two world wars. The prejudice appeared in a number of varieties and was not confined to the unsophisticated rabble rouser. In 1922, Harvard President Abbott Lawrence Lowell announced an investigation into "the proportion of Jews at the college." In a twisted rationalization, the president and his committee to study the "problem" concluded that Harvard should limit the number of Jewish students admitted in order to decrease the discrimination against them![57]

The worldwide economic depression of the 1920s and 1930s only exacerbated anti-Semitism. The stereotype of the capitalist Jew was resurrected, and a fictional conspiracy of Jewish financiers was said to have caused the economic difficulties. Father Charles Coughlin, the Catholic "radio priest," perpetuated the fictional link between Bolshevism and Jewish conspiracy theories in his popular broadcasts of the 1930s.[58]

Despite the limitations on immigration imposed in this country after World War I, American Jewry increased from 3.5 million to nearly 5 million in the twenty years prior to World War II.[59] The growing number of Jewish voters was on the cutting edge of the great political party realignment of 1936. From the 1924 presidential election on, they voted in increasingly greater proportions for the Democratic candidate. The 1928 contest marked a turning point when Democratic hopeful Al Smith garnered 72 percent of the Jewish vote in his unsuccessful run for the White House. Smith, the urban reformer of immigrant stock, forged a bond with many American Jewish voters, who shared similar backgrounds and interests. His attacks on the Ku Klux Klan won praise from targets of the Klan's anti-Semitism. Smith also chose a Jewish campaign manager, Joseph Proskauer, to orchestrate his run for the presidency.[60]

BENJAMIN N. CARDOZO

In the midst of the anti-Semitism between the two world wars, President Herbert Hoover nominated the second Jew, Benjamin N. Cardozo, to sit on the United States Supreme Court. Cardozo was a scion of an established and prominent Sephardic Jewish family of New York. His uncle, Benjamin Nathan, the future jurist's namesake, was president of New York's Spanish-Portuguese synagogue. Many of Cardozo's relatives had held the position or served as rabbis for the same congregation.[61] Cardozo's mother died when Benjamin was only nine; but his father was a devout Jew, who worried over having to conduct his judicial duties as a member of the Supreme Court of New York state on Saturdays. "But in his own home he neglected no detail of ancient ritualistic custom as to prayers, to food, and to special observances of religious holidays."[62]

As was customary, Benjamin was bar mitzvahed at the age of thirteen but gave up many of the more orthodox rituals of his faith as an adult. He did not attend synagogue services but maintained his membership in the same Spanish-Portuguese congregation that generations of his family had served with distinction. He also retained his inherited voting rights in its affairs. As an adult, he observed some of the Jewish dietary laws, participated in the activities of the Jewish Educational Association, and became a trustee of the Hebrew University in Jerusalem. He embraced Zionism with neither the alacrity nor vigor of his predecessor on the Court, Justice Brandeis; but as storm clouds gathered over Europe, threatening another global conflict, Cardozo supported a Palestinian haven for his coreligionists.[63]

Cardozo's rejection of religious orthodoxy may have resulted from his inquiring mind, which manifested its brilliance even in his youth. With such intellectual acumen, Cardozo distinguished himself academically as an undergraduate and law student at Columbia University. A superlative career at the bar resulted in his election to the New York Supreme Court, the state's intermediate appellate tribunal. One month after his election to that court, Cardozo received an appointment to the highest court in the state, the prestigious New York Court of Appeals. In 1927 he assumed the chief judgeship of the court and served there until Hoover's call sent him to the United States Supreme Court five years later.

Since 1922, Cardozo's name had been suggested to presidents for nomination to the nation's highest court, but a variety of political, ideological, and judicial factors intervened to thwart his appointment. Even President Hoover had passed over the New York jurist in selecting Supreme Court nominees prior to 1932.[64] Yet few men were as well-qualified by jurisprudential skill and experience to fill the chair of the "Yankee from Olympus," Associate Justice Oliver Wendell Holmes, Jr., who retired from the bench in January 1932.

In addition to considerations of the talents required to take what came to be called the "scholar's seat" on the Court, several "representative" factors entered Hoover's selection decision. The first was the geographic consideration. The Court, as it had been throughout its history, was top-heavy with easterners.[65] President Hoover envisioned potential political gains for his Republican party, which would soon have to defend its record in the midst of the Great Depression in the 1932 presidential election, if he recognized the West or South with a Supreme Court appointment. Holmes's resignation had sparked a public campaign on Cardozo's behalf, but Hoover was initially unwilling to put another native of the Empire State on the Court. (Chief Justice Charles Evans Hughes and Justice Harlan Stone, both New Yorkers, were already on the high bench.) But Senators Robert F. Wagner of New York and William E. Borah of Idaho urged the president to ignore geography and make history—as Zachariah Chafee would characterize Hoover's eventual nomination of Cardozo. Senator Borah argued to the president that the man he appointed to the Court would represent "every state, Idaho as well as New York. If you appoint Judge Cardozo, you will be winning the applause of the whole country and not merely one part."[66]

Newton D. Baker of Cincinnati, former President Wilson's secretary of war, was reportedly under consideration to fill the Holmes vacancy. Rabbi Stephen Wise, the prominent Jewish clergyman, phoned Baker and asked if he supported Cardozo for the position. Baker responded affirmatively and agreed to contact Hoover immediately about his position. He assured Dr. Wise, "I'll tell the President the appointment ought to be decided by mentality and not geography."[67]

The *New York Times*'s report of Hoover's list of putative candidates for the Court's empty seat focused on the geography factor by listing the potential nominees according to their home region. Cardozo's name was conspicuously absent from the list. A *Times* editorial on the same day, however, described the nationwide support for Cardozo that transcended geographic considerations.[68]

There is no evidence that President Hoover considered Cardozo's religious affiliation as a positive factor either in terms of electoral gains among Jewish voters or as recognition for the Jewish community. The latter point, particularly, was moot. Brandeis was still on the Court and a vigorous participant in its affairs. He would remain another seven years—one year beyond Cardozo's untimely death.

Although Hoover is said to have been devoid of any traces of anti-Semitism, he may have pondered the wisdom of having two Jews serving on the Court together just as he concerned himself with the problem of three New Yorkers on the bench at the same time. Then there was the variation on the old Harvard admissions argument that one too many Jews on the Court would increase anti-Semitism.[69]

Indeed, Hoover's ultimate decision to nominate Cardozo overcame the dictates of "representativeness," which imply some notion of a rough balance or proportionality on the Court. Cardozo's universally recognized merits outweighed Hoover's concerns that his nominee was from the "wrong" state or of the "wrong" religion. According to Professor David M. O'Brien's analysis, Hoover nominated Cardozo not only on the basis of the latter's "unimpeachable" reputation but because the president knew the nomination was "politically opportune" and "his confirmation secure."[70] In any event, the absence of the religion factor in Cardozo's appointment, therefore, had no impact on the concept of the Court's "Jewish seat." But as Rabbi Wise commented, American Jews could be proud that two of the greatest men in American legal history both were Jews and sat on the nation's highest court.[71]

As noted above, there is no evidence to suggest that Hoover intended his appointment of Cardozo as a gesture to attract Jewish voters to his candidacy in the 1932 presidential election. Even if he had entertained such a thought, the Depression and Al Smith's gain among Jews in 1928 would have combined to thwart such efforts. In fact, Franklin Roosevelt captured 82 percent of the Jewish vote in 1932, compared to only 18 percent for the unsuccessful incumbent. In F.D.R.'s landslide victory four years later, he increased his percentage of the Jewish vote to 85 percent. It rose to a nearly unanimous 90 percent in his unprecedented try for a third term and stabilized at that figure in his last bid for the presidency in 1944.[72] The overwhelming support for Roosevelt led Judge Jonah B. Goldstein to quip that the American Jew had three worlds:"Die velt [this world]; yene velt [the world to come]; and Roosevelt."[73]

American Jews can trace their influence on the national political scene to the Roosevelt administration. They were instrumental in, indeed indispensable to, the formation of the New Deal—a label coined by Bernard Baric, David Lilienthal, and Sam Rosenman. Benjamin V. Cohen and Thomas G. Corcoran breathed life into the program by drafting New Deal legislation. Many of Roosevelt's young "brain trusters" were protégés of the president's long-time friend and trusted adviser, Felix Frankfurter, professor of law at Harvard University. The eager band of New Dealers sent down from Boston were dubbed "Frankfurter's happy hot dogs."[74]

FELIX FRANKFURTER

The question of whether Felix Frankfurter would serve on the Court focused on "when" rather than "if." F.D.R. had promised the Harvard Law School professor that it was only a matter of finding the right time to appoint him to the Supreme Court. After an excruciatingly long period of five years without a Supreme Court vacancy, Roosevelt had two opportunities to begin reshaping the high bench in the first half of his second presidential term. He had appointed Hugo L. Black and Stanley F. Reed to fill those vacancies. The death of Justice Cardozo in 1938 at the age of sixty-eight, after only a half-dozen years of service on the Court, left F.D.R. with yet a third seat to be filled. Several months after Cardozo's demise, the *New York Times* reported that it was a well-known fact that Frankfurter would undoubtedly go to the Court eventually but that this current opening was reserved for a westerner. No mention was made of Frankfurter's religion.[75]

A Viennese Jew of German cultural heritage, Frankfurter and his family had immigrated to the United States in 1894 when Felix was twelve years old. Many of his relatives on his father's side of the family had been rabbis, and Frankfurter's father had studied for the rabbinate at one time. Although young Felix was raised as a practicing Jew and recalled a "religiously observant" boyhood, the Frankfurters were less than devout. For instance, the family did not strictly follow kosher dietary restrictions, and Felix's father would often sing Jewish chants to opera tunes on the less solemn holy days. Like Cardozo, Frankfurter abandoned formal religious services as a young man. Nevertheless, Frankfurter was proud of his Jewish heritage[76] and identified strongly with Jewish causes. With Louis Brandeis, he was a forceful and effective advocate of Zionism and other political causes dear to the hearts of both men.[77] Frankfurter battled against academic anti-Semitism in the form of quotas against Jewish students and faculty members at Harvard.[78] Again like Cardozo, Frankfurter returned to his Jewish roots at the end of his life, requesting that Jewish prayers be read at his funeral. He explained his request with characteristic feistiness: "I came into the world a Jew and I want to leave it as a Jew."[79]

Hoover's appointment of Cardozo in 1932 had postponed the selection of a westerner to the Supreme Court. In turn, F.D.R. felt compelled by geographic considerations to consider a judicial nominee who hailed from west of the Mississippi River. Midwestern and western governors and senators urged the president to appoint a native from their respective regions, which were still unrepresented on the Court.[80] Nonetheless, support for a noneasterner was not unanimous among midwestern senators. Senator George F. Norris of Nebraska wrote a glowing letter of support for Frankfurter to the president. Opinion polls of the American bar showed Frankfurter to be the preferred candidate for the Cardozo vacancy. Yet the demand for western representation on the Court remained, prompting Norris to declare that the geographic issue should not enter into the selection.[81]

Unlike in the case of Cardozo's appointment, however, F.D.R. took seriously *both* the geographic factor and the religious issue. As he explained to his postmaster general and confidant, Jim Farley:

F.F. wants to get on [the Court] in the worst way. Some months ago I had to tell him at Hyde Park that I just couldn't appoint him for many reasons. In the first place, the appointment has to go west. In the second, I told Felix that I could not appoint him in view of the anti-Semitic feeling. I couldn't appoint another Jew, but if Brandeis should resign or die, I told Frankfurter I would appoint him that same day without hesitation.[82]

Apparently, some members of the Jewish community feared an intensification of anti-Semitism should Frankfurter be appointed to the Court while Brandeis continued to serve. Wait until Brandeis left the Court was their advice, and a group of prominent Jews was delegated to speak to F.D.R. to urge him not to select Frankfurter at that time.[83] Secretary of the Interior Harold Ickes wrote in his diary of September 18, 1938, that Tom Corcoran claimed that the president had decided to name Frankfurter to the Court but that "the rich Jews [were] objecting."[84]

Ickes eventually made his own pitch to the chief executive in Frankfurter's behalf. The secretary of the interior pleaded that geography should not enter into the decision. With rather odd reasoning, Ickes recorded in his diary that he told F.D.R. that the West was certainly not adequately represented on the Court but neither had it been in the presidency. Moreover, placing Frankfurter on the high bench would assure its Rooseveltian bent long after F.D.R. left office.[85]

Ickes's arguments in Frankfurter's favor found a sympathetic ear in the Oval Office. Roosevelt presumed (erroneously as it turned out) that his trusted friend and adviser, Frankfurter, would consistently practice New Deal liberalism on the Court. Moreover, a seat on the nation's highest tribunal would be the perfect reward for his past loyalty and service to the president. Finally, the Harvard law professor was a superb scholar in the Story, Holmes, Cardozo mold.[86]

Still, in the months that passed between Cardozo's death in July 1938 and Congress's reconvening in January of the next year, F.D.R.

agonized over the religion question. In late November 1938, Attorney General Homer Cummings forwarded a list of potential nominees to the president and included among the data each candidate's age and religious affiliation. The tragedy and violence of Germany's *Krystallnacht* earlier in November 1938 had made Frankfurter's Jewishness more worrisome to Roosevelt. He continued to wonder if the Court should have two Jews from Massachusetts among its membership. Yet the pressure to appoint Frankfurter continued unabated from those within and outside the administration. On January 4, 1939, the president phoned his friend at Harvard; and after a conversation that reflected F.D.R.'s schizophrenia over the decision, conveyed the good news to Frankfurter that his name would be sent to the Senate for appointment to the Supreme Court.[87]

From the beginning, Frankfurter's religion was an issue in his confirmation hearings. The Senate Judiciary Committee declared at the outset that it did not want to discuss such a factor in investigating Frankfurter's fitness to serve on the Court. Nevertheless, crackpot witnesses incessantly raised the issue while denying that they were anti-Semitic.[88] One witness, who opposed Frankfurter's nomination, read a telegram that asked: "Why not an American from Revolution times instead of a Jew from Austria?" Senator Norris responded dismissively: "An American from Revolution times would be too old."[89] Anti-Semitism could not derail Frankfurter's obviously meritorious nomination, and the Senate approved his appointment by unanimous voice vote after expeditious hearings.

Religion played a complex role as a representative factor in Roosevelt's decision to nominate Felix Frankfurter to the Supreme Court. F.D.R. had no need to attract Jewish votes; they were his for the asking. Indeed, he might have wanted to repay Jewish voters for their past electoral support and cement their allegiance in his try for an unprecedented third term in 1940. The president's many recorded references to Frankfurter's eventual appointment to Brandeis's chair indicate that he was well-aware that a "Jewish seat" existed on the Court. Because Brandeis remained, F.D.R. had to overlook Frankfurter's religion to place him on the Court. (Still, Roosevelt knew that Brandeis could not remain on the Court forever.) As in Hoover's appointment of Cardozo, the president also ignored the geography factor. Frankfurter's demonstrable merit, his New Deal credentials, his long-time friendship with Roosevelt, and his overwhelming support from professional and political circles impelled the president to select him as Cardozo's replacement.

Yet Frankfurter believed that his religious affiliation played a part in both his selection and successful appointment. It was more related to world events than to domestic politics, however. He explained many years later:

In the context of world affairs in 1939, with all the brutal, barbaric behavior of

Germany and generally the infection that was caused thereby elsewhere in the spread of anti-Semitism, and not least in this country, for the President of the United States to appoint a Jew to the Supreme Court had such significance for me to make it impossible to have said "no."[90]

In February 1939, just a little over one month after Frankfurter's appointment, Justice Brandeis retired from the Supreme Court, leaving his protégé the only Jew on the high bench. Frankfurter would serve there with distinction for the next twenty-three years. During his tenure on the Court, the Jewish population in America rose from just under 4.8 million to a little over 5.5 million. Yet the Jewish percentage of the total American population declined from an all-time high of 3.65 percent in 1940 to 3.07 percent in 1960.[91] The Jewish population followed the trend of the rest of Americans in migrating from the northeastern and northcentral states to the South and the West. By the end of the half century between 1930 and 1980, over 75 percent of American Jewry lived in ten metropolitan areas: New York, Los Angeles, Philadelphia, Chicago, Miami, Washington, Boston, Baltimore, Detroit, and Cleveland. The Greater New York area alone would become home to one-fifth of the *world*'s Jewry.[92]

In presidential politics of the same era, Jews maintained their strong electoral support for Democratic presidential candidates. Harry S Truman received 75 percent of the Jewish vote in his memorable upset of Republican Thomas E. Dewey. The popular Dwight D. Eisenhower attracted some Jewish votes from the Democratic column, but his opponent, Adlai E. Stevenson, Jr., polled 64 percent and 60 percent of the Jewish vote, respectively, in his two unsuccessful attempts to reach the White House. Jewish voters flocked back to the Democratic ticket headed by John F. Kennedy in 1960. Nationwide, he attracted 82 percent of the Jewish vote,[93] and a California poll showed 91 percent of that state's Jewish voters supporting Kennedy as compared to only 73 percent of California Catholics.[94]

ARTHUR J. GOLDBERG

In August 1962, ill health forced Felix Frankfurter to retire from his beloved Supreme Court. Thus, President Kennedy had a second Court vacancy to fill. He had awarded the first to his long-time friend and political supporter, Deputy Attorney General Byron R. White. J.F.K. told his adviser, Arthur Schlesinger, Jr., that he had also considered Paul Freund, Arthur Goldberg, and William Hastie before he chose White. When Justice Frankfurter retired, Kennedy reconsidered his original list of potential nominees and upon Robert Kennedy's recommendation, added Archibald Cox's name to it. Ultimately, the president turned to Secretary of Labor Arthur J. Goldberg. Schlesinger reported that Kennedy confided:

"I think we'll have appointments enough for everybody."[95] Of course, his assassination in 1963 thwarted such plans.

Frankfurter's replacement was the son of Russian Jews, who had immigrated to Chicago, where the future justice was born in 1908. Information on Goldberg's religious upbringing is scarce; but upon his appointments to the Court and then to the United Nations, the press reported that he was a member of a Reform temple in Washington, observed the Jewish holy days, and described himself as a Zionist.[96]

The young Goldberg was typical of many first-generation Jewish-Americans, who worked their way through higher education and often entered professions unattainable for their immigrant parents. Goldberg's father had delivered produce by horse and buggy in Chicago; but his son, Arthur, put himself through college and then graduated first in his class from Northwestern Law School, where he was editor-in-chief of the law review.[97] He became a prominent labor lawyer and his success paved his way to the office of general counsel of the United Steel Workers, the American Federation of Labor, and the Congress of Industrial Organizations.[98] Soon after the 1960 presidential election, John Kennedy named Goldberg to the post of secretary of labor, where he was serving when Kennedy sent him to the Court in 1962.

J.F.K. deliberated barely a day before announcing that Goldberg was his choice to replace the retiring Justice Frankfurter. At a news conference, the president cited Goldberg's experience in law, his accomplishments at the bar, his character, temperament, and ability, his "scholarly approach to law," and his "deep understanding of our economic and political system" as the reasons for nominating the secretary of labor to be an associate justice.[99]

At least privately, Goldberg's religious affiliation had surfaced as an issue in his initial appointment by Kennedy to the cabinet. After Kennedy had made the offer, Goldberg and his wife, Dorothy, discussed the pros and cons of accepting the position. As Mrs. Goldberg wrote several years later:

another consideration was . . . being a Jew. There were Jewish senators and representatives, but no Jews in the Cabinet. Perhaps there was an obligation when a door was opened to keep one's foot in it, so that it might open even a little wider for others. . . . I asked Art if the names Abe Ribicoff, Wilber Cohen, Arthur Goldberg were possibly considered for political appearance. [Mr. Goldberg replied:] "Put that out of your mind. Kennedy thinks of nothing but the office and the right person for the office."[100]

Theodore Sorensen's memoirs of Kennedy confirm Mr. Goldberg's view. The former assistant to J.F.K. reported that he thought it was necessary to inform the president-elect that all three proposed associates for the White House staff were of "Jewish ancestry." Kennedy replied: "So what? They tell me this is the first Cabinet with two Jews, too. All I care about is whether they can handle it." Sorensen also wrote that in considering Goldberg for the Supreme Court position that ultimately went to White, the president was unconcerned about having two Jews on the Court at the same time.[101]

Nevertheless, Kennedy had given some thought to the implications of Goldberg's religion for a Court appointment. *Washington Post* editor, and long-time Kennedy friend and confidant, Benjamin Bradlee recalled that in discussing the first Supreme Court nomination that J.F.K. had to consider, the president mentioned "Arthur Goldberg favorably, and implied strongly that Goldberg would be on the Supreme Court inevitably. 'But not to fill Frankfurter's seat,' he [Kennedy] added. 'That's too obvious and cute.' "[102]

Time magazine was probably most on target in explaining the presidential change of mind, which put Goldberg on the Court to replace Frankfurter. The week after Goldberg's nomination, the periodical listed his qualifications "as an eminent and successful lawyer, as a liberal of the activist New Frontier type, and as a Jew (Frankfurter was the court's only Jewish member, and political doctrine demanded that his successor be a Jew)."[103]

The Senate confirmed Goldberg with only one opposing vote. His confirmation hearings before the Judiciary Committee had raised the issue of his religion only in passing—for example, mention of a letter of support from a Jewish interest group, reference to Goldberg's membership in a Jewish organization and that he belonged to a synagogue, and recognition of a rabbi, who sat with Mrs. Goldberg during the hearings. The tone of the debate was remarkably higher than Frankfurter's. Senator Sam J. Ervin, Jr., of North Carolina directed scholarly questions toward the nominee on the judicial role, for instance, and exhibited his mastery of constitutional law that would be evident again on the more momentous occasion of the Watergate hearings twelve years later.[104]

The lessening of attention paid to the religious affiliation of Brandeis, Frankfurter, and Goldberg in their respective Senate hearings for appointments to the Court is indicative of the diminution of overt anti-Semitism in this country as the twentieth century progressed.[105] Nevertheless, just as the country took for granted the fitness of Jews to serve on the nation's highest tribunal, it also seemed to take for granted that one seat should be reserved for them on the Court. Although President Kennedy may have considered such an arrangement "obvious and cute," he apparently bowed to the perceived necessity of keeping at least one Jew on the Supreme Court. Like the other potential candidates whom J.F.K. considered, Goldberg was highly capable and an ideological soul mate of the Kennedy administration. Yet his religion most likely gave him the final and swift push to the top of the president's list. With Goldberg's succession of Frankfurter, the president implicitly acknowledged what the media explicitly recognized—a "Jewish seat" on the Supreme Court.

Justice Goldberg served on the Court a mere three years before reluctantly accepting President Lyndon Johnson's offer to be United States Ambassador to the United Nations. L.B.J. indicated that Goldberg's religion played a role in his decision to send him to the U.N. Underscoring the geographic, racial, and religious factors in American politics, Johnson declared: "When a Southerner can sit in the White House, when a Negro can aspire to the highest offices in the land, when a man of deep Jewish background can be spokesman of this country to the world—that's what America is all about."[106] Tom Wicker, *New York Times* editorialist, suggested a possible electoral motivation in Johnson's appointment of Goldberg to the U.N. Wicker presumed that it probably would "pay handsome domestic political dividends among the nation's 5,500,000 Jewish voters [sic]."[107] Johnson had equaled F.D.R.'s 1940 and 1944 tallies of 90 percent of the Jewish vote in his 1964 landslide election victory over Barry Goldwater, despite the latter's declared pride in the fact that he was half Jewish.[108] No one knew in 1965 that Johnson's foreign policy fiasco in Vietnam would force him out of the 1968 election and make his potential gains among Jewish voters a moot point.

ABE FORTAS

Abe Fortas's name surfaced immediately in the press's speculative discussions of Goldberg's successor. Obviously, he was of the "right" religion. Born to Orthodox Jewish parents, who had immigrated to the United States from England, Fortas was raised in Memphis, Tennessee, a city with a minuscule Jewish community. The youngster became a superior student and accomplished violinist. At the age of fifteen, he was graduated second in his class from a Memphis public high school and earned a scholarship to a small Presbyterian liberal arts college in his home town. As a child, Fortas had been exposed to the Orthodox faith of his parents at home and attended synagogue regularly; but, like Frankfurter and Cardozo before him, he abandoned regular attendance as a young adult. To some, he appeared to be an agnostic. Yet he was fully aware of his Jewish heritage.[109] He once said that he considered himself "a Jew all the way through, from top to bottom—I can no more separate my Jewishness from anything that I do than I could unmake the rest of my education or separate out my emotional components."[110]

Based on Fortas's stellar performance as an undergraduate, both Harvard and Yale Law Schools offered him scholarships. (A $50 difference per month in the Yale stipend resulted in Fortas's choice of New Haven over Cambridge.) The future justice's consistency as a scholar continued in law school. By his senior year, he was editor in chief of the *Yale Law Journal*, a position usually reserved for the student achieving the top academic rank in the class.[111]

An offer to join the Yale law faculty capped Fortas's laudable law school career. Before he could begin his teaching duties, however, he left for Washington to plunge into the New Deal as a member of the legal staff of the Agricultural Adjustment Administration. William O. Douglas called him from there to the Securities and Exchange Commission in 1934. During these years, Fortas managed to hold his faculty position at Yale while participating in the whirlwind life of a New Dealer. He eventually left academics, however, to work under the tutelage of Harold Ickes as general counsel of the Public Works Administration. The formidable Ickes was so impressed with Fortas's work that in 1942 he promoted him to be his undersecretary of the interior. Fortas continued to serve in the Roosevelt administration throughout the war. When the conflict ended, he joined his former Yale law professor, Thurman Arnold, as a partner in the new firm of Arnold & Fortas, which was to become one of the capital's most successful and prominent law firms.[112]

One of the many contacts Abe Fortas made during his New Deal years was with a young congressman from Texas, Lyndon Johnson. In July 1965, the *New York Times* reported that Fortas's "close relationship with the President," in addition to his "immense prestige in the legal profession," made him a likely candidate for the Court.[113] Indeed, the close personal and professional relationship between the president and Fortas continued even after the latter went to the Court and contributed to the charges of impropriety that ultimately resulted in Fortas's resignation from the bench in 1969.

L.B.J.'s memoirs describe his reasons for nominating Fortas to be associate justice:

I was confident that the man [Fortas] would be a brilliant and able jurist. He had the experience and the liberalism to espouse the causes that both I and Arthur Goldberg believed in. He had the strength of character to stand up for his own convictions, and he was a humanitarian.[114]

Johnson added that Fortas had been "a distinguished lawyer in Washington for over thirty years." The former president also mentioned that he had previously offered Fortas a cabinet post in his administration.[115]

For public consumption, Johnson understandably did not offer to delineate the role played by Fortas's religion in the decision to send him to the Court. Yet it was clearly on his mind in the personnel maneuver that shifted Goldberg to the U.N. and elevated Fortas to the Court.[116] In addition to his previous statement regarding a Jew serving as America's ambassador to the United Nations, Johnson is on record as reflecting on religion and ethnicity as factors in Court appointments. Lady Bird Johnson's diaries recall that the Fortases and the Johnsons were enjoying a summer evening on the Truman Balcony when the question was raised about the Arab reaction to Goldberg going to the U.N. According to Mrs. Johnson, the president responded that "we couldn't let anyone dictate to us—whether a Jew or a Catholic or a Negro or a person of whatever ethnic background—who sat on the Supreme Court or held any other government job."[117] Although the president's statement, or his wife's recollection of it, is rather muddled, it appears that L.B.J. wanted a free rein to recognize with appointments the religious and ethnic minorities he listed in his comment.

Moreover, Johnson's attorney general, Nicholas Katzenbach, solidified the historical tradition of the "Jewish seat" on the Supreme Court in the president's mind. In a memorandum delivered to Johnson six days before the announcement of the Fortas nomination, Katzenbach took note of the history of the "Jewish seat," but argued that "most Jews share with me the feeling" that religion should not be the main criterion for the position. He added, however, that at least one Jewish justice should be appointed before the presidential election year of 1968. Katzenbach concluded, "On balance, I think if you appoint a Jew he should be so outstanding as to be selected clearly on his own merits as an individual."[118] The attorney general thought Abe Fortas would be the perfect nominee.

The popular press was more explicit than ever before in recognizing the role of the religion factor in a justice's nomination. The *New York Times*, *Time* magazine, and the *Christian Science Monitor* all made references to Fortas filling the Court's "Jewish seat" vacated by Goldberg. All three publications referred to the seat as a "tradition."[119] As Robert Shogun summarized in his book on Fortas,

the precedent [of a Jewish seat] was of dubious logic and validity but of substantial political importance. It had been established by Woodrow Wilson's appointment of Louis D. Brandeis in 1916 and Lyndon Johnson was not about to become the first President in half a century to break that tradition.[120]

When Johnson made his abortive effort to promote Fortas to chief justice in 1968 (some say because he might enjoy naming the first Jewish chief justice in the Court's history[121]), the president reportedly reminded Senate minority leader Everett Dirksen of Illinois that he should support the nomination lest he antagonize Jewish voters and Jewish financial contributors in an election year.[122]

Despite such alleged sub-rosa considerations of Fortas's Jewishness, his Senate confirmation hearings reflected little concern about his religious faith. The record of his hearings shows even fewer references to Fortas's religious affiliation than to Goldberg's in his hearings three years earlier.[123] The Senate consented to Fortas's nomination with less than a handful of "nay" votes—all cast by Republican senators.[124]

Johnson's decision to nominate Fortas to be associate justice in many respects paralleled President Kennedy's selection of Arthur Goldberg for the Court. Both judicial nominees possessed meritorious academic records and had distinguished themselves in the legal profession and government service. Both were politically and ideologically aligned with their appointing presidents. They each had a professional relationship with the chief executive; Fortas had a long-standing personal friendship with Johnson as well. Finally, Goldberg's replacement of Frankfurter and Fortas's subsequent filling of the Goldberg vacancy ensured that the Court would continue to have one Jewish justice among its nine members. That fact was decisive in the two presidents' decisions to send them to the Court. Apparently, neither Kennedy nor Johnson wanted to ignore the "Jewish seat" tradition. They could have their cake and eat it too by appointing otherwise acceptable justices, who were members of the "right" religious faith.

Justice Fortas's stormy end to his brief tenure on the Court which came amid charges of judicial impropriety stemming from his acceptance of a $20,000 annual stipend from multimillionaire industrialist Louis Wolfson, encapsulated the zenith and the nadir of the "Jewish seat" tradition. Had his nomination to be chief justice come to fruition, he would have been the first Jew to serve in the center chair. Ironically, his forced resignation from the bench brought the "Jewish seat" to an abrupt end. Neither of President Richard M. Nixon's two unsuccessful nominees to fill the Fortas vacancy (namely, Clement Haynsworth and G. Harrold Carswell) was Jewish. Nor was his ultimately successful appointee, Harry A. Blackmun. Perhaps the controversy swirling about Washington for a year over the Fortas affair and the Senate's rejection of Nixon's first two nominees diverted attention from the "Jewish seat." Press accounts of Blackmun's appointment noted that he was the fourth Protestant nominated by Nixon to the Court.[125] But there was little public discussion of the fact that the "Jewish seat" remained unrecognized.

SUMMING UP THE "JEWISH SEAT"

Frank Mankiewicz, aide to the late Robert F. Kennedy and George McGovern's campaign manager, did comment on Nixon's dismal record in appointing Jews to government office and offered it as a reason why good Jews should not vote for Nixon in his reelection effort in 1972. Mankiewicz argued: "He's the guy who's taken the Jew off the Supreme Court. . . . There's no Jew in the Subcabinet, there's no Jew on the White House staff except for Henry Kissinger, and he doesn't work at it."[126]

President Reagan's 1987 nomination of Federal Appeals Court Judge

Douglas Ginsburg after the Senate's rejection of Robert Bork renewed discussion of a reemergence of the Supreme Court's "Jewish seat" because Ginsburg would have been the first Jewish member of the Court since Fortas's resignation in 1969. Nevertheless, as Reagan indicated at the time, Ginsburg's impressive professional credentials, his conservative ideology, and philosophy of judicial restraint were the major considerations in his nomination. His religious affiliation, however, could have been a strategic factor in winning Senate confirmation. On the whole, Jews had opposed Bork's nomination. Ginsburg's ideology was at least as conservative as Bork's, but Jews might have been less inclined to oppose a member of their own faith.[127] Such conjecture will forever remain in the realm of Supreme Court trivia because of the nominee's surprising revelations regarding his past marijuana use, both as a student and as a law professor, which resulted in his withdrawal from consideration.

What accounts then for the apparent demise of the "Jewish seat" on the Court? The tautological response is that Nixon and his successors did not nominate any Jews to the Supreme Court. But just as the political climate in this country promoted the establishment of the "Jewish seat," factors in that same climate arguably fostered its decline.

Among possible reasons for the collapse of the "Jewish seat" is the electoral factor. Nixon's percentage of the Jewish vote in his 1960 and 1968 bids for the White House was 18 percent and 17 percent, respectively.[128] He had little motivation to reward the Jewish community for its support, and perhaps he despaired of ever wooing Jewish voters from their traditional home since 1928 in the Democratic camp. In his landslide victory of 1972, he did manage to double his support among Jews, but this probably resulted from a reaction against McGovern rather than a positive affirmation of Nixon's presidency.[129]

In addition, by the time Presidents Ford and Reagan had opportunities to make appointments to the Court, another "representative" consideration had crept into the selection process. President Ford ultimately chose John Paul Stevens, a white male Protestant, but not before considering (with public pressure from his wife, Betty) the possibility of appointing the first woman to the Court. In President Reagan's first appointment— that of Sandra Day O'Connor—the gender factor took precedence.

Although the Jewish community lacks a landmark event to mark its assimilation into America's political and social mainstream, such as the election of President Kennedy for Catholics, it had by the middle of the twentieth century "become intimately interwoven with all phases" of American life.[130] Intermarriage of American Jews and Gentiles, while an alarming development for Jewish demographics, contributed to this assimilation.[131] As in the case of the "Catholic seat," this achievement of assimilation may have removed the political necessity of Jewish representation on the high court.[132]

During the twentieth century, Judaism became one of the "big three religions in America." Although constituting only 3 percent of the population, American Jewry was granted one-third of the recognition with Protestants and Catholics. "Symbols of this new status abounded. A minister, a priest, and a rabbi sat on the dais at every civic function, including the inauguration of a president; radio and television apportioned time equally to each of the three faiths."[133] American Jews especially delighted in the increased use of the descriptive term "Judeo-Christian." "This concept raised the Jew to full partnership—and senior partner at that!"[134]

As with the nine Catholic appointments, religion was never the *primary* factor in a president's selection of a Jew to sit on the Supreme Court. Yet, from the appointment of the first Jew to the Court, Judaism played a "representative" role in presidential selections. Wilson apparently was ready and willing to run the gauntlet of anti-Semitism to recognize American Jewry with the otherwise meritorious and politically acceptable Louis Brandeis. With their respective appointments of Cardozo and Frankfurter, Hoover and Roosevelt both overlooked the dictates of proportional "representativeness," which would have allowed only one Jew to serve on the Court at a time. Yet F.D.R. was obviously aware that Frankfurter would be the perfect replacement for Brandeis. (The latter's reluctance to retire forced an earlier decision to send Frankfurter to the Supreme Court.) By the time Frankfurter left the Court in 1962, observers were referring by name to the "Jewish seat," and J.F.K. must have felt the political pressures inherent in such references when he selected Goldberg. Just three years later, the "Jewish seat tradition" was so compelling that L.B.J. had to look no further beyond his Jewish friend, adviser, and ideological kin, Abe Fortas, the perfect choice.

The political and social development of American Jewry is inextricably linked to the foregoing presidential decisions in selecting Jewish justices. Likewise, the same evolution of the American Jewish community, to the point of assimilation with the American polity, resulted in the removal of the Court's "Jewish seat"—significantly, with very few cries of protest from Jewish-Americans.[135]

NOTES

1. Thomas Karfunkel and Thomas W. Ryley's *The Jewish Seat* (Hicksville, N.Y.: Exposition Press, 1978) examined Jewish Supreme Court appointments in light of the history of anti-Semitism in the United States, but the study did not explicitly address the role of "representativeness" in these appointments.

2. Stephen D. Isaacs, *Jews and American Politics* (Garden City, N.Y.: Doubleday, 1974), pp. ix–x.

3. Daniel J. Elazar, *Community and Polity: The Organizational Dynamics of American Jewry* (Philadelphia: The Jewish Publication Society of America, 1976), p. 15.

4. Abraham J. Karp, *Haven and Home: A History of the Jews in America* (New York: Schocken Books, 1985), p. 9.

5. Ibid, pp. 26–27.

6. Ibid., pp. 29, 60; Rufus Learsi, *The Jews in America: A History* (Cleveland: World, 1954), pp. 101, 211.

7. Nathanial Weyl, *The Jew in American Politics* (New Rochelle, N.Y.: Arlington House, 1968), p. 37.

8. "A substantial majority" of the 15,000 American Jews supported Van Buren. Ibid.

9. Ibid., pp. 37–38.

10. Learsi, *The Jews in America*, p. 96.

11. See the most recent biography, *Judah P. Benjamin: The Jewish Confederate* by Eli N. Evans (New York: The Free Press, 1988).

12. Weyl, *The Jew in American Politics*, pp. 50–51.

13. Karp, *Haven and Home*, p. 342; Evans, *Judah P. Benjamin*, pp. xi–xii.

14. Learsi, *The Jews in America*, p. 97; Weyl, *The Jew in American Politics*, p. 51.

15. Evans, *Judah P. Benjamin*, pp. 83–84; Weyl, *The Jew in American Politics*, p. 51; Henry J. Abraham, *Justices and Presidents: A Political History of Appointments to the Supreme Court*, 2d ed. (New York: Oxford University Press, 1985), p. 111.

16. A. L. Todd, *Justice on Trial: The Case of Louis D. Brandeis* (Chicago: The University of Chicago Press, 1964; Phoenix Edition, 1968), p. 256.

17. Evans, *Judah P. Benjamin*, p. xiii. Evans believes that Fillmore had promised a Supreme Court seat to a southerner who could "represent" the Fifth Circuit (Alabama and Louisiana) and Benjamin perfectly fit the job description.

18. Karp, *Haven and Home*, pp. 83, 113.

19. Ibid., pp. 170–71; Learsi, *The Jews in America*, pp. 270–71.

20. Karp, *Haven and Home*, p. 114.

21. Ibid., pp. 138–39 (emphasis added).

22. Learsi, *The Jews in America*; Karp, *Haven and Home*, p. 342.

23. Weyl, *The Jew in American Politics*, pp. 66–67.

24. Learsi, *The Jews in America*, pp. 172–73.

25. Weyl, *The Jew in American Politics*, p. 67.

26. For example, the author's parents discovered that their Jewish friends were unable to make reservations at a small resort motel on the west coast of Florida because the proprietor refused to accommodate Jews and announced his policy with a "Christian Clientele Only" notice in his brochures. This was in the 1950s.

27. Weyl, *The Jew in American Politics*, p. 37.

28. Most standard surveys of Jewish history in America recount the story of the doomed Leo Frank. See Karp, *Haven and Home*, pp. 268–69; Learsi, *The Jew in America*, pp. 289–90; Weyl, *The Jew in American Politics*, pp. 87–92.

29. Quoted in Weyl, *The Jew in American Politics*, pp. 90–91.

30. Ibid., p. 91. On March 11, 1986, the Georgia Board of Pardons and Paroles granted a posthumous pardon to Leo Frank for his murder conviction over seventy years earlier. *Washington Post*, March 12, 1986, p. 3.

31. See Chapter 2.

32. William S. Berlin, *On the Edge of Politics: The Roots of Jewish Political Thought in America* (Westport, Conn.: Greenwood Press, 1978), pp. 27–29 (emphasis added).

33. Todd, *Justice on Trial*, p. 31.

34. Ray Stannard Baker, *Woodrow Wilson: Life and Letters, Facing War, 1915–1917* (New York: Greenwood Press, 1968), pp. 112–13.

35. Josephus Daniels, *The Wilson Era: Years of Peace—1910–1917* (Chapel Hill: The University of North Carolina Press, 1944), p. 543.

36. Arthur S. Link, *Wilson: Confusions and Crises, 1915–1916*, vol. 4 of *The Papers of Woodrow Wilson* (Princeton, N. J.: Princeton University Press, 1964), p. 325.

37. Todd, *Justice on Trial*, p. 69.

38. Daniels, *The Wilson Era*, p. 543.

39. Quoted in Alpheus Thomas Mason, *Brandeis: A Free Man's Life* (New York: Viking, 1946), p. 491.

40. See Todd, *Justice on Trial*, Ch. 4, for an intriguing discussion of Lodge's political dilemma in deciding whether to support the Brandeis nomination. Lodge's distinctions among the three arguments appear on pp. 88–89.

41. Quoted in Link, *Wilson*, pp. 358–59.

42. Quoted in Leonard Baker, *Brandeis and Frankfurter: A Dual Biography* (New York: Harper & Row, 1984), p.101.

43. *New York Times*, January 29, 1916, p. 1. Todd revealed that the conservative *Times* found itself in an uncomfortable position. The paper opposed many of Brandeis's beliefs, but its publisher, Adolph S. Ochs, was Jewish. p. 74

44. Todd, *Justice on Trial*, pp. 70–71.

45. Ibid., p. 256.

46. Isaacs, *Jews and American Politics*, p. 151. A similar statistical breakdown for the 1912 election is unavailable and, therefore, prevents a comparison of Jewish support for Wilson across the two contests.

47. Todd, *Justice on Trial*, p. 71.

48. Quoted in Arthur Walworth, *Woodrow Wilson*, 3d ed. (New York: W. W. Norton, 1978), fn. 9, p. 273.

49. Isaacs, *Jews in America*, p. 19.

50. As reported by Todd, *Justice on Trial*, pp. 137, 259. Todd does not indicate who prepared the memo for Wilson.

51. See Chapter 2.

52. It is interesting to note that one source viewed Brandeis as a representative Jew in his *lack* of Jewish identification (see note 32), while Taft thought Brandeis attempted to be more representative of his coreligionists by becoming *more* Jewish through embracing Zionism. Baker noted that advocating Zionist causes was not the means of becoming more representative of American Jewry, at least of prominent American Jews, most of whom were anti-Zionist. Baker, *Brandeis and Frankfurter*, p. 100.

53. Quoted in full in Todd, *Justice on Trial*, pp. 77–82.

54. All of the quotations in the following paragraph are from Boston newspapers found in the Brandeis Papers, University of Louisville, Reel #45.

55. Lewis J. Paper, *Brandeis* (Englewood Cliffs, N.J.: Prentice-Hall, 1983), p. 214.

56. Berlin, *On the Edge of Politics*, p. 21.

57. Karp, *Haven and Home*, p. 271. For a detailed analysis of quotas against Jews in higher education, see Marcia Graham Synnott, "Anti-Semitism and American Universities: Did Quotas Follow the Jews?" in *Anti-Semitism in American History*, David A. Gerber, ed. (Urbana: University of Illinois Press, 1986).

58. Learsi, *The Jews in America*, pp. 293–97.

59. Ibid., p. 289.

60. Isaacs, *Jews and American Politics*, pp. 151–55.

61. George S. Hellman, *Benjamin N. Cardozo* (New York: McGraw Hill, 1940), pp. 3–13. Hellman's tome offers a comprehensive biography of Cardozo. Briefer, but more recent, treatments of Cardozo's life and religious upbringing include: Stanley C. Brubaker's award-winning "Benjamin Nathan Cardozo: An Intellectual Biography" (Unpublished Ph.D. dissertation, University of Virginia, 1979); Andrew Kaufman, "Benjamin Cardozo" in Leon Friedman and Fred Israel, eds., *The Justices of the United States Supreme Court, 1789–1969* (New York: Chelsea House, 1969); G. Edward White, *The American Judicial Tradition: Profiles of Leading American Judges* (New York: Oxford University Press, 1976); and Richard A. Posner's *Cardozo: A Study in Reputation* (Chicago: University of Chicago Press, 1990).

62. Hellman, *Benjamin N. Cardozo*, p. 13.

63. Ibid., pp. 163–66.

64. For a thorough description and analysis of the history of the Cardozo nomination, see Ira H. Carmen's article, "The President, Politics and the Power of Appointment: Hoover's Nomination of Mr. Justice Cardozo," in 55 *Virginia Law Review* 4 (May 1969): 616–59.

65. Ibid., p. 627.

66. Joseph P. Pollard, *Mr. Justice Cardozo: A Liberal Mind in Action* (New York: The Yorktown Press, 1935), pp. 281–83.

67. Hellman, *Benjamin N. Cardozo*, p. 200.

68. *New York Times*, January 18, 1932, p. 2.

69. Carmen, "The President, Politics and the Power of Appointment," p. 641; Hellman, *Benjamin N. Cardozo*, p. 202.

70. David M. O'Brien, *Storm Center: The Supreme Court in American Politics*, 2d ed. (New York: W. W. Norton, 1990), p. 67. Compare Carmen's conclusion that Hoover was not a "sophisticated politician" and "disregarded ideological and political commitments" in nominating Cardozo on the basis of his "craftsmanship and scholarship." Carmen's ultimate conclusion that follows the conventional merit-based explanation of Cardozo's nomination is rather puzzling given his thorough treatment of the political machinations surrounding Hoover's decision.

71. *New York Times*, February 16, 1932, p. 3.

72. Isaacs, *Jews and American Politics*, pp. 151–52.

73. Quoted in Karp, *Haven and Home*, p. 278.

74. Isaacs, *Jews in American Politics*, pp. 60–65, 241.

75. *New York Times*, January 6, 1939, p. 1.

76. Liva Baker, *Felix Frankfurter* (New York: Coward-McCann, 1969), pp. 18–19. Also see Robert A. Burt's *Two Jewish Justices: Outcasts in the Promised Land* (Berkeley: University of California Press, 1988), p. 38.

77. See Bruce Allen Murphy's *The Brandeis/Frankfurter Connection: The Secret Political Activities of Two Supreme Court Justices* (New York: Oxford University Press, 1982), for a fascinating account of the political advocacy of this judicial duo.

78. See Leonard Baker, *Brandeis and Frankfurter*, Ch. 11.

79. Ibid., pp. 491–92.

80. Liva Baker, *Felix Frankfurter*, p. 202.

81. Alfred Lief, *Democracy's Norris: A Biography of a Lonely Crusade* (New York: Stackpole Sons, 1939), p. 515.

82. James A. Farley, *Jim Farley's Story: The Roosevelt Years* (New York: McGraw-Hill, 1948), pp. 161–62. Roosevelt's reference to Frankfurter's desire to go on the Court raises the question of his self-advocacy for the Cardozo spot. The editor of the Roosevelt/Frankfurter correspondence argued that the latter never expected to be appointed to Cardozo's seat, especially since F.D.R. had told him that the vacancy had to go to someone else. And Frankfurter began to submit other names of possible nominees to the president. Max Freedman, ed., *Roosevelt and Frankfurter: Their Correspondence 1928–1945* (Boston: Little, Brown, 1968), p. 481. Joseph P. Lash, however, in *From the Diaries of Felix Frankfurter* (New York: W. W. Norton, 1975), pp. 63–66, wrote that there is false humility in Frankfurter's account that he did not covet the Cardozo seat on the Court.

83. Liva Baker, *Felix Frankfurter*, p. 202. Leonard Baker has labelled the story of the Jewish delegation going to F.D.R. to dissuade him from appointing Frankfurter "New Deal gossip." *Brandeis and Frankfurter*, p. 359.

84. Harold L. Ickes, *The Secret Diary of Harold L. Ickes*, vol. 2 (New York: Simon and Schuster, 1954), p. 470.

85. Ibid., p. 550–52.

86. Leonard Baker, *Brandeis and Frankfurter*, p. 358.

87. See Abraham, *Justices and Presidents*, p. 219, for a delightful account of Roosevelt's phone call to Frankfurter.

88. See *The Supreme Court of the United States: Hearings and Reports on Successful and Unsuccessful Nominations of Supreme Court Justices by the Senate Judiciary Committee 1916–1972*, compiled by Roy M. Mersky and J. Myron Jacobstein, "Felix Frankfurter," vol. 4 (Buffalo: W. S. Hein, 1975).

89. Quoted in Leonard Baker, *Brandeis and Frankfurter*, p. 366.

90. Ibid., p. 365.

91. Karp, *Haven and Home*, Appendix 1.

92. Ibid., p. 309.

93. Isaacs, *Jews and American Politics*, p. 152.

94. Weyl, *The Jew in American Politics*, p. 165.

95. Arthur M. Schlesinger, Jr., *A Thousand Days: John F. Kennedy in the White House* (Boston: Houghton Mifflin, 1965), p. 698. J.F.K. told Schlesinger that he did not want "to start off with a Harvard man and a professor" [Freund was a Harvard law professor] because "we've taken so many Harvard men that it's damn hard to appoint another." Ibid. According to Robert Kennedy, his brother passed over Paul Freund because he did not know him as well as he knew Byron White and Arthur Goldberg. See O'Brien, *Storm Center*, p. 48. See Chapter 4 for an explanation of why Kennedy did not nominate Hastie.

96. *New York Times*, July 21, 1965, p. 1; August 30, 1962, p. 1.

97. Victor Lasky, *Arthur J. Goldberg: The Old and the New* (New Rochelle, N.Y.: Arlington House, 1970), pp. 13–14.

98. Charles Moritz, *Current Biography Yearbook 1961* (New York: H. W. Wilson, 1961), pp. 178–79.

99. Quoted in Harold W. Chase and Allen H. Lerman, eds., *Kennedy and the Press* (New York: Thomas Y. Crowell, 1965), p. 311.

100. Dorothy Goldberg, *A Private View of a Public Life* (New York: Charterhouse, 1975), p. 2.

101. Theodore C. Sorensen, *Kennedy* (New York: Harper & Row, 1965), pp. 253, 273.

102. Benjamin C. Bradlee, *Conversations with Kennedy* (New York: W. W. Norton, 1975), pp. 69–70.

103. *Time*, September 7, 1962, p. 10.

104. See Mersky and Jacobstein, *The Supreme Court of the United States*, vol. 6, "Arthur Goldberg."

105. Karfunkel and Ryley suggested such a correlation in *The Jewish Seat*, p. 130.

106. *Time*, July 30, 1965, p. 11.

107. *New York Times*, July 21, 1965, p. 2. Wicker erred in referring to "5,500,000 *voters*" (emphasis added). That figure was the total Jewish *population* in America.

108. Isaacs, *Jews and American Politics*, p. 152; Weyl, *The Jew in American Politics*, p. 166.

109. Robert Shogun, *A Question of Judgment: The Fortas Case and the Struggle for the Supreme Court* (Indianapolis: Bobbs-Merrill, 1972), pp. 30–31. See also Bruce Allen Murphy's *Fortas: The Rise and Ruin of a Supreme Court Justice* (New York: William Morrow, 1988), p. 4.

110. Quoted in Isaacs, *Jews in American Politics*, p. 21.

111. Shogun, *A Question of Judgment*, p. 33.

112. Ibid., pp. 39–56.

113. *New York Times*, July 29, 1965, p. 1.

114. Lyndon B. Johnson, *The Vantage Point: Perspectives of the Presidency* (New York: Holt, Rinehart and Winston, 1971), pp. 544–45.

115. The former president did not mention that in 1948 he had called on Fortas, an acquaintance from New Deal days, for legal assistance in a disputed primary election for the Texas Democratic senatorial nomination. The young Fortas's efforts at the Supreme Court bar in Johnson's behalf resulted in the stay of a lower federal court's restraining order that would have kept L.B.J. off the ballot. See Murphy, *Fortas*, Ch. 4.

116. Ibid., pp. 168–69.

117. Lady Bird Johnson, *A White House Diary* (New York: Holt, Rinehart and Winston, 1970), p. 299.

118. Quoted in Murphy, *Fortas*, p. 175.

119. *New York Times*, July 29, 1965, p. 1; *Time*, August 6, 1965, p. 18.

120. Shogun, *A Question of Judgment*, p. 109.

121. Fred Graham suggested such a motive in his *New York Times Magazine* article, "The Many-Sided Justice Fortas," June 4, 1967, p. 88.

122. Shogun, *A Question of Judgment*, p. 151.

123. See Mersky and Jacobstein, *The Supreme Court of the United States*, vol. 7, "Abe Fortas."

124. Those GOP senators opposing the Fortas nomination were: Carl T. Curtis of Nebraska, Strom Thurmond of South Carolina, and John Williams of Delaware. Abraham, *Justices and Presidents*, p. 284.

125. *New York Times*, April 18, 1970, p. 10.

126. Quoted in Isaacs, *Jews and American Politics*, pp. 189–90.

127. See my commentary "With Ginsburg, a return to high court 'Jewish seat,' " *Orlando Sentinel*, November 2, 1987.

128. Isaacs, *Jews and American Politics*, pp. 152–53.

129. Ibid. See pp. 182–97 for an analysis of the Jewish vote in the 1972 election.

130. Learsi, *The Jews in America*, p. 327.

131. Weyl, *The Jew in American Politics*, pp. 301–02.

132. Judge Stephen Reinhardt of the United States Court of Appeals for the Ninth Circuit has made an emotional appeal for renewed Jewish representation on the Supreme Court in part because he contends that there is no Jewish leadership in either the legislative or executive branch—a debatable conclusion given the number of influential Jewish senators and cabinet members during the past three decades. Among them are Senators Jacob Javits (R.–N.Y.), Abraham Ribicoff (D.–Conn.), Warren Rudman (R.–N.H.), Arlen Specter (R.–Penn.), Howard Metzenbaum (D.–Ohio), Carl Levin (D.–Mich.), Ernest Gruening (D.–Alas.), William Cohen (R.–Maine), and cabinet members Goldberg, Ribicoff, and Edward Levi. (Indeed, Levi, as attorney general in the Ford administration, participated in the selection of John Paul Stevens for the Supreme Court.) In addition, Reinhardt also emphasizes the psychological importance of a Jewish justice who could "serve as a symbol of hope for Jewish youth." One might question, however, the implications of Reinhardt's conclusion that the high court "has now been closed to them [Jews] . . . for an entire generation." There is simply no evidence to indicate that Jews have been deliberately excluded from the Court. See Stephen Reinhardt, "Jewishness and Judging: A Judge's Thoughts on *Two Jewish Justices*," 10 *Cardozo Law Review* 2345 (1989): 2357.

133. Karp, *Haven and Home*, p. 370.

134. Ibid.

135. Judge Reinhardt is one of the few voices demanding a return to Jewish representation on the Supreme Court, but he admits that the Jewish community has been notably silent on the issue. He writes: "The recent aborted nomination of Judge Douglas Ginsburg failed to result in the rush of Jewish support anticipated by the administration. Instead, Jews generally adopted a cautious wait-and-see attitude." Reinhardt, "Jewishness and Judging," at 2356–7.

Chapter 4 _____

Race: A "Black Seat"?

The second representative factor to be examined in this study—race—offers a slightly different set of challenges and opportunities for determining the relationship between it and appointments to the Supreme Court. Unlike the factor of religion, which provided at least a handful of illustrations for both Catholic and Jewish religious affiliation, the racial category includes a sole appointment—that of black civil rights attorney and public servant, Thurgood Marshall, in 1967.

Nonetheless, because the appointment of the Court's only black justice occurred so relatively recently, and in an era of obvious concern over racial issues in this country, a wealth of evidence exists for drawing conclusions on the link between race and President Lyndon B. Johnson's historic elevation of Marshall to the nation's highest court. Therefore, this chapter focuses on the more recent demographic, sociological, geographic, and electoral developments of American blacks.

BLACK AMERICANS IN THE TWENTIETH CENTURY

One of the landmark events for black American development in the twentieth century was the black exodus from the South. Before the turn of the century, over 90 percent of black Americans lived below the Mason-Dixon Line. Above the line, states had abolished slavery in the early nineteenth century. Economic factors, however, may have outweighed humanitarian considerations in the northern abolition movement. Waves of European immigrants were an alternate source of cheap labor; and because relatively few groups in the North directly benefited from slave labor, there was less pressure to preserve it. Ironically, opposition to blacks in the North increased after the abolition of slavery. Particularly during periods of economic depression, violence often erupted between blacks and whites when they competed for the same jobs.[1]

Nevertheless, blacks did not face the rigid restraints of Jim Crow in the North; and by World War I, blacks began moving north in increasing numbers. Although a lull occurred in black migration from the South during the Great Depression, World War II had the same effect on black demographics as the war in 1917. In the 1940s, the net migration of blacks from the South to cities in the North and on the West Coast was nearly 1.6 million[2] At the beginning of World War II, 27 percent of black Americans lived outside the South; by the start of the Korean War, that figure had increased to 37 percent. Almost half of the black population in the United States was settled outside the South by 1960.[3] Only in the 1970s, when blacks began to move into the South rather than out of it, did this demographic trend begin to reverse itself.[4]

Such geographical shifts in the black population have had a direct impact on black political power in the United States. Although "white primaries," literacy tests, "grandfather clauses," poll taxes, and other more violent measures effectively thwarted the black vote in the South during the first half of the twentieth century, blacks usually exercised their right to vote in the North and West with virtually no interference. Moreover, they "moved into such big-city states as New York, Pennsylvania, Illinois, and Michigan, which carry large numbers of electoral votes. In these states the major city contains a black voting population whose ballots could mean the difference between success and failure in a national election."[5]

To be sure, presidential aspirants had paid little heed to black political interests until potential black influence on the outcome of national elections became a reality. On this score, blacks share a common background with Catholics and Jews, who won the attention of White House hopefuls in proportion to the electoral potency of the two religious groups.

Presidents in the first decades of the twentieth century largely ignored, or actually worked against, black interests. Theodore Roosevelt made a symbolic gesture to Negro constituents by inviting the black leader Booker T. Washington to dine with him at the White House. Washington served as political adviser to both T.R. and his successor William Howard Taft and was somewhat successful in urging several Negro appointments on the two presidents. Robert H. Terrell served as judge of the municipal court in the District of Columbia from 1901 to 1921. Charles W. Anderson was collector of internal revenue in New York from 1905 to 1915. In 1911 William H. Lewis received an appointment as assistant attorney general and served two years in that office. These were the highest federal judicial and executive appointments of blacks in this country up to that time. Still, blacks received little beyond such symbolic recognition from the White House.[6]

As with American Catholics and Jews, the New Deal era was a watershed in the political history of Negro Americans. Though the civil rights revolution was still some thirty years away, the sincere interest of prominent New Dealers in the status of black Americans provided an entree for blacks into politics. The motivations of the Roosevelt administration resulted from a mixture of higher ideals and baser electoral considerations. Its

concern was part of the larger humanitarian interest in the welfare of all the underprivileged in American society. At the same time, the Negro vote had reached sizable proportions in a number of Northern cities, creating an additional motivation for the attention to Negro welfare among New Deal politicians.[7]

Blacks had more to gain from New Deal policies than most other Americans. Subject to "last hired, first fired" employment practices, blacks suffered even more than other groups from the severe economic depression of the 1930s. Because blacks were unemployed at a higher rate than other Americans, they benefited in higher proportions from the government relief programs established under F.D.R.'s New Deal. By Roosevelt's landslide reelection in 1936, black voters had made a dramatic shift from their traditional political home in the party of Abraham Lincoln to the Democratic party, joining other ethnic groups, Catholics, and Jews in an electoral realignment that forged the New Deal coalition.[8]

THE BLACK VOTE

Though still small in absolute numbers as a result of the South's continuing practice of disenfranchisement, the black vote continued to provide strategic support for F.D.R. in his final two runs for the White House. In Roosevelt's unprecedented third campaign for the presidency in 1940, the vote was relatively close in several northern and border states, where the majority of black votes were concentrated (the states included Illinois, Indiana, Maryland, Michigan, Missouri, New York, Ohio, and Pennsylvania). Only two of these states registered in the Republican column of Wendell Wilkie, but a slight switch in votes would have altered the results in each state, except Maryland. Such a switch would have given Wilkie 153 more electoral votes and pulled him within striking distance of the incumbent. Herbert Brownell, National Committee Chairman of the Republican party, calculated that a switch of only 303,414 votes in fifteen states outside the South would have made Thomas Dewey the victor by eight electoral votes in the 1944 presidential election. The black vote held the potential of switching several states from one column to the other.[9]

The year 1944 marked another momentous event for the black vote in the United States. In the case of *Smith v. Allwright*,[10] the Supreme Court declared the "white primary" unconstitutional and, in doing so, enfranchised 750,000 black citizens.[11] The 1948 election was the first presidential campaign since Reconstruction in which the plight of the American black played an appreciable role. For example, the Democratic party's adoption of a strong civil rights plank at its national convention sparked the angry walkout by southern "Dixiecrats," and overwhelming support from the black electorate was decisive in Harry Truman's "snatching victory from the jaws of defeat." Henry L. Moon, the public relations director for the National Association for the Advancement of Colored People (NAACP), had argued in his book *Black Balance of Power*, published in early 1948, that the black vote in several strategic states could determine the outcome of a close national election. Truman's upset victory over Republican Thomas Dewey added credence to Moon's thesis.[12]

When one recalls that his victory would not have have been possible without the electoral votes of California, Illinois, and Ohio, and that he managed to carry those states by narrow margins of 17,000, 33,000, and 7,000 votes respectively, it is readily apparent that the overwhelmingly pro-Truman preference of Negro voters was indispensable in placing the three states in the Democratic column.[13]

By 1952, evidence indicated that more than 1 million blacks were registered to vote in the South.[14] Black political participation, stifled since Reconstruction, reemerged in the decade after World War II, with candidates vying for black votes in the North and South. A 1953 study of eight northern industrial cities (Chicago, Cincinnati, Cleveland, Detroit, Kansas City, New York City, Pittsburgh, and St. Louis) showed that Adlai Stevenson polled a larger percentage of black votes in 1952 than did President Truman in 1948. Stevenson's success among black voters marked a high point of black support for the Democratic party in the eight cities studied.[15]

In the Eisenhower/Stevenson rematch four years later, the GOP made an effort to attract blacks back to the Republican fold. The Republican overtures, combined with Governor Stevenson's more moderate platform in his second run for the White House, produced the desired result for the incumbent president. An NAACP survey of election returns from predominantly black sections of 63 cities across the country showed a 19.9 percent gain among black voters for President Eisenhower.[16] Anticipating a close presidential election in 1960, an article written just prior to the race concluded that neither party could "afford to ignore the numerical weight of the Negro vote."[17]

The Democratic candidate, Senator John F. Kennedy, heeded such advice; he "campaigned vigorously for the black vote, and his narrow victory would not have been possible without it."[18] The "strange bed-fellows" nature of the Democratic coalition found J.F.K. in the uncomfortable position of attempting to support the erupting civil rights revolution, while placating southern segregationists, who represented a potential bottleneck to his legislative program in Congress. With the Kennedy administration's implied, if not expressed, support, the drive to register black voters in the South continued and nearly doubled the number of black registrants from 1 to 2 million by 1964.[19]

At least 70 percent of these more than 2 million black voters in the South exercised their right to vote in the 1964 presidential election. The overwhelming majority of those votes contributed to President Lyndon B. Johnson's landslide victory over Senator Barry Goldwater. The black vote in Florida was illustrative of its general impact on the election's outcome, particularly in the South: Johnson won a narrow victory in the Sunshine State; only 37,000 votes separated him from his Republican opponent. The fact that between 97 and 99 percent of Florida's estimated 211,000 black voters cast their ballots for L.B.J. was decisive. Professor Everett Carl Ladd calculated that if all black votes were simply subtracted, Johnson would have lost Florida, Virginia, Tennessee, and Arkansas; and North Carolina would have just barely swung to his column. Ladd conceded, however, that the civil rights issue also prompted defections from the Democratic candidate on the part of outraged whites, who traditionally had formed the backbone of the Solid South.[20]

THE CIVIL RIGHTS REVOLUTION

The so-called civil rights revolution in the United States was in full swing when Lyndon Johnson was elected to his own presidential term, and it was intertwined with the issue of black suffrage and American electoral politics. Part of the revolution itself was dedicated to recapturing the vote for blacks disenfranchised since the end of Reconstruction. In turn, full and meaningful participation by blacks in the electoral process was intended to reduce, and finally eliminate, a color-based caste system in this country.

Throughout the twentieth century, blacks had resorted to a number of strategies to end the U.S.'s version of apartheid. The moderate NAACP adopted a policy of carrying the good fight to the nation's courts. Starting in the 1930s, it successfully began to chip away at the "separate-but-equal" doctrine as applied to graduate and professional schools.[21] The United States Supreme Court finally dealt the death blow to its 1896 *Plessy* ruling in its 1954 landmark decision in *Brown v. Board of Education*.[22] The case symbolized the culmination of two decades of judicial struggle and ironically transferred the Negro movement from the courts to the streets. The decade following the *Brown* decision was marked by bus boycotts, Freedom Rides, sit-ins, marches, and a whole host of other acts of civil disobedience that turned uncivil with the black urban riots of the mid-1960s.

During this period, the federal government responded with legislation that increasingly addressed the issues raised by the civil rights movement. Thus Congress joined the Court, albeit timidly at first, in attempts to redress black grievances. The 1957 Civil Rights Act, which, among other provisions, established the Civil Rights Commission and procedures to protect the individual's right to vote, aided the federal government in bringing suits against five southern states to eliminate voting barriers for blacks.[23] As the first major piece of civil rights legislation since Reconstruction, the 1957 act packed a symbolic punch as well. The Civil Rights Act of 1960 added teeth to the voting guarantees for blacks in the 1957 act. But, on the whole, the 1960 act, like its predecessor three years earlier, was still more symbolic than substantive. It took the incomparable political acumen of President Johnson, and the emotional reaction to President Kennedy's assassination in 1963, to push the comprehensive Civil Rights Act of 1964, which the Kennedy administration had drafted, through Congress.

The 1964 act provided for, among other things, the extension of the life of the Civil Rights Commission; the proscription of employment discrimination on the basis of race, color, sex, religion, or national origin; the prohibition of racial discrimination by voting registrars; judicial procedure to desegregate state and local government facilities; the exclusion of federal funding for public or private programs that discriminated on the basis of race, color, or national origin; and the proscription of race, religion, color, or national origin discrimination in public accommodations that are linked to interstate commerce.

As black protests continued, President Johnson submitted a bill to Congress, which was to drive the final nail into the coffins of those who would deny blacks the right to vote in this country. The bill was enacted as the Voting Rights Act of 1965 and provided the legal mechanisms for overturning all legal roadblocks to black exercise of the franchise.[24]

BLACKS ON THE FEDERAL COURTS

The appointments of blacks to the lower federal courts, and ultimately to the Supreme Court, have followed the same slow and agonizing trail that American blacks blazed in their twentieth-century efforts to attain civil rights and liberties. Theodore Roosevelt's aforementioned 1901 appointment of Robert H. Terrell to the District of Columbia Municipal Court may be considered the first presidential appointment of a black judge. As noted above, the presidency of Franklin Roosevelt was the first to offer sincere concern for black interests, and F.D.R. has the distinction of appointing the first black judge to a federal bench. In 1937 he selected William H. Hastie for the United States District Court for the Virgin Islands to serve a four-year term.[25]

Black advances in federal judicial appointments coincided with increased black participation and clout in American electoral politics. In 1945, President Truman nominated Irvin C. Mollison to the United States Customs Court. Mollison thus became the first black judge to be appointed to the federal bench in the *continental* United States and the first federal judge to be appointed to a life term.[26]

During his hard-fought 1948 campaign for the presidency, Harry Truman welcomed the aid of William Hastie. The latter had resigned his seat on the Virgin Islands District Court in 1939, after two years of service, to accept the deanship of the Howard University Law School. Hastie had done his undergraduate work at Amherst College, where he was elected to Phi Beta Kappa and was graduated magna cum laude and was valedictorian of his class. He received his law degree from Harvard and served on the editorial board of the *Harvard Law Review*, much to the chagrin of some southern students. During World War II, Hastie attempted to represent black interests as an aide to Secretary of War Henry L. Stimson.[27] By 1945 the National Lawyers Guild (NLG) was urging Attorney General Tom Clark to push Hastie's appointment to the U.S. Circuit Court of Appeals in the District of Columbia. Clark assured the NLG that Hastie's name was under consideration for nomination to the federal bench. But later that year, President Truman appointed him governor of the Virgin Islands.[28]

As the 1948 presidential campaign heated up, and Truman worried that Henry Wallace's Progressive party would siphon crucial black votes from his candidacy, Hastie offered to take a leave from his Virgin Islands governorship in order to woo black ballots for the incumbent president. Hastie traveled to city after city, meeting with his fellow Negroes and rallying them to Truman's camp. The Virgin Island's governor called his contribution to Truman's dramatic victory over heavily favored Thomas Dewey "relatively unimportant." Thurgood Marshall begs to differ: "He got the votes."[29] Politicians who witnessed Hastie's campaign skills testified to his effectiveness. Hastie's recent biographer, Gilbert Ware, has described the governor's role in Truman's success: "It is certain that Truman did not win on black votes alone. It is equally certain that he would not have won without them."[30]

Truman is quoted as telling Hastie as the campaign drew to a close: "Bill, you may think nobody here knows all the towns you've been in and all the church groups and barbecues you've spoken at during these past weeks. But I know. And I'm grateful. And I'll always remember."[31] Truman rewarded Hastie one year later with a nomination to the United States Court of Appeals for the Third Circuit. After a delay of ten months, while the Senate Judiciary Committee investigated his background and grilled him about his affiliations with "left-wing" organizations, the full Senate gave its unanimous consent to Hastie's recess appointment. In doing so, it made Hastie the first black federal judge on an Article III court, the first black to occupy a seat on a federal appellate court, and the highest-ranking black member of the federal judiciary.[32]

During his two terms as president, Dwight Eisenhower appointed no blacks to the federal trial or appellate courts. As a presidential candidate in 1960, Senator John F. Kennedy articulated the concern of some national leaders that blacks should be represented in the federal judiciary. In a campaign address in August 1960, to the American Bar Association, Kennedy asserted: "I assure you that in a new Democratic Administration there will be far better representation, on the basis of merit, of persons of all our racial groups, including particularly those who in the past have been excluded on the basis of prejudice."[33] In 1961 President Kennedy appointed the first black as a trial court judge with life tenure, James B. Parsons, to the U.S. District Court for the Northern District of Illinois. Kennedy named another black, Wade H. McCree, Jr., to the U.S. District Court (Eastern District of Michigan) in 1961. President Johnson would promote McCree to the Sixth Circuit Court of Appeals in 1966. (Jimmy Carter appointed him as solicitor general in 1977.) L.B.J. named another black, Spottswood W. Robinson III, a U.S. District Court Judge since 1963, to the U.S. Circuit Court for the District of Columbia in 1966.[34] In all, Johnson appointed five blacks to the U.S. District Courts.[35]

THURGOOD MARSHALL

In addition to Kennedy's two successful appointments of Negroes to the U.S. District Courts before his death (i.e., Parsons and McCree), he nominated Thurgood Marshall for the Second Circuit Court of Appeals in September 1961. Internal and external pressure on the Kennedy administration was a factor in its selection of Marshall for the federal appellate bench. In his first few months in office, J.F.K. was urged to carry through on his campaign promise to appoint a qualified black to an authoritative position in government. In particular, the NAACP stressed that Kennedy should nominate Thurgood Marshall to fill the first available Supreme Court vacancy. Within the administration, Attorney General Robert Kennedy opposed Marshall's nomination for the circuit court,[36] arguing that the political cost of getting Marshall confirmed over the objections of southern segregationists in the Senate would be prohibitive. Marshall recalls a tête-à-tête with Bobby Kennedy, who wanted him to take a district court appointment instead. Growing impatient with Marshall's insistence, Kennedy said, "You don't seem to understand. It's this [the district court job] or nothing." Marshall replied, "I do understand.

The trouble is that you are different from me. You don't know what it means, but all I've had in my life is nothing. It's not new to me. So goodbye." With that, the future justice walked out on the attorney general.[37]

Indeed, Marshall's backers could muster an impressive list of reasons for making him the second Negro to sit on the U.S. Court of Appeals. An honors graduate of the "black Princeton," Lincoln University in Pennsylvania, Marshall had received his law degree from Howard Law School, where he was graduated first in his class. In the 1930s, Howard attracted to its faculty such black legal luminaries as Charles Houston, William Hastie, and James Nabrit, who planned and engineered the legal assault on segregation in this country. An observer of, and sometimes participant in, their strategy sessions, Marshall became one of their star pupils.[38]

Just seven years after his graduation from Howard, Marshall was appointed special counsel of the NAACP Legal Defense and Educational Fund. The list of cases he successfully argued in that capacity before the Supreme Court comprises most of the major judicial victories in the civil rights movement of the 1940s and 1950s including *Smith v. Allwright, Sipuel v. University of Oklahoma, Shelley v. Kraemer, Sweatt v. Painter, McLaurin v. Oklahoma State Regents,* and, most important, *Brown v. Board of Education.*[39]

With pressure from black voters increasing, Louis Martin, President Kennedy's chief black adviser, persuaded the president to overrule his brother's opposition and name Marshall to the circuit court. But just as Bobby Kennedy predicted, the Senate responded with an immediate roadblock; the Judiciary Committee delayed the confirmation hearings for eight months.[40] There is some dispute over the nature of a rumored deal that may have occurred between the Kennedys and Senate Judiciary Committee Chairman James O. Eastland. Arthur M. Schlesinger, Jr., Kennedy aide and biographer, intimated that a quid pro quo was involved in Eastland's ultimate acceptance of Marshall's appointment. Just before the administration sent Marshall's nomination up to the Senate (along with two other black nominees for district judgeships), Kennedy appointed W. Harold Cox, a southern segregationist and Eastland's college roommate, to be a federal district judge in Mississippi. Schlesinger noted that Eastland's racist remark to R.F.K.—"tell your brother that if he will give me Harold Cox I will give him the nigger"—may be apocryphal. (The nasty comment has been well-documented, however.) But at the very least, Schlesinger believed that the appointment of Eastland's old college friend "helped soften Eastland for Marshall."[41]

Finally, in September 1962, nearly a year and a half after Marshall's initial nomination, the full Judiciary Committee approved the appointment (with four dissenting votes); and on September 11, the full Senate confirmed Marshall's appointment by a vote of 54–16. The "yea" votes were split nearly evenly between Democratic and Republican senators. All 16 negative votes were cast by southern Democrats.[42]

During his "1,000-day" presidency, J.F.K. had two opportunities to fill vacancies on the Supreme Court. The first vacancy occurred with the retirement of Justice Charles Whittaker in early 1962. Among the names on Kennedy's "short list" was Judge William Hastie, who was in the midst of his distinguished career on the Third Circuit Court of Appeals. Chief Judge William Denman of the Ninth Circuit Court of Appeals had twice offered Hastie's name to President Eisenhower for Supreme Court seats that eventually went to John Marshall Harlan II and William J. Brennan, Jr.[43] Thus, even before Kennedy's consideration of Hastie in 1962, he had earned the historic distinction of the first black to be recognized as a possible Supreme Court nominee. In a 1964 interview, Robert Kennedy described the consideration given Hastie's candidacy for the Whittaker seat:

I had originally been for putting a Negro on [the Court]. . . . My first recommendation was Hastie. I went up and saw [Chief Justice Earl] Warren about Hastie. He was violently opposed to having Hastie on the Court. . . . He said, "He's not a liberal, and he'd be opposed to all the measures that we are interested in, and he would just be completely unsatisfactory."[44]

Justice William O. Douglas, an old Kennedy friend, told the attorney general that Hastie would be "just one more vote for Frankfurter."[45]

The "best and the brightest" of the Kennedy White House inner circle gave careful consideration to the racial, political, and professional merits of a potential Hastie nomination. Robert Kennedy remembered that no one among his brother's advisers was opposed to Hastie on racial grounds. There was opposition, however, based on politics. Some thought the appointment of a black at that time would simply seem too political, "too obvious." Kennedy's adviser, Clark Clifford, counseled the president that "it would be a mistake for him to reach out just to put a Negro on the bench." Clifford characterized Hastie's judicial record as "reasonably good" but not outstanding. The attorney general countered that "obviousness" was not a valid reason for rejection. He argued that Hastie

was a good judge, and that it was an appropriate time. . . . If you were going to consider the five or six best judges of the Circuit Court, you'd put him there. So that was the basis of it. . . . I didn't know when another vacancy would come, and I thought that it would mean so much overseas.[46]

In order to settle the judicial merit question, Assistant Attorney General Nicholas Katzenbach conducted a thorough study of Hastie's opinions and pronounced them "competent and pedestrian." Katzenbach later recalled, "When [I said] I thought his opinions were rather pedestrian, this just killed him with President Kennedy."[47]

Notwithstanding Katzenbach's recollection, the political ramifications seemed to have weighed more heavily against Hastie. J.F.K. confided to Arthur Schlesinger at the time that "it was just too early" to appoint Hastie, though the president counted on more vacancies in the future, for which Hastie could receive an appointment. He also intended to nominate Harvard Law Professor Paul Freund and his Secretary of Labor Arthur Goldberg, who had been passed over when J.F.K. chose his long-time friend and Deputy Assistant Attorney General Byron R. White to replace Whittaker.[48] Of the trio that Kennedy anticipated sending to the high bench, only Arthur Goldberg received the honor. He garnered the only other nomination that fate allowed Kennedy to make to the Court before his assassination.

Thus, the political argument against Hastie followed this reasoning, as expressed by James E. Clayton in his book on the Supreme Court:

If the President should appoint Hastie, critics would say it was a move to get the Negro vote. Regardless of Hastie's qualifications, the President felt this would put him [Hastie] in a difficult position on the Court. He would be attacked constantly on the ground that he was there solely because of his race and not because of his ability. Both the President and the Attorney General decided that these difficulties might not exist if the President should decide later in his term of office to appoint a Negro.[49]

The realities of congressional politics further dampened the Kennedy administration's enthusiasm for a Hastie nomination. J.F.K. had recently been on the losing side of a bruising battle with the Congress, which had defeated the administration's proposal for creating a Department of Housing and Urban Development. The congressional mood in 1961 would not tolerate Kennedy's intention to appoint Robert C. Weaver, an eminent economist, as secretary of the new department and the nation's first black cabinet member.[50]

Lyndon Johnson seized the opportunity that Kennedy had hoped would be his in a more propitious political climate. True to his masterful command of most political situations (the Vietnam War being the obvious and fatal exception in Johnson's long career), L.B.J. apparently carefully orchestrated the nomination of the first black Supreme Court justice. The man he groomed for the appointment was Thurgood Marshall, not William Hastie, whom Johnson chose to consider too unknown.[51] In the summer of 1965, the president spoke to Judge Marshall about accepting the position of solicitor general of the United States. There was speculation at the time that service in the Department of Justice's third-ranking post was to be an interim step for Marshall to mount the Court eventually.

In a 1970 interview, former President Johnson admitted such an implicit intention on his part:

I did not tell Marshall of my intentions at this time. But I fully intended to eventually appoint him to the Court. I believed that a black man had to be appointed to that body. . . . I wanted him to serve as Solicitor General as an advocate to prove to everyone, including the President, what he could do.[52]

Johnson apparently had confided his plans to his wife, and perhaps to Congressman Carl Albert (D.–Okla.). Early in July 1965, Lady Bird Johnson recorded in her diary that her husband had spoken to Albert about efforts on behalf of blacks. Mrs. Johnson wrote:

Lyndon admires Judge Thurgood Marshall and spoke of the possibility of asking him to be Solicitor General, and then if he proved himself outstanding perhaps when a vacancy on the Supreme Court opened up, he might nominate him as a Justice—the first of his race.[53]

On July 13 the president announced his nomination of Marshall to be solicitor general. The Senate Judiciary Committee displayed none of the recalcitrance it had demonstrated three years earlier over Marshall's judicial appointment. Instead, the committee completed its hearings in one day, and the full Senate confirmed the nomination on August 11 "without objection."[54]

Less than two years later, on June 14, 1967, major U.S. newspapers heralded the fulfillment of Johnson's plan. Virtually all headlines broadcast the news that L.B.J. had named the "first Negro" to the United States Supreme Court. Just twenty-four hours after Justice Tom C. Clark's retirement from the Court (as a result of his son Ramsey's becoming attorney general), President Johnson had made his historic announcement that Marshall merited appointment to the nation's highest tribunal by virtue of his "distinguished record" in the law. Further stressing Marshall's professional credentials and judicial experience and implicitly acknowledging the importance of race in his decision, Johnson continued: "He is the best qualified by training and by very valuable service to the country. I believe it is the right thing to do, the right time to do it, and the right man and the right place."[55]

Although Marshall's legal and judicial experience and demonstrable liberal inclinations rounded out the reasons for Johnson's selection of him for the Court, the indisputable and obvious primary factor was Marshall's color. Or as Justice William O. Douglas bluntly wrote in his autobiography: "Marshall was named simply because he was black, and in the 1960s that was reason enough."[56] Railing against such considerations in presidential motivations, syndicated columnist Joseph Kraft argued that Marshall's appointment symbolized only "the outmoded principle of ethnic representation, and for years to come his seat will probably be a Negro seat."[57]

Nevertheless, most of the press recognized that Johnson's nomination of the first black Supreme Court justice would give "the Johnson Administration one more claim to the loyalty of blacks in general, along with such legislation as the Civil Rights Act of 1964 and the Voting Rights Act of 1965."[58] (Of course, in electoral terms, such support would matter little after L.B.J. bowed out of the 1968 presidential contest in March of that year.) Just recently, however, it came to light that Johnson believed at the end of his life that his appointment of Marshall and other blacks to high office destroyed his electoral chances. In a sealed 1977 interview that Marshall granted to Columbia University and allowed quoted for the first time in 1990, the justice said of L.B.J., "He thought that moving me here [the Supreme Court] was what killed him off." When asked if his appointment was more critical than the Vietnam War in damaging Johnson's electoral chances, Marshall responded that the former president told him the week before he died that he felt that "they [Johnson's enemies] used the Vietnam War as the excuse."[59] Johnson's propensity for hyperbolic distortions of reality, so evident during his political career, may have been exacerbated by an impending sense of his own death. Yet, on the day that the Senate confirmed Marshall's nomination to sit on the Supreme Court, President Johnson reportedly told the nation's first black justice, "Well, congratulations, but the hell you caused me. Goddammit, I never went through so much hell."[60]

Despite Johnson's privately expressed gloom over his appointment of Marshall, black leaders and white political pundits alike acknowledged the symbolic value of Johnson's act. A member of the former category, Whitney M. Young, Jr., rhapsodized:

This is an event of tremendous significance for Negro citizens. It is an example of the heights which are open to kids in the ghetto. There was a time when a Negro youth could aspire only to becoming a boxing champ or singer. The doors to positions of power and influence were tightly shut. But now we see Negroes in Congress, in the cabinet, in high administrative positions, and now, with Marshall's appointment, in the most important spot in the judicial system. His appointment is proof that, whatever the obstacles, Negroes can fight their way to the top.[61]

L.B.J., in his own memoirs, echoed Young's sentiments. After cataloguing the "distinguished black men and women" whom he had named to high governmental offices during his presidency, the former president concluded: "I . . . deeply believed that with these appointments Negro mothers could look at their children and hope with good reason that someday their sons and daughters might reach the highest offices their government could offer." But Johnson's recollection that he appointed blacks to authoritative government offices because of "their competence, wisdom, and courage, not for the color of their skin"[62] is a half-truth at best.

Both support for, and opposition to, Marshall's appointment centered on his race. Other issues were peripheral. As Court correspondent Fred Graham observed of the confirmation process: "Rarely was the nominee's race mentioned, though it was largely the point at issue."[63] Nevertheless, the Senate moved with what might be called "deliberate speed," confirming Marshall by a 69–11 vote after a little over two-month delay. "Although all but one of Mr. Marshall's critics were from the Deep South, they insisted that their opposition was unrelated to the fact that he . . . [would] be the first Negro to sit on the Supreme Court." Opponents' *overt* objections to Marshall centered on his anticipated "judicial activism."[64] Racist though the motivations of Marshall's critics may have been, time has proved the opponents correct in predicting his judicial posture once seated on the Court.

Whether the lack of more opposition was a result of "Johnson's adroitness in conditioning the public for what he intend[ed] to do" (as columnist Clayton Fritchey suggested at the time of Marshall's appointment)[65] or a general sign of changing times and changing attitudes toward race in this country is a question perhaps best answered indirectly by Justice Marshall himself. At a 1968 reception, held by high-ranking blacks in the Johnson administration to pay tribute to their mentor, Marshall commended the president: "The people in this room have just one purpose—to say 'Thank you, Mr. President.' You didn't wait. You took the bull by the horns. You didn't wait for the times. You made them!"[66]

Presidents Truman and Kennedy had broken the race barrier by appointing the first black federal circuit court and district court judges with life terms. Still, neither they nor the intervening chief executive, Dwight Eisenhower, attempted to appoint the first black to the highest bench. The civil rights revolution paved the way for Lyndon Johnson to take such an initiative. Like other historic presidential actions, the times were right, and Johnson had the political skills to make the most of his times.

BLACKS ON THE SUPREME COURT

What factors will determine whether Thurgood Marshall's appointment to the Court established a "black seat"? Two practical considerations, among others, will play a role in the answer: the number of blacks in the legal profession and the number of blacks in the judiciary. Such factors obviously increase the pool from which presidents might choose black Supreme Court justices in the future.

United States Census Bureau figures paint the statistical portrait of the struggle of black Americans to penetrate the barriers of the white legal establishment in this country. In 1890 only 431 black lawyers were reported among the employed Negro population in this country. By 1910 that figure had nearly doubled to 798. Of course, the Jim Crow system was a major factor in severely limiting black opportunities to lead successful legal careers. Until 1936, blacks were not admitted to "white" law schools on a regular basis. Until 1943, applicants to the American Bar Association had to list their color on the application forms. And until 1946, no blacks served on the faculties of predominantly white law schools.[67]

As World War II approached, 1,925 black lawyers were recorded in this country. In other words, there was one black lawyer for every 13,000 blacks. The judicial and legislative aspects of the civil rights revolution had a profound effect on the academic legal community. By 1960 census figures indicated that there were 2,004 black lawyers; the total was 3,406 by 1970. The latter figure comprised about 1.0 percent of the total number of American lawyers. By 1979 the percentage had increased to nearly 2.5 percent or an estimated 12,000 blacks out of 478,000 American attorneys. Two years later, the estimated number of black lawyers was 13,594, which represented slightly less than 4 percent of the total.[68]

In the 1960s and 1970s, the number of black law students increased nearly eightfold, from about 700 (or 1 percent of all American law students in accredited schools) to 5,503 (or about 4.7 percent) in 1976–77.[69] By just three years later (1979–80), however, both the number and percentage of blacks enrolled in J.D. degree programs had fallen to 5,257 and 4.2 percent, respectively.[70]

In obtaining judicial posts, blacks have fared better at the federal than the state level. In 1980 *The National Roster of Black Judicial Officers* reported 505 black judges in state judiciaries (or 2 percent of state court judges).[71] The percentage of black judicial officials at the federal level in 1980 was more than double the state figure—about 5 percent or 94 federal judges and magistrates.[72] By 1985, statistics for black judges at both levels of government demonstrated slight gains with 465 black state court judges (3.8 percent), including 9 black judges on state high courts (2.7 percent) and 33 black judges (4.7 percent) on intermediate appellate courts. In 1985 there were 53 black federal judges, constituting 7 percent of the federal judiciary.[73]

President Jimmy Carter was largely responsible for increased representation of blacks on the federal bench. During his one term in the White House, he appointed more black federal judges than the combined total of all his predecessors. He named nine blacks to the circuit courts (including Amalya Kearse, the first female black federal appellate court judge) and twenty-eight blacks to the district courts. The 1978 Omnibus Judgeship Act, which created 152 new federal judgeships, aided Carter's record performance in black appointments. Moreover, he made a concerted effort, through his Circuit Court Nominating Commissions (established by executive order in 1977 but abolished during Reagan's first term), to appoint minorities and women to the federal bench.[74] His controversial judicial affirmative action policy prompted arguments that he was emphasizing "representativeness" to the detriment of merit, while failing to eliminate partisanship from the judicial selection process (another avowed goal of his commissions). The wisdom of Carter's policy aside, he did create a potential pool of experienced candidates for the Supreme Court for a future president with similar ideological views. In contrast, of President Reagan's 346 nominees to the federal courts in his eight years in office, only seven were black. (Six were appointed to the district courts and one to the court of appeals.)[75]

In addition to such practical considerations of finding qualified and experienced black candidates for the Supreme Court, there lies a deeper question for the issue of "representativeness," namely, whether presidents in the future will feel compelled by the racial factor to have at least one black justice on the Court. Despite his unwavering support for affirmative action, Justice Marshall has argued that there should not be a permanent "black seat" on the Supreme Court. When asked if he should be replaced by another black justice, Marshall replied recently, "I don't think there should be another 'Negro' justice. I think the next justice should be a qualified person."[76] (He then noted the apparent death of the "Jewish seat," although he incorrectly traced its demise to Justice Goldberg's departure from the Court in 1965. As described in Chapter 3, Abe Fortas, another Jewish justice, took Goldberg's seat; but no Jew has served on the Court since Fortas's resignation in 1969.) Yet Marshall really seemed to be arguing against mere tokenism by qualifying his initial statement somewhat: "I would propose that they get a good person. The best person they can find, and I would hope that would be a Negro. But a good one. Not a [William] Lucas," whom the Senate rejected as President Bush's choice for assistant attorney general for civil rights.

When questioned in 1985 about the future of the so-called black seat on the Court, Marshall's liberal colleague and best friend, Justice William J. Brennan, Jr., commented that he thought efforts would be made to maintain such a seat. But he added, "Then fifty years from now, we won't even notice the color of a fellow's skin. And that's how it should be."[77]

As for the near future, however, presidents still have two key motivations that have impelled them to establish and maintain other "representative" seats on the Court. Although the black vote was not a decisive factor in Ronald Reagan's two overwhelming victories in the 1980 and 1984 presidential races, in a close election, such as that of 1976, it could well hold the balance of power.[78] Blacks constituted only 10 percent of the voting age population in the United States during the 1980s, but a significant portion of this population is concentrated in states traditionally rich in electoral votes: California, New York, Texas, Ohio, and Illinois.[79]

Despite the fact that several of these "Frost Belt" states in the Midwest and Northeast will lose electoral votes because of population declines, blacks and Hispanics will comprise the largest minority groups in booming "Sun Belt" states, like California, Texas, and Florida, which will see an increase in their number of electoral votes after the 1990 census. Thus, blacks will be strategically situated to influence presidential elections. Combined with increasing voter registration and turnout for blacks, geographic concentration renders them disproportionately more powerful than their percentage in the voting population suggests.[80]

In addition to electoral considerations, presidents may still view blacks in the United States as a "sub-community"[81] that has failed to achieve the degree of political and social assimilation that Catholics and Jews have and which, therefore, continues to need and demand special treatment to redress historical inequities in Supreme Court appointments and elective offices. American blacks were excluded completely from the political arena until relatively recently. Although rapid and measurable progress has been achieved in removing barriers to that arena, a more obvious and difficult obstacle to black assimilation in this country remains. "The Negro community is perhaps the most distinctive sub-community in America because its racial identity is an element in all its equations."[82] The very title of the National Urban League's annual report, *The State of Black America* (rather than Americans), may symbolically reflect the separateness still felt by black citizens in the United States. In fact, a 600-page, $2.7 million study published by the National Research Council in 1989 on the status of blacks in American society concluded gloomily that "full assimilation of blacks in a 'color blind' society is unlikely in the foreseeable future."[83]

Moreover, on college campuses, for example, there is convincing evidence of the existence of a dynamic that stresses, indeed encourages, a "politics of differences" rather than commonalities rooted in equality between and among racial, ethnic, and cultural groups.[84] Cultural diversity programs currently in vogue in university curricula, as well as extracurricularly, while well-intentioned, may only serve to accentuate the differences among groups and thwart assimilation. In addition, the persistent support for affirmative action programs, as evinced by Congress's attempt to pass the Civil Rights Act of 1990 and the Supreme Court's surprising extension of such programs at the end of its 1990 term in *Metro Broadcasting, Inc. v. Federal Communications Commission*,[85] indicates a continuing desire to allow the use of race as a factor in a wide variety of decisions in the business and academic worlds. Decisions over whom to appoint to the nation's highest court will unlikely be immune from such pressures.

Nevertheless, if Justice Marshall's seat becomes vacant during the current Republican administration, President Bush might be hard pressed to find an otherwise qualified, ideologically compatible black to take the position. Clarence Thomas, a conservative black member of the U.S. Court of Appeals for the District of Columbia, reportedly made the short list of four candidates when Bush was considering a replacement for Justice Brennan in July 1990. According to unnamed senior White House officials, however, Attorney General Richard Thornburgh and White House Counsel C. Boyden Gray, who advised the president in his ultimate choice of Judge David Souter, successfully argued that Thomas should be allowed "to settle in, to get some experience. He will be around for a long time." Moreover, Thomas, who is only forty-two and who was just appointed to the federal bench in early 1990, faced stiff opposition to his appellate court nomination because liberals accused him of attempting to dismantle affirmative action programs as chairman of the Equal Employment Opportunity Commission during the Reagan administration.[86]

Perhaps the best scenario for the president to follow would be to nominate a well-qualified, moderately conservative black, whose race might blunt ideological attacks as Justice O'Connor's gender and Justice Scalia's ethnic heritage arguably did. What Bush would want to avoid at all costs is a replay of the unsuccessful nomination of William Lucas to be assistant attorney general for civil rights, when his race, ideology, and qualifications muddled the debate. The process for filling a seat on the nation's highest tribunal demands better from all its participants.

NOTES

1. William J. Wilson, *The Declining Significance of Race in America* (Chicago: The University of Chicago Press, 1978), pp. 46–48.

2. Ibid., pp. 65–69.

3. Harry A. Bailey, Jr., ed., *Negro Politics in America* (Columbus, Ohio: Charles E. Merrill, 1967), pp. 3–4.

4. Henry J. Abraham, *Freedom and the Court: Civil Rights and Liberties in the United States*, 5th ed. (New York: Oxford University Press, 1988), p. 397.

5. Bailey, *Negro Politics in America*, p. 4.

6. August Meier and Elliott M. Rudwick, *From Plantation to Ghetto: An Interpretive History of American Negroes* (New York: Hill and Wang, 1966), pp. 169–70, 181, 187. Perhaps presidents considered Booker T. Washington a "safe" Negro as a result of his advocacy of an "equal but separate" position for Negroes in American society—an argument that provoked bitter controversy among his own people. See Herbert J. Storing, ed., *What Country Have I?* (New York: St. Martin's Press, 1970), p. 57. Meier and Rudwick noted the irony in the fact that "the *sine qua non* in receiving Washington's endorsement for political office was to declare constantly that, for Negroes, office-holding was unwise or unimportant." p. 187.

7. Meier and Rudwick, *From Plantation to Ghetto*, p. 36.

8. Ibid., p. 212. James L. Sundquist's *Dynamics of the Party System* (Washington, D.C.: The Brookings Institution, 1973), offers statistical evidence and clear analysis of the realignment of the 1930s in Ch. 10, pp. 183–217.

9. Robert E. Martin, "The Relative Political Status of the Negro in the United States," in Bailey, *Negro Politics in America*, pp. 30–31.

10. 321 U.S. 649 (1944).

11. William R. Keech, *The Impact of Negro Voting* (Chicago: Rand McNally, 1968), p. 219.

12. Meier and Rudwick, *From Plantation to Ghetto*, p. 219.

13. Oscar Glantz, "The Negro Voter in Northern Industrial Cities," in Bailey, *Negro Politics in America*, p. 331.

14. Charles Aiken, ed., *The Negro Votes* (San Francisco: Chandler, 1962), p. 8.

15. Martin, "The Relative Political Status of the Negro," p. 352.

16. Henry L. Moon, "The Negro Vote in the Presidential Election of 1956," in Bailey, *Negro Politics in America*, pp. 353–54.

17. Glantz, "The Negro Voter in Northern Industrial Cities," p. 352.

18. Meier and Rudwick, *From Plantation to Ghetto*, pp. 227–28.

19. Ibid., p. 228.

20. Everett Carl Ladd, "Negro Politics in the South: An Overview," in Bailey, *Negro Politics in America*, p. 244.

21. For example, see *Missouri ex. rel. Gaines v. Canada*, 305 U.S. 337 (1938); *Sipuel v. University of Oklahoma*, 322 U.S. 631 (1948); *Sweatt v. Painter*, 339 U.S. 629 (1950); and *McLaurin v. Oklahoma State Regents*, 339 U.S. 637 (1950).

22. 347 U.S. 483.

23. My brief narrative of the history of civil rights legislation also relies on the excellent descriptive detail in Abraham's *Freedom and the Court*, pp. 346–65.

24. Bailey, "Governmental Outputs to the Sub-community," in Bailey, *Negro Politics in America*, pp. 378–79.

25. George W. Crockett, Jr., Russell R. DeBow, and Larry C. Berkson, *National Roster of Black Judicial Officers, 1980* (Chicago: American Judicature Society, 1980), p. 2.

26. Ibid.

27. Gilbert Ware, *William Hastie: Grace Under Pressure* (New York: Oxford University Press, 1984), passim.

28. Jonathan J. Rusch, "William M. Hastie and the Vindication of Civil Rights" (unpublished M.A. thesis, University of Virginia, 1978), pp. 86–88.

29. Quoted in Ware, *William Hastie*, pp. 215–16.

30. Ibid., pp. 217–20.

31. Quoted in Rusch, "William M. Hastie," p. 95.

32. Ibid., pp. 95–101.

33. Quoted in Beverly Blair Cook, "Black Representation in the Third Branch," 1 *Black Law Journal* 2 and 3 (1971): 269.

34. Ibid., p. 269. John R. Schmidhauser, *Judges and Justices: The Federal Appellate Judiciary* (Boston: Little, Brown, 1979), p. 59.

35. Sheldon Goldman, "Reaganizing the Judiciary: The First Term Appointments," 68 *Judicature* 9–10 (April–May): 319.

36. Randall W. Bland, in *Private Pressure on Public Law: The Legal Career of Justice Thurgood Marshall* (Port Washington, N.Y.: Kennikat Press, 1973), p. 118,

reports that the attorney general *supported* a Marshall nomination, but Marshall himself recalls otherwise. See Marshall interview in Juan Williams, "The Triumph of Thurgood Marshall," *The Washington Post Magazine*, January 7, 1990, p. 27.

37. As quoted in ibid.

38. Bland, *Private Pressure on Public Law*, pp. 5–6.

39. Ibid. For references to cases see notes 10, 21, and 22; *Shelley v. Kraemer*, the "restrictive covenants" case, 334 U.S. 1 (1948).

40. Williams, "The Triumph of Thurgood Marshall," p. 27.

41. Arthur Schlesinger, Jr., *Robert Kennedy and His Times* (New York: Ballantine Books, 1978), pp. 330–31. See Victor S. Navasky's *Kennedy Justice* (New York: Atheneum, 1977), Ch. 5, for a detailed account of the Kennedy administration's appointments of Cox and other segregationist federal judges in the South. Navasky revised the liberal explanation of the appointments, which maintained "that Kennedy cynically or shrewdly, depending on how you saw it traded Coxes to the South for Thurgood Marshalls up north." Navasky argued that "the bad Southern choices were the products of the pre-existing judicial selection system which the Kennedys inherited and more or less perpetuated without much question, at least during the first half of the Kennedys' tenure," p. 256.

42. Bland, *Private Pressure on Public Law*, pp. 119–20; Schlesinger, *Robert Kennedy*. See also U.S. Congress, Senate, Vote on Thurgood Marshall nomination to U.S. Court of Appeals for Second Circuit, 87th Cong., 2nd sess., 11 September 1962. *Congressional Record* 108:19055.

43. Rusch, "William M. Hastie," pp. 115–16.

44. Quoted in Schlesinger, *Robert Kennedy*, p. 404.

45. Ibid.

46. Ibid., p. 405.

47. Ibid.

48. Arthur Schlesinger, Jr., *A Thousand Days: John F. Kennedy in the White House* (Boston: Houghton Mifflin, 1965), p. 51.

49. James E. Clayton, *The Making of Justice: The Supreme Court in Action* (New York: Dutton, 1964), p. 51.

50. Henry J. Abraham, *Justices and Presidents: A Political History of Appointments to the Supreme Court*, 2d ed. (New York: Oxford University Press, 1985), p. 274; Schlesinger, *Robert Kennedy*, p. 334.

51. Rusch, "William M. Hastie," p. 119.

52. Quoted in Bland, *Private Pressure on Public Law*, pp. 129–30.

53. Lady Bird Johnson, *A White House Diary* (New York: Holt, Rinehart and Winston, 1970), p. 294.

54. Bland, *Private Pressure on Public Law*, p. 130. See also U.S. Congress, Senate, Action on Thurgood Marshall nomination for solicitor general, 89th Cong., 1st sess., 11 August 1965, *Congressional Record* 111:19743.

55. *New York Times*, June 14, 1967, p. 1.

56. William O. Douglas, *The Court Years, 1939–1975, The Autobiography of William O. Douglas* (New York: Vintage Books, 1981), p. 251.

57. Quoted in *Current Biography Yearbook 1989*, Charles Moritz, ed. (New York: H. W. Wilson, 1989), p. 380.

58. *New York Times*, June 14, 1967, p. 1.

59. Quoted in Williams, "The Triumph of Thurgood Marshall," p. 28.

60. Ibid.

61. (Philadelphia) *Sunday Bulletin*, July 16, 1967, p. 19.

62. Lyndon Johnson, *The Vantage Point: Perspectives of the Presidency* (New York: Holt, Rinehart and Winston, 1971), pp. 178–79.

63. *The New York Times*, September 3, 1967, p. 16.

64. Ibid.

65. (Philadelphia) *Sunday Bulletin*, June 25, 1967, p. 1.

66. Quoted in Lady Bird Johnson, *A White House Diary*, p. 758.

67. Geraldine R. Segal, *Blacks in the Law* (Philadelphia: University of Pennsylvania Press, 1983), pp. 1, 211–12.

68. Reported in "Black Law Schools: The Continuing Need," 16 *Southern University Law Review* 249 (1989): 250 (note 7).

69. Segal, *Blacks in the Law*, pp. 6, 211–12.

70. Reported in "Black Law Schools," p. 278. The most up-to-date statistics available from the U.S. Department of Education indicated that in 1986–87, 1,753 blacks received law degrees out of the 36,056 granted. *Digest of Education Statistics 1989* (Washington, D.C.: Government Printing Office, 1989), p. 251. That figure constituted 4.8 percent.

71. Crockett, DeBow, and Berkson, *National Roster of Black Judicial Officers*, p. 4.

72. Segal, *Blacks in the Law*, p. 226.

73. *The Success of Women and Minorities in Achieving Judicial Office: The Selection Process* (New York: Fund for Modern Courts, Inc., 1985), pp. 13–15.

74. For an empirical examination of the Carter commissions, see Larry C. Berkson and Susan B. Carbon, *Federal Judicial Selection During the Carter Administration, The United States Circuit Judge Nominating Commission: Its Members; Procedures, and Candidates* (Chicago: American Judicature Society, 1980).

75. Sheldon Goldman, "Reagan's Judicial Legacy: Completing the Puzzle and Summing Up," 72 *Judicature* 6 (April–May 1989): 318–30.

76. Marshall's thoughts on the "black seat" are reported in Williams, "The Triumph of Thurgood Marshall," p. 29.

77. Personal interview, Washington, D.C., April 1, 1985.

78. James D. Williams, ed., *The State of Black America, 1983* (National Urban League, 1983), p. 272.

79. Dianne M. Pinderhughes, "The Black Vote: The Sleeping Giant," in James D. Williams, ed., *The State of Black America, 1984* (National Urban League, 1984), p. 71.

80. Ibid., p. 76.

81. Bailey, *Negro Politics in America*, p. 1. Bailey borrowed the term from Floyd Hunter, *Community Power* (Garden City, N.Y.: Doubleday, 1963), Ch. 5.

82. Ibid.

83. See Gerald D. Jaynes and Robin M. Williams, Jr., eds. *A Common Destiny: Blacks and American Society* (Washington, D.C.: National Academy Press, 1989).

84. Shelby Steele, "The Recoloring of Campus Life: Student Racism, Academic Pluralism, and the End of a Dream," *Harper's*, February 4, 1989, p. 49; Diane Ravitch, "Multiculturalism," *The American Scholar*, Summer 1990: 337–54.

85. The Civil Rights Act of 1990, vetoed by President Bush, would have reversed several of the 1989 Supreme Court decisions that narrowed the scope

of affirmative action programs in employment. The decision in the *Metro Broad-casting* case upheld by a narrow 5–4 vote the federal minority preference plan for boosting minority ownership of radio and television stations in order to increase diversity of programming.

86. See *New York Times*, July 25, 1990, p. 6; *Newsweek*, July 30, 1990, pp. 16–17.

Chapter 5

Gender: A "Woman's Seat"?

As a "representative" factor in presidential considerations for appointments to the United States Supreme Court, gender is obviously more similar to race than it is to religion in the history of nominations examined in this study. Like the racial factor, gender offers but a single case for analysis—the appointment of Sandra Day O'Connor by President Ronald Reagan in 1981.

Yet, like race, the serious and formal consideration of gender by a president in selecting Court members is so recent, and follows so closely the political upheavals of the 1960s and 1970s, that a relatively detailed body of evidence exists on which to form a conclusion on the establishment and future of a "woman's seat" on the Supreme Court. Therefore, like the preceding chapter's approach to race, this chapter concentrates on the recent political, electoral, and sociological trends affecting American women.

THE "WOMEN'S VOTE"?

Feminists hoped that a "women's vote" would materialize after the extension of the franchise to females through passage of the Nineteenth Amendment in 1920. In anticipation of such bloc voting behavior, male political leaders were initially responsive to women's issues in the years immediately following the ratification of the women's suffrage amendment. For example, the Democratic party's 1920 platform adopted twelve of the fifteen provisions advocated by the newly founded League of Women Voters. Warren G. Harding, the successful Republican candidate for president that year, supported equal pay for women, an eight-hour work day, maternity and infant-care legislation, and the establishment of a federal department of social welfare. Both Democrats and Republicans named an equal number of men and women to their national committees, though women could still not breach the inner sanctum of the smoke-filled rooms where the real power lay. By the middle of the "Roaring Twenties," however, the male political establishment had retreated from its position of actively wooing women's votes.[1]

The reason for the decrease in both parties' activities to attract the female vote was simple. Contrary to the fervent hopes of the suffragists, who fought so long and hard for the vote, "no identifiable 'women's vote' emerged . . . following the extension of the suffrage in 1920."[2] In the 1920 election, just a few months after ratification of the Nineteenth Amendment, only about one-third of the eligible women voted for president.[3] Of course, some lack of participation was due to the administrative difficulties of trying to register newly enfranchised women in the short amount of time before the 1920 November election. Another factor in the low turnout of women was the disenfranchisement of black females in the South. In addition, most women obviously were not in the "habit" of voting. Social and political mores did not welcome them to their new level of citizenship.[4]

Ironically, with the attainment of suffrage, American women lost their one unifying issue;[5] and they were not viewed as having interests distinct from the male electorate. The fact that wives apparently took their voting cues from their husbands did not further the argument that women should be treated as a separate voting bloc. Therefore, the lack of representation of women in government was simply not an issue for the half-century after passage of the women's suffrage amendment.[6] In Congress, for example, of the more than 10,000 individuals who have served there since 1789, only a little over 100 have been women. Nearly half of the female representatives in Congress have achieved their positions as widows of deceased male legislators. Jeannette Rankin, the first female congressman, however, was elected in her own right to the House of Representatives from Montana in 1916. She was an indefatigable supporter of the suffrage amendment on the House floor.[7]

Like Catholics, Jews, and blacks, women managed to attain an unprecedented amount of political recognition under the administration of Franklin Roosevelt. Thanks in part to efforts of incomparable First Lady Eleanor Roosevelt, a record number of more than fifty women, including Secretary of Labor Frances Perkins, were appointed during Roosevelt's White House tenure of more than twelve years.[8]

FLORENCE ALLEN: FIRST LADY OF THE LAW

F.D.R. also appointed the first woman to the prestigious federal courts of appeals. Labeled "First Lady of the Law" for her pioneering career as a female jurist, Florence Allen was named to the Sixth Circuit Court of Appeals by President Roosevelt in 1934. Before becoming the first woman to serve on a federal constitutional court, Allen had been the first female elected to a state supreme court judgeship. Prior to her landmark election to Ohio's highest tribunal, she had served for two years on a county level court of general jurisdiction in the Buckeye State.[9]

In addition to her judicial experience, Allen possessed respectable academic credentials that were especially noteworthy considering the rampant and overt gender discrimination in legal education in the first half of the twentieth century. Harvard Law School, for example, did not admit women until 1952. The University of Chicago's superb law school, which boasted such distinguished faculty members as Roscoe Pound, did admit women, and Allen enrolled there to pursue her law degree. But she encountered sexism and transferred to New York University, from which she was graduated second in her class in 1913.

With Allen's academic and professional successes, it is no wonder that President Herbert Hoover's attorney general, William Mitchell, considered her for appointment as the Supreme Court's first female member. In 1929 he wrote to the president: "I should like very much to appoint a woman to a distinguished position if I could find a distinguished woman to appoint."[10] One year later, upon the death of Justice Edward T. Sanford, *The Christian Science Monitor* editorialized "that the time has come when the presence of a woman jurist upon the supreme bench must be recognized as an altogether normal and likely development." In addition to several male candidates for the Sanford vacancy, the *Monitor* suggested Ohio Supreme Court Justice Florence Allen and Mrs. Mabel Walker Willebrandt, former U.S. assistant attorney general. The editorial sensibly maintained that "a woman should [not] be appointed to the Supreme Court because she is a woman, but . . . no thoughtful commentator should either overlook or disregard a jurist merely because she is a woman."[11]

The *Monitor*'s sentiments were far ahead of their time. As Professor Beverly B. Cook suggested in her article on women Supreme Court candidates, "The sex attribute itself was the disqualification which kept women out of the pool of [Supreme Court] eligibles."[12] Cook also perceptively argued that Hoover's successor in the White House, Franklin Roosevelt, had no political capital to gain from an elevation of Allen to the nation's highest court. The numerous, but relatively small, women's interest groups, who urged Allen's nomination to the Supreme Court, did not constitute enough votes to persuade F.D.R., the consummate practitioner of realpolitik.[13]

Yet support from women's organizations had been instrumental in getting Allen at least as far as the United States Court of Appeals. Allen's biographer, Jeannette Tuve, found in Allen's papers that 238 individuals,

3 labor organizations, 81 social and political organizations, and 32 lawyers drafted endorsements for Allen's nomination to the appellate court in 1934. As was the case throughout Allen's professional career, a good portion of these letters likely came from women and their organizations.[14]

Such support combined with a vocal female faction within the New Deal coalition, an activist first lady, and Allen's professional credentials to make her the first woman to reach a federal appellate bench. The administration tried to emphasize that Allen had earned her appointment by her credentials and not by her gender. Still, Attorney General Homer Cummings and Assistant Attorney General Harold M. Stephens, both of whom were close to Allen and her family, admitted that their most difficult mission in obtaining confirmation of Allen's appointment was to prevent rejection on the basis of the candidate's sex. Allen later wrote in her autobiography that Roosevelt had appointed her to the federal bench for "shock effect" and revealed in an interview with her biographer that she did not consider F.D.R. committed to the appointment of women to the federal judiciary.[15]

F.D.R. maintained that gender was not a barrier to appointments in his administration,[16] and Allen and her supporters continued her campaign to become the first female Supreme Court justice. Their hopes were dashed when each of Roosevelt's near-record nine appointments to the high court went to a male. Even if Allen's sex was not a direct bar to her appointment, it precluded her from obtaining many of the qualifications that Roosevelt's appointees possessed. Harvard and Yale, the alma maters of Frankfurter and Reed, respectively, did not admit women in Allen's generation. Columbia Law School, where Douglas had received his law degree, accepted women only for its summer program. For all intents and purposes, a congressional career or a stint in the upper levels of the Department of Justice were unlikely vocational paths for Allen and her female cohorts. (Hugo Black was a senator when he went to the Court; James Byrnes had a long congressional career on his resume; Frank Murphy was a nationally known politico in the Democratic party and member of the Roosevelt administration in several capacities; Robert Jackson served as solicitor general and attorney general before his appointment to the Court.) Allen's strongest credential was her long and distinguished career as a jurist, but judicial experience was not high on Roosevelt's list of appointment criteria. And, gender aside, Allen's political and partisan purity were not as demonstrable as F.D.R.'s ultimate choices.[17]

A recent biography of Allen convincingly documented the campaign to urge nomination of Allen to the Supreme Court in the 1930s and three subsequent decades.[18] After Roosevelt's death, women were less sanguine about the odds of an Allen appointment to the Court. They did not attempt to push for her nomination during President Truman's first search for a justice. Ironically, the position went to another Ohio resident, Truman's friend and former Senate colleague, Harold H. Burton. The next year, 1946, women attempted to organize a letter-writing campaign to urge the president to name Allen to the latest opening on the Court; but that vacancy, the chief justiceship, went to a male, Fred M. Vinson.

Throughout this period, each Supreme Court opening had prompted speculation that the president might seize an opportunity to make an historic appointment of Allen to the nation's highest tribunal. In the late 1940s, Allen gained another supporter, who had access to the president, India Edwards, the executive director of the Women's Division of the Democratic National Committee. She took Allen's case directly to the Oval Office, where she pleaded with Truman to fill either the Murphy or Rutledge vacancy with the top woman judge in the country. The president assured Edwards that he thought it was a good idea to have a woman on the Court—especially one of Judge Allen's demonstrable capability, and he told Edwards that he would discuss the matter with Chief Justice Fred Vinson. Edwards recorded her vexation when Truman later reported to her

that the Chief Justice and his conferees [his eight male associates] would not willingly have a woman as a Justice. She would make it difficult for them to meet informally with robes, and perhaps shoes, off, shirt collars unbuttoned and discuss their problems and come to decisions. I am certain that the old line about their being no sanitary arrangement for a female Justice was also included in their reasons for not wanting a woman, but President Truman did not mention this to me.[19]

Allen's partisan ties, tenuous though they might have been, were to the Democratic party. Therefore, her chances of going on the Court during the Republican reign of President Eisenhower seemed even more remote. But this fact did not dampen the enthusiasm of a new Allen cheerleader, Rosalind Bates, president of the International Federation of Woman Lawyers. In a 1954 newsletter to her fellow Federation members she exclaimed: "Would it not be wonderful if President Eisenhower is sufficiently overwhelmed by wires to realize the value of Judge Florence Allen on the Supreme Court!"[20] Despite her advanced age, 73, Allen allowed one more campaign on her behalf for the vacancy on the Court created by the retirement of Justice Stanley F. Reed (at age 72) in 1957. Once more, women's groups, led by the National Association of Women Lawyers and the Business and Professional Women's Clubs, deluged the president, the attorney general, and members of the Senate Judiciary Committee with letters of support for Allen. Attorney General Herbert Brownell frankly admitted that Allen's age was now the biggest factor working against her appointment. Whatever the reasons precluding an

Allen nomination, the 1957 vacancy went to Charles E. Whitaker. Judge Allen retired from the appeals court bench in 1959, one year after Eisenhower's appointment of her Sixth Circuit colleague, forty-three-year-old Potter Stewart.

The conclusion that F.D.R. had little or no electoral incentive to nominate the first woman Supreme Court justice is equally applicable to his two immediate successors in the White House. To reiterate, "women were not regarded as a politically relevant group until the feminist movement of the middle and late 1960s."[21] Women continued to report to polling places in lower rates than men in the immediate post–World War II era. Between 1948 and 1968, however, women did increase their voting turnout by 14 percent. The differences between female and male rates of voting participation narrowed to 3 percent in the presidential elections of 1964 and 1968.[22]

THE WOMEN'S MOVEMENT OF THE 1960s AND 1970s

The civil rights movement and antiwar protests of the turbulent 1960s are often viewed as catalysts for the feminist revolution that began during that incomparable decade of political and social activism. "Woman as nigger" was a shorthand expression for the second-class citizenship that women shared with blacks and against which they railed in their respective movements to attain parity with the white male establishment in this country.[23]

A precursor of the women's liberation movement appeared early in the decade with the establishment of the Commission on the Status of Women by President Kennedy in 1961. The commission published a report, *American Woman*, which outlined the inequalities still faced by women more than forty years after they had received the vote. The federal commission spawned similar agencies in all fifty states. In addition to producing studies about the current status of women in the United States, these government agencies drew together concerned women who might not otherwise have united to address women's issues.[24]

Two other events in the first half of the 1960s stimulated activity in the women's movement. In 1963, Betty Friedan published her bombshell feminist work, *The Feminine Mystique*, which prompted a whole generation of American women to question its lot in life as "traditional" homemakers and mothers. The next year witnessed the passage of the 1964 Civil Rights Act, with its Title VII that included sex in its categories of proscribed employment discrimination. (Reportedly, Representative Howard W. Smith of Virginia had suggested the addition of the gender category in hopes that his colleagues would reject Title VII in its entirety. The dubious legislative strategy backfired for Smith but inadvertently aided the feminist cause.)[25]

Such social and political events spurred the foundation of the National Organization of Women (NOW) in 1966. Under the leadership of Betty Friedan, its first president, the group began to press for equal rights for women. The issues pursued in its first manifesto ranged from equal employment opportunities for women to legalization of abortion. Such contentious issues were bound to breed factionalization. NOW soon lost its conservative members on the abortion controversy, and more radical elements revolted against the perceived centralization and elitism of the organization. Notwithstanding these splits, by 1973, NOW counted 500 local chapters and 50,000 members under its banner. To lobby for women's causes and promote female participation (both as voters and candidates) in electoral contests at all levels of the governmental system, NOW members helped form the National Women's Political Caucus in 1971.[26] Some success for the Caucus was evident in statistics for female members of state legislatures across the country. Twenty-five years after World War II, women held only 3 percent of the seats in state legislative assemblies. Just three years after the inception of the Caucus, that percentage had climbed to 8.[27]

A focal point for the modern feminist movement in the 1970s was the Equal Rights Amendment (ERA). Militant suffragists had proposed the first ERA to the Constitution in 1923; and it had been introduced at every subsequent session of the Congress. Since 1943, it had read: "Equality of rights under the law shall not be denied by the United States or any State on account of sex." Reluctant to see the demise of protective legislation for women, the League of Women Voters opposed the amendment. But by the 1970s, such legislation was viewed as detrimental to women's achievement of complete equality, and feminists supported the ERA with renewed vigor. They achieved a congressional victory in 1970 when the House of Representatives passed the amendment. The Senate followed suit two years later. In 1972, twenty-eight states ratified the ERA but the feminist victory celebrations were short-lived.[28] Led by Phyllis Schlafly, opponents of the ERA mustered their forces to stymie the amendment's ultimate ratification. Despite Congress's grant of a thirty-nine-month extension period, the ERA fell three states short of the thirty-eight required for passage.

Nonetheless, the women's movement counted among its victories in the 1970s the Supreme Court's *Roe v. Wade*[29] ruling of 1973, categorically striking down state and federal barriers to abortions in the first trimester of pregnancy and harnessing other barriers in the second and third trimesters. Feminists considered the landmark decision a blow for so-called reproductive freedom. In the realm of education, women cheered the passage of Title IX of the Education Amendments of 1972, which ordered elimination of gender discrimination in federally funded educational programs.[30]

WOMEN IN THE LEGAL PROFESSION AND
THE JUDICIARY

Education was one of the primary areas where the effects of the social and political transformation wrought by the women's movement were most visible. Annual surveys of college freshmen throughout the country revealed a stunning reversal in perceptions about women's roles in society and career choices among both young men and women. In 1970, for example, one-half of college males and more than one-half of college females responded in a survey that "the activities of married women are best confined to the home and family." Just five years later, only one-third of the men and less than one-fifth of the women responded affirmatively to that statement. Statistical evidence indicates that behavior began to reflect the opinions expressed in surveys. Between 1970 and 1975, the proportion of women receiving doctoral degrees nearly doubled from 11 percent to 21 percent. The proportion of women entering the nation's law schools soared by an astonishing 300 percent over the same period.[31]

The civil rights movement and the feminist revolution had undoubtedly spurred the increase in women law students and lawyers. A 1970 census estimate showed 12,655 female lawyers or 4.5 percent of the total 264,752 lawyers in the United States. A decade later, the Bureau of Labor Statistics reported that women constituted 61,000 or some 13 percent of the estimated 478,000 attorneys in this country.[32] The proportions of women in the legal profession were far less than the 52.2 percent of the American population that females constituted in 1970. Nevertheless, borrowing from the popular cigarette commercial jingle of the early 1970s, one could say to aspiring women lawyers, "You've come a long way, baby!" Indeed, a long way from 1869, when the Illinois Supreme Court refused to license Myra Bradwell to practice law, despite a lower court's assurances that she was of good character and had passed the required examination. The United States Supreme Court upheld the Illinois high court's decision four years later, with Justice Joseph P. Bradley writing in a concurring opinion: "The harmony, not to say the identity, of interests and views which belong, or should belong, to the family institution is repugnant to the idea of a woman adopting a distinct and independent career from that of her husband."[33] Then citing the decrees of nature formulated by the Almighty, Bradley continued his dictum: "The paramount destiny and mission of women is to fulfill the noble and benign offices of wife and mother. This is the law of the Creator."[34]

Undaunted, women pressed for the removal of gender classifications from state licensing statutes and achieved some success in the 1870s. As the twentieth century loomed, women gained admission to state bars, and some secured admittance to practice before the federal courts. In 1879, Belva Lockwood of Texas became the first woman admitted to the

United States Supreme Court bar. Yet the percentage of women attorneys in the United States remained minuscule. The Department of Labor reported that women constituted 1 percent of all American lawyers in 1910. By 1930, that figure had slightly more than doubled to 2.1 percent. At the start of the women's movement in the 1960s, it was still just 2.7 percent.[35]

Hence, the pool of female attorneys from which judicial appointments could have been made was prohibitively small. In fact, Esther Morris, the first woman to serve on the bench in the United States, was not a lawyer. Marilla Ricker became the first woman with legal training to reach any court when she was appointed U.S. commissioner in the District of Columbia in 1884. Two years later, Carrie Kilgore, the first female graduate of the University of Pennsylvania Law School, became the first law-trained woman to served in a state judiciary. By the dawn of the twentieth century, no other women had served on a state court nor had they ascended to the federal benches.[36]

Florence Allen began her long list of "firsts" as a female jurist by becoming the first woman to be elected, rather than appointed, to a judicial post other than justice of the peace. Her 1921 election to the Court of Common Pleas in Cuyahoga County, Ohio, launched her successful judicial career. From the county court of general jurisdiction, she waged a victorious campaign to reach the Ohio Supreme Court, where she was serving in 1934 when President Roosevelt made her the first woman U.S. appellate court judge.

Several woman had preceded Allen to the federal judiciary in the first decades of the twentieth century. In 1918, Kathryn Sellers was named juvenile court judge for the District of Columbia, and two years later Mary O'Toole was appointed to a municipal court judgeship for the District. President Calvin Coolidge named Genevieve R. Cline to the U.S. Customs Court in 1928. Two years later, Annable Matthews was appointed to the U.S. Board of Tax Appeals. Until 1949, a woman had yet to serve on a U.S. District Court. Finally in that year, President Harry Truman named Burnita Shelton Matthews to the federal District Court for the District of Columbia.[37]

No other woman (beside Judge Allen) served on the U.S. Courts of Appeals until 1968, when President Lyndon Johnson appointed Shirley Hufstedler to the Ninth Circuit tribunal. A top-ranked graduate of the Stanford University Law School, Hufstedler had served on the Los Angeles County Superior Court from 1961 to 1966, when she had received an appointment from Governor "Pat" Brown to the California Court of Appeals.[38] She was serving there when she received her federal appointment.

By the beginning of the 1970s, fewer than 200 women attorneys served on the nation's state courts. But during that decade, the number increased by quantum leaps. In early 1980, statistics indicated that 11 women lawyers were serving on the states' highest courts, 32 on the intermediate appellate courts, 183 on general jurisdiction trial courts, and 322 on courts of limited or special jurisdiction[39] for a total of 548 women lawyers serving in state judiciaries.

By the summer of 1980, 10 women were on the federal Courts of Appeals and 31 on District Courts. As with blacks, the increase in women on the federal judiciary resulted from President Jimmy Carter's affirmative action policies in judicial appointments. Prior to Carter's election to the White House in 1976, only 8 women had served on federal district or appellate courts.[40]

The modern women's movement prompted presidents to give more serious consideration to female candidates for the Supreme Court. The newly organized women's interests groups in the 1960s urged President Johnson to consider women for the vacancy that L.B.J. ultimately filled with Arthur Goldberg. In 1971, the National Women's Political Caucus drafted a list of qualified women jurists, law professors, and members of Congress for President Nixon's consideration in choosing members of the nation's highest court.[41] For the two vacancies left by the retirements of Justices Hugo Black and John Marshall Harlan II in 1971, Nixon included Judge Mildred Lillie of the California State Court of Appeals among the names on the short list that he sent to the American Bar Association's (ABA) Committee on Federal Judiciary for rating. Much to Nixon's dismay (especially after his frustration in watching his nominations of both Clement Haynsworth and G. Harrold Carswell go down to defeat in the Senate), the ABA's committee gave Judge Lillie a rating of "unqualified."[42] Nixon ultimately filled the vacancies with Lewis F. Powell, Jr. and William H. Rehnquist.

After Nixon's resignation in the wake of the Watergate scandal, President Gerald Ford had one opportunity to name a Supreme Court justice, and feminists engaged in speculative discussions over which of several prominent women might get the nod. Former President Ford recorded in his memoirs that he specifically ordered his attorney general, Edward Levi, to include women in his list of potential candidates.[43] At various times in the decision process, the names of women under consideration included Housing and Urban Development Secretary Carla Hills (outspoken First Lady Betty Ford's personal choice), U.S. District Court Judge Cornelia Kennedy of Michigan, and U.S. Court of Appeals Judge for the Ninth Circuit Shirley Hufstedler.[44] Sandra Day O'Connor, then a newly elected Arizona judge, was also on the list.[45]

In a 1985 interview, Ford's eventual choice for the Court, Seventh Circuit Court of Appeals Judge John Paul Stevens, recalled that "there was sentiment for a woman" at the time of his appointment. He also remembered the opposition he faced from NOW. But he remarked that it was his "impression" that presidential advisers Edward Levi and Philip Buchen did not want the representative factors of religion or gender to play a role in filling the Douglas vacancy.[46]

SANDRA DAY O'CONNOR

The 1980s ushered in a decade of increasing concern among male politicians to capture the female vote. During the post–World War II era, women had boosted their voting turnout, and the modern feminist movement had generated issues around which women could rally. The 1980 presidential election found both candidates engaging in one-upmanship on promises to increase the number of female appointments in their respective administrations.[47]

Republican candidate Ronald Reagan announced in October of the 1980 campaign that he would fill one of his first Supreme Court vacancies with "the most qualified woman he could find." He rejected "tokenism" or the "setting [of] false quotas" but stated his recognition of the fact "that within the guidelines of excellence, appointments can carry enormous symbolic significance."[48]

Justice Potter Stewart's unexpected retirement from the Court in mid-1981 gave Reagan his first opportunity to fulfill his campaign pledge, and he seized the initiative. Attorney General William French Smith offered the president a list of some twenty-five candidates. Nearly half the potential nominees were women. Among them were the eventual appointee, Arizona Court of Appeals Judge Sandra Day O'Connor; U.S. Court of Appeals Judge for the Sixth Circuit, Cornelia Kennedy; Chief Justice of the Michigan Supreme Court, Mary Coleman; and U.S. Court of Appeals Judge for the Second Circuit, Amalya E. Kearse, the first black female federal court judge, who had been appointed by President Carter.[49]

Judge O'Connor survived the winnowing process to appear on the final list of about five putative candidates. As Justice O'Connor has described the process, the administration then conducted a thorough investigation of her background and credentials to determine if she was ideologically "acceptable" to the president. In fact, she recently quipped that the investigation into her years as a legislator and jurist in Arizona was so complete that the "Arizona government shut down" while those in it were interviewed about her.[50]

The administration had good reason to find O'Connor's background more than acceptable in terms of ideology and merit. A high school graduate at sixteen, Sandra Day completed her undergraduate course and law degree at Stanford University in just five years. She was graduated magna cum laude and inducted into the prestigious law student honorary, the Society of the Coif. She and her future colleague on the Court, William H. Rehnquist, were top students in their Stanford Law

School class and earned positions on the *Stanford Law Review*.

Despite her exemplary academic record, Sandra Day collided with the gender discrimination extant in the legal profession in the 1950s and was unsuccessful in finding a law firm that would hire a female associate. In fact, her only job offer from the private practice realm was for a legal secretary's position. Today, at the pinnacle of her profession, Justice O'Connor expresses "no bitterness" about the roadblocks she encountered in her early career. Yet she admits to having come to a first-hand "realization that opportunities [for women] were limited." Although she was surprised at the professional discrimination that she faced, having encountered no sexism at Stanford, she simply turned to the public sector to pursue her career. In hindsight, she now recognizes the increased opportunities she had as a public servant that she might well have missed in a private law firm.[51]

After pausing to raise her three sons, Mrs. O'Connor served as an assistant attorney general in Arizona. In 1969 she was elected to the state Senate; and, just three years after taking her seat, she was elected majority leader by her party. She was the first woman to hold such a position in this country.[52] Turning to a judicial career in 1974, she won election to the Maricopa Superior Court. In 1980 the Democratic governor of Arizona, Bruce Babbitt, nominated her to the state's intermediate appellate court. After serving just eighteen months on the Arizona Court of Appeals, President Reagan plucked her from this relative obscurity to assume her historic position on the highest court in the land.

The administration's investigation into Mrs. O'Connor's legislative and judicial record had revealed a moderate conservatism compatible with the president's views on various issues and in step with his judicial philosophy of restraint and deference to state legislatures and judiciaries.[53] But in his announcement of Mrs. O'Connor's nomination, President Reagan stressed that she met "the very high standards" that he would require of all his judicial appointees.[54] Nevertheless, the ABA Committee on Judiciary had given the first woman Supreme Court nominee a qualified endorsement. The committee applauded her judicial temperament and integrity, which met "the highest standards"; but the ABA panel noted her limited judicial experience and declared that it was not "as extensive or challenging as that of some other persons who might be available for appointment."[55] University of Virginia Law professor G. Edward White and others frankly admitted that a man with O'Connor's sparse background would have been an unlikely nominee for the high court.[56]

Hence, gender was the primary and decisive factor (followed closely by ideological compatibility and merit) in Justice O'Connor's historic nomination to the Court. She accepts the reality that gender was a prime element in her selection. Reagan's announced goal of selecting a female for the Court was as well-known to Justice O'Connor as to other Americans. She also recognizes that the women's movement had raised "public consciousness" and awareness about the plight of women in this country. The time was ripe for her appointment. Women's groups warmly greeted Reagan's announcement that a woman would finally penetrate the previously male-dominated "marble palace," and Mrs. O'Connor received supportive mail from women's interest groups during the confirmation process. And times had changed on the Court itself: whereas Chief Justice Vinson had reported to President Truman on a potential nomination for Florence Allen in 1949 that the all-male Court would be unwilling to accept a female justice, Justice O'Connor states emphatically that she was "cordially" and "kindly" welcomed by her brethren. She adds, "The Court was willing to have a new member of any sex."[57]

For a discussion of "representativeness," it is important to stress the symbolism of Justice O'Connor's service on the Court for her and other women. Fighting the inevitable and ever-present specter of tokenism, O'Connor has reported that she feels a tremendous responsibility to perform her job well so that people will recognize that women properly belong in such high-level positions. After her first four years on the Court, she noted: "It's been touching to see how women of all ages have responded to the appointment of a woman to this Court; with an outpouring of appreciation that it happened and a feeling of encouragement that the appointment gave them."[58]

The success of the women's movement in creating the "right time" for a female Supreme Court appointment is closely related to electoral factors. If the movement raised the consciousness of the general public regarding women's issues, it also raised the consciousness of politicians about the possibility of a "women's vote" for the first time since the 1920s. Women's advocacy groups tried to promote the image of a solid female voting bloc, which male politicians would do well to court as candidates and placate as officeholders. Two days before the 1980 presidential election, an ad hoc group called WARN (Women Against the Republican Nominee) ran a full-page ad in the *New York Times*. It read: "There is a women's vote. We may not yet have a candidate we're wholeheartedly for, but we do have one we're against—because he's against everything we need for equality."[59] In announcing his intention to name a female Supreme Court justice, candidate Reagan had referred to the "false and misleading" accusation that he was "somehow opposed to full and equal opportunities for women in America."[60] His announcement, similar to his famous "there-you-go-again" response to critics, was aimed at defusing such feminist attacks.

The feminists' "warnings" against a Reagan victory in 1980 were ineffective. Of the nearly 46 million women who voted in the contest,

46 percent cast their ballots for Reagan, while 45 percent voted for Carter. Still, feminists took heart that the studies of the 1980 election indicated that women were voting in equal percentages to men and displaying more sophistication and independence in their voting preferences. Moreover, women's movement leaders were quick to label the 8 percent disparity in male and female support for Reagan a "gender gap." (Between 1960 and 1972, Gallup polls had found no significant gender differences in preferences for presidential candidates.[61])

Studies in the mid-1980s of women's voting patterns questioned the stability of the gender gap and argued that it was too early to speak in terms of a "women's vote." Nevertheless, such studies acknowledged that the gender gap was at least "a media event, one which—whatever its empirical validity—clearly trouble[d] Reagan."[62] For ascertaining presidential motivations in Court appointments, this final point is determinative. If Reagan feared a feminist backlash against his perceived lack of sympathy for women's causes (and his statements reveal such a fear), he had a prime electoral reason to demonstrate his good faith among female voters by naming the first woman Supreme Court justice. Indeed, his strategy may have contributed, in part, to his electoral gains among female voters, a clear majority of whom voted for Reagan in 1984.[63]

WOMEN ON THE SUPREME COURT

Commentators on the O'Connor appointment were quick to call the chair she filled on the Court "the woman's seat."[64] What of its future? Presidential considerations of electoral factors in appointing woman justices may depend upon whether they continue to perceive female voting behavior in terms of a "women's vote." The putative gender gap of the 1980s seemed to persist along partisan lines; in every election during the decade, women voted 6 to 8 percentage points more Democratic than men. Moreover, in every election since 1980, women have voted in greater numbers than their male counterparts. In 1988, for example, 6.8 million more women than men voted in the presidential election.[65]

On the equitability score, women have made remarkable political and social strides in the decade and a half since Jeane Kirkpatrick lamented:

Half a century after the ratification of the nineteenth amendment, no woman has been nominated to be president or vice-president, no woman has served on the Supreme Court. Today, there is no woman in the cabinet, no woman in the Senate, no woman serving as governor of a major state, no woman mayor of a major city, no woman in the top leadership of either party.[66]

In the intervening years, Geraldine Ferraro won the 1984 Democratic vice-presidential nomination, and Sandra Day O'Connor was named to the Supreme Court. Elizabeth Dole served two years in the Bush cabinet as secretary of labor and before that served in the Reagan cabinet as secretary of transportation, along with two other women, Margaret Heckler (secretary of health and human services) and Ann McLaughlin (secretary of labor). In 1990 Lynn Martin was named as Dole's successor in the Bush cabinet. Kirkpatrick herself was U.S. ambassador to the United Nations until her resignation in 1984. Two women currently hold seats in the U.S. Senate: Nancy Kassebaum (R.–Kan.) and Barbara Mikulski (D.–Md.). Ann Richards (D.–Tex.), Barbara Roberts (D.–Org.), and Joan Finney (D.–Kan.) serve as state governors. In fact, eighty-five women ran for state offices in 1990, and fifty-one were elected. They include six women lieutenant governors, ten secretaries of state, three attorneys general, and twelve state treasurers.

It is clear that women are moving into the mainstream of political life in the United States. Still, scholars also argue that women "are not fully integrated into the political world."[67] In her insightful work on the integration of women in politics, Virginia Sapiro maintained that women will not be able to overcome separation from the "public" realm of politics until social norms of their "private" realm are transformed. As a basic example, Sapiro points to the traits of passivity and emotionalism that many women are socialized to develop and which are unacceptable in the male-dominated world of politics.[68] The negative reaction to U.S. Representative Pat Schroeder's (D.–Colo.) tearful announcement that she would not seek the Democratic nomination for president in 1988 is illustrative.

Until women overcome such barriers to complete social, political, and economic integration, presidents may feel motivated to offer them "representation" on the Court. Like blacks, as females continue to make inroads in the legal profession and in the judiciary, they will provide larger pools of potential Supreme Court candidates from which presidents may draw. Including Justice O'Connor, President Reagan appointed twenty-nine women to the federal judiciary during his eight years in office. By comparison, his predecessor, Jimmy Carter, named a total of sixty-four women to the federal bench in just four years.[69] Women have also made some slight progress on state courts. Between 1980 and 1985, the total number of women lawyers serving on state judiciaries increased from 548 to 873. In 1985, twenty-three women served on state courts of last resort (6.8 percent of all judges at that level).[70] During approximately the same period (1980–85), the percentage of law degrees awarded to women jumped by almost 10 percent (from 10,754 out of 35,647 or 30.2 percent in 1980 to 14,529 out of 36,172 or 39.0 percent in 1986).[71] As the number of female recipients of law degrees rises, so too will the number of female attorneys. It is estimated that one-third of all lawyers by the year 2000 will be women.[72] Women are also registering small, but perceptible, gains among the nation's most influential law firms, which traditionally have served as stepping stones to prestigious judgeships. In the late 1970s, women occupied less than 1 percent of the partnership ranks in leading law firms. By 1988, women accounted for about 8 percent of the partners in the country's 247 largest law firms.[73]

Comprising over half of the population, women will surely remain on the Supreme Court even after the concept of the "woman's seat" is obsolete. As Justice O'Connor has noted, there will always be a woman on the Court. Her confident expectation that there will be more female justices to follow in her footsteps will all but certainly become a fact of the judiciopolitical process. Indeed, federal Appeals Court Judge Edith Jones, a forty-one-year-old conservative Texan, reportedly was the runner-up to Judge David Souter as President Bush's choice to replace Justice Brennan in the summer of 1990. She had the obvious advantages of gender and geography in her favor, and White House Counsel C. Boyden Gray described the president's decision between the two as "very, very close. I think in the president's mind, in [Attorney General Richard] Thornburgh's and my mind, it almost didn't matter because both were so good. It was a good choice, not a bad choice."[74] In explaining what ultimately tipped the balance to Souter, Gray said: "I think there was some sense that this scholarly approach he [Souter] brings to bear in the future might get lost in the political shuffle. The next time around, are you going to be able to have the luxury of choosing this caliber of candidate for whom there is no obvious political gain?"[75] Still, Jones's "so-near-and-yet-so-far" experience bodes well for the future appointment of women to the high court.

NOTES

1. Bella Abzug with Mim Kelber, *Gender Gap* (Boston: Houghton Mifflin, 1984), pp. 29–30.

2. Susan J. Carroll, *Women as Candidates in American Politics* (Bloomington: Indiana University Press, 1985), p. 3.

3. Abzug, *Gender Gap*, p. 109.

4. See John J. Stucker's article, "Women's Political Role," *Current History* (May 1976): 212–13, for elaboration of these three factors limiting female voting turnout.

5. Abzug, *Gender Gap*, p. 109.

6. Carroll, *Women as Candidates*, p. 3.

7. Abzug, *Gender Gap*, pp. 154–55.

8. Ibid., p. 30.

9. Jeannette E. Tuve's biography of Allen, *First Lady of the Law* (Lanham, Md.: University Press of America, 1984), provides a well-researched and fascinating account of this remarkable woman. Many biographical facts are also contained in Beverly B. Cook's article, "Women as Supreme Court Candidates: From Florence Allen to Sandra Day O'Connor," in 65 *Judicature* 6 (December–January 1982): 314.

10. Quoted in John R. Schmidhauser, *Judges and Justices: The Federal Judiciary* (Boston: Little, Brown, 1979), p. 59. (The letter is among the Hoover Judicial Selection Correspondence File in the Herbert Hoover Papers, Hoover Presidential Library, Schmidhauser, p. 102, fn. 24.)

11. *The Christian Science Monitor,* March 12, p. 18.

12. Cook, "Women as Supreme Court Candidates," p. 323.

13. Ibid.

14. Tuve, *First Lady of the Law,* p. 323.

15. Reported in ibid., pp. 110–11.

16. Reported in the *New York Times,* January 14, 1938, p. 4. Cited in ibid., p. 125.

17. Allen's biographer concluded that she was too closely aligned with women's issues of the past rather that the broader liberal agenda of the New Deal. Moreover, Tuve pointed out that Allen's finest political hours had been recorded in nonpartisan campaigns. Her ties to the Democratic party were growing weak by the mid–1930s. Tuve, *First Lady of the Law,* pp. 169–70.

18. Ibid., see generally pp. 162–71.

19. Quoted in ibid., p. 164. Amazingly, after Sandra Day O'Connor's appointment to the Court more than thirty years later, brief stories appeared in the press speculating about plumbing arrangements that would have to be made for the first female justice.

20. Quoted in ibid., p. 167.

21. Keith T. Poole and Harmon Zeigler, *Women, Public Opinion, and Politics: The Changing Political Attitudes of American Women* (New York: Longman, 1985), p. 1.

22. Marjorie Lansing, "The American Woman: Voter and Activist," in Jane S. Jaquette, ed., *Women in Politics* (New York: John Wiley, 1974), pp. 7–8.

23. Jo Freeman, *The Politics of Women's Liberation* (New York: David McKay, 1975), p. 28.

24. Vicky Randall, *Women and Politics* (New York: St. Martin's Press, 1982), p. 148.

25. Ibid., p. 148; Freeman, *The Politics of Women's Liberation,* p. 53.

26. Randall, *Women and Politics,* p. 148.

27. Stucker, "Women's Political Role," p. 233.

28. Judith Evans, "USA," in Joni Lovenduski and Jill Hills, eds., *The Politics of the Second Electorate* (London: Routledge & Kegan Paul, 1981), pp. 36–37.

29. 410 U.S. 113 (1973).

30. Stucker, "Women's Political Role," p. 233. In the 1984 case of *Grove City College v. Bell,* 465 U.S. 555, the Supreme Court narrowly interpreted Title IX to apply only to the specific program or activity that received federal funds and not necessarily to the institution as a whole. After several unsuccessful attempts, Congress managed to enact legislation overturning *Grove City* in 1988. President Reagan vetoed the bill but was overridden.

31. William H. Chafe, *Women and Equality: Changing Patterns in American Culture* (New York: Oxford University Press, 1977) p. 16.

32. Geraldine R. Segal, *Blacks in the Law: Philadelphia and the Nation* (Philadelphia: University of Pennsylvania Press, 1983), p. 203.

33. *Bradwell v. Illinois,* 83 U.S. 130 (1873).

34. Ibid.

35. Larry Berkson, "Women on the Bench," 65 *Judicature* 6 (December–January): 288–89.

36. Susan B. Carbon, "Women in the Judiciary: An Introduction," 65 *Judicature* 6 (December–January 1982): 285.

37. Berkson, "Women on the Bench," p. 292. Also see Larry C. Berkson and Donna Vandenberg, *National Roster of Women Judges, 1980* (Chicago: American Judicature Society, 1980), p. viii.

38. For a brief biography of Hufstedler see Esther Stineman's *American Political Women: Contemporary and Historical Profiles* (Littleton, Colo.: Libraries Unlimited, 1980), pp. 80–82.

39. Berkson, "Women on the Bench," p. 293.

40. Elaine Martin, "Women on the Federal Bench: A Comparative Profile," 65 *Judicature* 6 (December–January 1982): 307–08. See also Martin's "Men and Women on the Bench: Vive La Difference?" 73 *Judicature* 4 (December–January 1990): 204–08.

41. Cook, "Women as Supreme Court Candidates," p. 324.

42. Henry J. Abraham, *Justices and Presidents: A Political History of Appointments to the Supreme Court*, 2d ed. (New York: Oxford University Press, 1985), pp. 20–21.

43. Gerald Ford, *A Time to Heal* (New York: Harper & Row and Readers Digest Association, 1979), p. 335.

44. Ibid.; *New York Times*, November 19, 1975, p. C16.

45. David M. O'Brien, *Storm Center: The Supreme Court in American Politics*, 2d ed. (New York: W. W. Norton, 1990), p. 86.

46. Personal interview, Washington, D.C., September 12, 1985. (Justice Stevens emphasized that he never discussed the criteria in his appointment with either Levi or Buchen.)

47. Cook, "Women as Supreme Court Candidates," p. 323.

48. Reagan's full statement is quoted in Elder Witt, *A Different Justice: Reagan and the Supreme Court* (Washington, D.C.: Congressional Quarterly, 1986), p. 33.

49. *Time*, July 20, 1981, p. 11.

50. Personal interview, Washington, D.C., May 14, 1985.

51. Ibid.

52. Cook, "Women as Supreme Court Candidates," p. 322.

53. Barbara A. Perry and Henry J. Abraham, "The Reagan Supreme Court Appointees," paper presented at annual Fall Forum, Louisiana State University-Shreveport, November 16, 1990.

54. *New York Times*, July 8, 1981, p. 12.

55. Quoted in the *Washington Post*, September 9, 1981, p. 1.

56. (Charlottesville, Va.) *Daily Progress*, July 8, 1981, p. 8.

57. O'Connor interview.

58. Quoted in Joan S. Marie, "Her Honor: The Rancher's Daughter," *The Saturday Evening Post*, September 1985, p. 43.

59. Abzug, *Gender Gap*, p. 87.

60. Witt, *A Different Justice*, p. 33.

61. Abzug, *Gender Gap*, pp. 80–90.

62. See Poole and Zeigler, *Women, Public Opinion, and Politics*, p. 88, and passim, for an intriguing analysis of women's political attitudes. The authors raise

significant doubts about the cohesiveness of the women's bloc. But, of course, feminists continue to perpetuate the concept of a women's vote and gender gap, which add to women's perceived political potency.

63. Reported in James Q. Wilson's *American Government: Institutions and Policies* (Lexington, Ma.: D. C. Heath, 1989), p. 104.

64. See, for example, Cook's insightful summary of factors leading to O'Connor's selection in "Women as Supreme Court Candidates," passim.

65. Paul Taylor, "Politics of Gender 1990: Shift in Issues May Benefit Women," *Washington Post*, June 10, 1990, p. 16.

66. Jeane Kirkpatrick, *Political Women* (New York: Basic Books, 1974), p. 3.

67. Virginia Sapiro, *The Political Integration of Women: Roles, Socialization, and Politics* (Urbana: University of Illinois Press, 1983), pp. 7–8. Poole and Zeigler, *Women, Public Opinion, and Politics*, p. viii.

68. See Sapiro, *The Political Integration of Women*, for development of her complex theory.

69. Sheldon Goldman, "Reagan's Judicial Legacy: Completing the Puzzle and Summing Up," 72 *Judicature* 6 (April–May 1989): 318–30.

70. From a survey conducted by the Fund for Modern Courts, reported in *The Success of Women and Minorities in Achieving Judicial Office: The Selection Process* (New York: 1985), pp. 9–10.

71. Reported in U.S. Department of Education's *Digest of Education Statistics 1989* (Washington, D.C.: Government Printing Office, 1989), p. 239.

72. Donna Fossum, "Women in the Legal Profession: A Progress Report," 67 *American Bar Association Journal* (May 1981): 582.

73. Reported by Jill Abramson, "For Women Lawyers, An Uphill Struggle," *New York Times Magazine*, March 6, 1988, pp. 36, 75. For a superb analysis of how women must overcome traditional male "gatekeepers" to advance in the legal and judicial professions, see Beverly Blair Cook, "Women Judges in the Opportunity Structure," in *Women, the Courts, and Equality*, Laura L. Crites and Winifred L. Hepperle, eds. (Beverly Hills, Calif.: Sage Publications, 1987), Ch. 6.

74. *Washington Post*, July 25, 1990, p. 6.

75. Ibid.

Chapter 6 _____

Conclusion: Should the Supreme Court Be "Representative"?

Religion, race, and gender have played a measurable role in nearly a dozen of the more than 100 successful Supreme Court appointments since the founding. In the realm of religion, a study of the so-called Catholic seat revealed that Catholicism was not a factor in the appointment of the Court's first two Catholics (Chief Justice Roger Taney and Associate Justice Edward White). In fact, given the widespread anti-Catholicism prevalent in nineteenth-century United States, Taney's and White's religious affiliation was a potential handicap outweighed by presidential considerations of ideological compatibility and merit. Justice Joseph McKenna's appointment in 1898 and Justice White's promotion to chief justice in 1910, on the other hand, exemplified two nominations in which Catholicism was the deciding factor, but only after the respective presidents had established the candidates' basic professional and political "acceptability." The selection of Justice Pierce Butler for the Court in 1922 demonstrated the use of Catholicism as an explicit concern by presidential advisers in initially establishing the pool of potential candidates for nomination.

Justice Frank Murphy's appointment marked the zenith of the "Catholic seat," for his religion was one of the top two or three reasons for President Franklin Roosevelt's selecting him for the Court. The seven-year gap between Murphy's death and Justice William Brennan's appointment left Catholics without "representation" on the high court. Brennan's Catholic religious affiliation was undoubtedly of some concern to President Eisenhower, but the factor was a lower priority for Ike than for F.D.R. when naming Murphy. The gradual assimilation of Catholics into the political mainstream, marked most dramatically by John F. Kennedy's

1960 presidential election victory, demonstrably tempered and may even have removed the electoral and equitability motivations from presidential considerations of Catholics for the Court. Judge Antonin Scalia's Roman Catholic religious affiliation played no more than a minor role in President Reagan's decision to name him to the high court in 1986. With Justice Anthony Kennedy, the most recent Catholic appointee, religious affiliation was a virtual irrelevancy, except perhaps as an indicator of his impeccable moral character, which was absolutely essential to the success of his nomination in the wake of the Ginsburg disaster over his use of marijuana.

Although slightly more complicated in its history and, therefore, less easy to categorize than the "Catholic seat," the "Jewish seat" followed several similar paths in its development. Many Jews and Gentiles viewed Woodrow Wilson's appointment of the first Jewish justice—Louis Brandeis in 1916—as recognition for the increasingly influential Jewish population. But Brandeis's religious affiliation was patently and primarily a handicap to overcome. Brandeis was still on the Court when Hoover named Cardozo in 1932, and there is no evidence that the president considered his meritorious appointee's religious affiliation in an effort to attract Jewish votes by offering additional "representation" on the Court to the Jewish community. If anything, Cardozo's religion was a detrimental factor in Hoover's eyes.

Franklin Roosevelt recognized that his and Justice Brandeis's friend, Felix Frankfurter, would be the obvious replacement for the Court's first Jewish justice. Yet Brandeis's seat on the Court did not become vacant as early as F.D.R. expected, and Frankfurter served with his judicial idol one month before ill health forced Brandeis's retirement. Frankfurter remained the Court's sole Jewish member until his own retirement in 1962, occupying what by then had come to be labeled the "Jewish seat." In an apparent allusion to that seat, President Kennedy had stated that naming Secretary of Labor Arthur Goldberg to succeed Frankfurter was "too obvious and cute." Nevertheless, J.F.K. followed what, arguably, had become a tradition and expectation of having at least one Jew on the Court. His successor, President Johnson, did the same in his appointment of Justice Fortas. Yet, above all, both Kennedy and Johnson chose ideological soul mates, whose views were well-known to them through personal and professional associations. That Goldberg and Fortas were Jewish completed the desired set of credentials for the seats they filled.

The "Jewish seat" was vacated by Fortas's resignation from the Court in 1969. It has been absent ever since, and the likelihood of a revival of the "Jewish seat" along its past "representational" lines is remote. Like Catholics, American Jews have assimilated into politics and society to such a degree that presidents may no longer feel the need to offer them "representation" on the Court.

The categories of race and gender provide only one appointment each for analysis. Still, the appointments of Justices Thurgood Marshall and Sandra Day O'Connor are illustrative of presidential attempts explicitly to "represent" on the Court two groups that had been so long excluded from the political and societal mainstream. The presidential extension of such judicial recognition to blacks and women as their electoral potency increased was not, of course, coincidental. Presidents Johnson and Reagan were following past chief executives who had offered "representation" to religious groups as their potential voting power became a factor in national politics. It is all but certain that the recently established "black seat" and "woman's seat" will remain as a fact of sociopolitical life unless and until blacks and women achieve fuller and more meaningful integration into the American polity—thereby removing the need to offer a "representative" seat on the high court.

INFLUENCE OF "REPRESENTATIVE" FACTORS IN THE JUDICIAL SELECTION PROCESS

The impact of religion, race, and gender factors on the selection of Supreme Court justices is distinctly a twentieth-century phenomenon. Such a conclusion is not surprising given the political coming-of-age of Catholics, Jews, blacks, and women in the past ninety years. But the degree of influence of these "representative" factors on presidential considerations of Court appointments is relatively small. In the religion realm, neither Catholicism nor Judaism was ever a *primary* factor in the relevant appointments. In Thurgood Marshall's and Sandra Day O'Connor's appointments, however, the "representative" concepts of race and gender were, in fact, the overriding presidential considerations—despite loud presidential disclaimers.

The recognition of race and gender followed persistent and sometimes radical, even violent, movements by blacks and women to achieve political and social parity. The more evolutionary trends in Catholic and Jewish assimilation account, in part, for the decreased impact of the religion factor in appointments. In addition, the constitutionally enshrined principle of separation of church and state would have made the nomination of a justice primarily on the basis of his religious affiliation highly problematic.

In the sixteen cases examined, "representativeness" was *a* factor in all but four instances (Roger Taney's, Benjamin Cardozo's, and Anthony Kennedy's appointments, and Edward White's appointment to associate justice). Yet, in only two appointments (Marshall's and O'Connor's) was the desire to "represent" a group on the Court the *primary* positive factor. This may seem an insignificant number compared to the 52

Supreme Court appointments made thus far in the twentieth century or to the 105 justices who have served on the Court. But the two race and gender examples constitute nearly one-quarter of the nine successful appointments to the Court effected in the past two decades.

The study of the factors of religion, race, and gender in Court appointments has revealed a link between their consideration by presidents and the social, political, demographic, and electoral development of the "represented" groups. In order to attract votes or perhaps to repay electoral support, presidents have provided Catholics, Jews, blacks, and women "representation" on the Supreme Court. Consideration of "representative" factors by a president occurs between the periods when a group receives no recognition in appointments because of its ostracism from the political and social mainstream and its assimilation into American society and politics, when the White House apparently no longer perceives the group as deprived of political rewards (such as public office) and, therefore, not due "representation" on the Court.

JUDGING THE USE OF THE "REPRESENTATIVE" CRITERIA

If the past is indeed prologue, future presidential use of "representative" criteria in Supreme Court appointments seems inevitable. Even President Reagan, who, with others in his administration, denounced most varieties of affirmative action, used gender as the primary criterion in his first Supreme Court appointment. In addition, President Bush reportedly considered the first Hispanic nominee for the seat vacated by Justice Brennan in 1990 before he ultimately chose Judge David H. Souter of the First Circuit Court of Appeals.[1] Bush also included a black (U.S. Circuit Court Judge Clarence Thomas) and a woman (U.S. Circuit Court Judge Edith Jones) on his short list. In fact, Jones was the runner-up to Souter. If "representative" factors are here to stay, do they conform with the broader requirements of the Supreme Court and its role in our governmental system?

As Chapter 1 noted, the "descriptive" or "passive" concept of representativeness can be used to characterize the bureaucracy as well as the judiciary, both of which fail to draw authority from democratic election of their members. The tension between democracy and bureaucracy was the subject of a table developed by Professors Samuel Krislov and David Rosenbloom, which contrasted the characteristics of democracy with those of the bureaucracy to measure their degree of compatibility.[2] Substituting the Supreme Court for bureaucracy, and making the appropriate descriptive changes, my modified table appears as follows:

Characteristics of Democracy	Characteristics of the Supreme Court
Equality	Elitism
Rotation in office	Lifetime tenure
Freedom	Adherence to precedent and formal rules
Pluralism	Homogeneity
Citizen participation	Participation based on expertise
Openness	Secrecy
Legitimacy based on elections	Legitmacy based on expertise

Of the above characteristics, only "elitism" and "homogeneity" necessarily would be altered by the occasional use of the "representativeness" criterion in choosing Supreme Court justices.[3] Such an alteration would not weaken the Court's ability to function, *if* the other necessary characteristics of an effective judicial body (such as life tenure, adherence to precedent and formal rules, expertise, and secrecy) remain intact.

Moreover, adding democratic features to the Court by making it less elite and homogeneous (that is, a bastion of male WASPs) could blunt frequently voiced criticism that because the Court is the least democratic of the branches, it has improperly become the final arbiter in constitutional disputes. Throughout the Court's history, critics have accused it of stepping beyond the bounds of interpreting the law to embrace the law-making function. Especially when it has exercised judicial review to invalidate a federal statute, the Court has been castigated (sometimes even by its own members) for aspiring to be a "super legislature." By becoming more balanced in its membership, the Court could at least stake a claim to being more open and legitimate.[4] As former Justice Brennan has observed, the sole end of making the Court diverse and reflective of America's heterogeneity was to foster legitimacy for it in the eyes of the American people.[5] Or as Justice O'Connor has expressed it, the Court only possesses the "power of the pen"; and, therefore, to gain public acceptance, it must not be of a "single image" or a "single mold."[6]

The table of characteristics is admittedly reductionist in its empirical description of the Court and its relation to democratic goals, but it is primarily intended to offer a broader foundation for judging presidential appointment strategies. The usual distinction drawn between "merit" and "representativeness"[7] is, at best, far too narrow and, at worst, simply inaccurate. It precludes a judicial candidate who is both meritorious *and* "representative" of a particular societal group. Undoubtedly, Presidents Johnson and Reagan might have found an even more qualified black or woman to name to the Supreme Court than Marshall or O'Connor,

respectively; but two political considerations barred arguably more meritorious appointments. First, Johnson and Reagan, following electoral in-
stincts, recognized blacks and then women before the full assimilation of
these groups into the legal profession and the state and federal judiciaries,
where their members might have gained more and broader expertise.
Second, the ideological/political compatibility factor no doubt moved
Johnson and Reagan away from some, perhaps more qualified, members
of the two groups.

Taken to its extreme, the logic that draws an unbreachable line between
merit and "representativeness" would also exclude all other factors beyond merit (e. g., political and ideological compatibility or friendship).[8]
In other words, if "representativeness" implies a lessening of merit, the
same can be said of political and ideological compatibility and certainly
friendship. Undoubtedly, the definition of merit itself is one of the most
contentious issues in judicial selection debates. Some argue that there is
no objective standard for merit as applied to Supreme Court nominees
or any other judicial candidate. Nonsense! As I always point out to my
students, professors are called upon everyday to evaluate the work of
their own students and peers in the academic world. In those evaluations,
they attempt to put personal or ideological biases aside in order to judge
written and oral presentations "on their merits."

In an effort to inject some objectivity into the evaluation of judicial
merit, I would propose the following professional and personal criteria
for potential Supreme Court nominees: strong educational background,
intelligence, clarity of expression, professional ability, judicial temperament, impeccable moral character, and diligence and conscientiousness.[9]
Although the individual components of such models may be difficult
to define, they are meant to take us beyond futile exercises in which
conservatives and liberals declare those of a similar ideological stripe
"meritorious."

Given the judicial role of the Court and its requirements of expertise,
independence, and public confidence, we should enshrine merit as a
prime criterion for Supreme Court selection. Nevertheless, other factors can, do, and should enter into the selection process. The criterion
of ideological and political compatibility is simply a cardinal fact of
political life and Supreme Court appointments. It does not *necessarily*
have to detract from a candidate's objective merit.[10] Moreover, it, too,
can add to the Court's legitimacy in the eyes of the public. During the
1984 presidential campaign, when Supreme Court appointments became
a hotly debated issue, Justice William Rehnquist argued that "there is no
reason in the world why a president should not . . . appoint people . . .
who are sympathetic to his political or philosophical principles." He
supported his claim by noting that the president is the "one official who
is elected by the entire nation" and, therefore, the public has "something

to say about the membership of the Court."[11]

In an interview one year later, Justice Rehnquist also acknowledged that "diversity is desirable" on the Court. He noted that the president is free to chart his own course in judicial selection, and that the chief executive should maintain merit "as a floor" for nominees. But "all things being equal," the president might indeed consider "representative" factors. Rehnquist emphasized that "no one should be excluded [from the Court] because of" factors such as religion, race, and gender.[12] (When questioned on this same point, Justice Stevens was equally emphatic, arguing that there should be a "total absence of disqualifying categories" for potential nominees.[13])

Like political and ideological compatibility, "representativeness" is a fact of political life and is destined not only to remain on the judicial appointment scene, but perhaps to complicate matters, as other groups (e. g., Asians and Hispanics) demand a place on the high bench and presidents attempt to meet their demands in return for electoral support. The Bureau of the Census reported in 1980 that of America's 600,000 lawyers, approximately 8,900 were of Spanish origin and 3,700 were Asian or Pacific Islanders. In a 1984 feature on the hiring of minority attorneys by law firms, the *American Bar Association Journal* quoted Robert Pickett, an administrative law judge in New Jersey, on the future of minorities in influential law firms in major urban areas. Pickett predicted that "as the political winds shift, these populations [of ethnic groups] will begin to demand that there be some representation of people who look like them in these large law firms."[14]

As a factor in Court appointments, "representativeness" by no means has to entail a diminution of the merit principle. Indeed, the sixteen appointees examined in this book met at least a minimum standard of merit, and some are considered among the "greats" who have served on the Supreme Court. Moreover, a public perception that the high bench is open to all groups in society and is as reflective of American pluralism as the nine seats will allow may be particularly crucial at this time in the nation's development. As the country grows more ethnically and racially heterogeneous, there are increasingly vocal demands to accommodate cultural diversity in all realms of life.[15] Although such demands have aroused ugly controversies, especially in the education field, the application of the diversity principle to the Supreme Court strikes me as a positive goal—again, as long as merit is at the threshold of any appointment. I reject, however, the "diversity for diversity's sake" argument so prevalent now among extremists in the multiculturalism debate.

In addition, Justice Powell argued in a 1986 interview that a member of a previously excluded group can bring insights to the Court that the rest of its members lack. He spoke of Justice Marshall's unique contribution to the Court because of his direct experience with racial segregation in this country. But Justice Powell stressed that such a member of the Court, chosen to reflect the "heterogeneous nature of the population," must be "qualified." He added: "This institution would be handicapped if less than meritorious individuals came to the Court."[16]

Use of the friendship criterion as the sole basis for appointments is the least defensible of the factors that lie beyond the merit principle. It smacks of cronyism and unprofessionalism, and may be most likely to produce unmeritorious justices. (Franklin Roosevelt's appointment of his friend, Felix Frankfurter, to the Court was a notable exception.) Like political and ideological compatibility and "representativeness," however, use of the friendship criterion in appointments may be an inevitable facet of the judicial selection process. But as Justice Stevens recently observed, its only justification is if it allows a president to have first-hand knowledge of a potential nominee's merits.[17]

Ultimately, where one stands on this issue may depend on the theory of constitutional analysis to which one subscribes. Those members of the "traditional" school—with its emphasis on a model of independent, expert judges finding law and interpreting it with utmost objectivity—would undoubtedly emphasize a purely merit-based judicial selection system. Conversely, those devotees of the so-called conventional or behavioralist schools recognize the political nature of the Court's endeavors as well as the appointment process, and would therefore consider inevitable the use of political considerations in judicial selection.

Justice Frankfurter once described the appointment of a Supreme Court justice as resulting from "the turn of a wheel."[18] But as Frankfurter well knew, the process is not nearly so random. Presidents are not carnival barkers spinning a wheel labeled with potential nominees' names and shouting, "Where she stops, nobody knows!" The public, and even the press, occasionally may be surprised by a president's selection decision (e. g., Brennan's appointment). But that does not mean that the president and his advisers had not taken into account the profound ramifications of selecting a judicial nominee who might remain on the Court long after his appointing chief executive has departed the Oval Office—and sometimes this earthly life. Not surprisingly, a variety of political considerations, occasionally in the form of "representative" factors, impinge upon that momentous decision. But presidents must carefully survey the political and judicial landscape to find ideologically compatible *and* professionally respected justices, for they may well participate in shaping the legacy of the Court and the nation.

NOTES

1. The potential Hispanic nominees mentioned in the media were Ferdinand

Fernandez, a former federal district court judge in California who was elevated to the circuit court in 1990, and Ricardo Hinojosa, a federal district court judge in Texas.

2. Samuel Krislov and David H. Rosenbloom, *Representative Bureaucracy and the American Political System* (New York: Praeger, 1981), pp. 23–34. Their table listed the following "requirements" for bureaucracy juxtaposed with those of democracy: hierarchy, seniority, command, unity, participation based on expertise, secrecy, and legitimacy based on expertise.

3. In terms of the social background characteristics of the majority of Court members throughout history, elitism and homogeneity have been hallmarks of the Supreme Court. See John R. Schmidhauser: "The Justices of the Supreme Court: A Collective Portrait," 3 *Midwest Journal of Political Science*, February 1959: 1–57; *The Supreme Court: Its Politics, Personalities, and Procedures* (New York: Holt, Rinehart and Winston, 1960), pp. 30–62; *Judges and Justices: The Federal Appellate Judiciary* (Boston: Little, Brown, 1979), pp. 41–101. For a brief composite profile of the 102 justices who sat on the Court to 1985, see Henry J. Abraham's *Justices and Presidents: A Political History of Appointments to the Supreme Court*, 2d ed. (New York: Oxford University Press, 1985), pp. 61–62.

4. Very few studies have attempted to quantify the illusive concept of legitimacy as it applies to the Court. As Walter Murphy has noted: "for all its apparent clarity and simplicity, political support is typically difficult to measure." But, see Walter Murphy, Joseph Tannenhaus, and Daniel L. Kastner's pioneering survey research study in this area, *Public Evaluation of Constitutional Courts: Alternative Explanations* (Beverly Hills, Calif.: Sage Publications, 1973).

5. Personal interview, Justice William J. Brennan, Jr., Washington, D.C., April 1, 1985.

6. Personal interview, Justice Sandra Day O'Connor, Washington, D.C., May 14, 1985.

7. See Chapter 1.

8. I return to Henry Abraham's quartet referred to in Chapter 1: objective merit, personal and political friendship, balancing "representation" on the court, and "real" political ideological compatibility. See his *Justices and Presidents*, pp. 3–70, for elaboration of the four criteria.

9. See ibid., for a similar litany which constitutes Abraham's merit model.

10. As in Robert Bork's unsuccessful nomination, however, controversy over his ideology completely obscured his meritorious credentials.

11. Quoted in the *Washington Post*, October 20, 1984, p. 6.

12. Personal interview, Justice William H. Rehnquist, Washington, D.C., September 24, 1985.

13. Personal interview, Justice John Paul Stevens, Washington, D.C., September 12, 1985.

14. Faye A. Silas, "Business Reasons to Hire Minority Lawyers," *American Bar Association Journal*, April 1984: 53.

15. Among a plethora of articles on this issue, see most recently, for example, Dinesh D'Souza, "The New Segregation on Campus," *The American Scholar* Winter 1991: 17–30.

16. Personal interview, Justice Lewis F. Powell, Jr., Washington, D.C., February 20, 1986.

17. Personal interview, Justice John Paul Stevens, Washington, D.C., September 12, 1985.

18. Frankfurter said of Judge Learned Hand: "To bemoan that the turn of the wheel did not put him on the Supreme Court grossly underestimates what he accomplished off it." "Learned Hand," 75 *Harvard Law Review* 1, November 1961: 4.

Appendix 1
Members of the United States Supreme Court, 1789–1991

NAME OF JUSTICE AND SEAT OCCUPIED*	APPOINTING PRESIDENT	STATE FROM WHICH APPOINTED	COURT TENURE
CHIEF JUSTICE:			
John Jay	Washington	N.Y.	1789-95
John Rutledge	"	S.C.	1795 (Unconfirmed)
Oliver Ellsworth	"	Conn.	1796-1800
John Marshall	Adams	Va.	1801-35
Roger B. Taney	Jackson	Md.	1836-64
Salmon P. Chase	Lincoln	Ohio	1864-73
Morrison R. Waite	Grant	"	1874-88
Melville W. Fuller	Cleveland	Ill.	1888-1910
Edward D. White	Taft	La.	1910-21
William H. Taft	Harding	Conn.	1921-30
Charles E. Hughes	Hoover	N.Y.	1930-41
Harlan F. Stone	F. Roosevelt	"	1941-46
Fred M. Vinson	Truman	Ky.	1946-53
Earl Warren	Eisenhower	Cal.	1953-69
Warren Burger	Nixon	Minn.	1969-86
William H. Rehnquist	Reagan	Ariz.	1986-
SEAT #2:			
John Rutledge	Washington	S.C.	1789-91
Thomas Johnson	"	Md.	1791-93
William Paterson	"	N.J.	1793-1806
Henry B. Livingston	Jefferson	N.Y.	1806-23
Smith Thompson	Monroe	"	1823-43
Samuel Nelson	Tyler	"	1845-72
Ward Hunt	Grant	"	1872-82
Samuel Blatchford	Arthur	"	1882-93
Edward D. White	Cleveland	La.	1894-1910
Willis Van Devanter	Taft	Wyo.	1910-37
Hugo L. Black	F. Roosevelt	Ala.	1937-71
Lewis F. Powell, Jr.	Nixon	Va.	1972-87
Anthony Kennedy	Reagan	Cal.	1988-
SEAT #3:			
William Cushing	Washington	Mass.	1789-1810
Joseph Story	Madison	"	1811-1845
Levi Woodbury	Polk	N.H.	1845-51
Benjamin Curtis	Fillmore	Mass.	1851-57

Appendix 1 (continued)

NAME OF JUSTICE AND SEAT OCCUPIED	APPOINTING PRESIDENT	STATE FROM WHICH APPOINTED	COURT TENURE
SEAT #3 (cont.):			
Nathan Clifford	Buchanan	Maine	1858-81
Horace Gray	Arthur	Mass.	1881-1902
Oliver Wendell Holmes	T. Roosevelt	Mass.	1902-32
Benjamin N. Cardozo	Hoover	N.Y.	1932-38
Felix Frankfurter	F. Roosevelt	Mass.	1939-62
Arthur Goldberg	Kennedy	Ill.	1962-65
Abe Fortas	L. Johnson	Tenn.	1965-69
Harry Blackmun	Nixon	Minn.	1970-
SEAT #4:			
James Wilson	Washington	Penn.	1789-98
Bushrod Washington	Adams	Va.	1798-1829
Henry Baldwin	Jackson	Penn.	1830-44
Robert C. Grier	Polk	"	1846-70
William Strong	Grant	"	1870-80
William B. Woods	Hayes	Ga.	1880-87
Lucius Q. C. Lamar	Cleveland	Miss.	1888-93
Howell E. Jackson	Harrison	Tenn.	1893-95
Rufus W. Peckham	Cleveland	N.Y.	1895-1909
Horace H. Lurton	Taft	Tenn.	1909-14
James. C. McReynolds	Wilson	"	1914-41
James F. Byrnes	F. Roosevelt	S.C.	1941-42
Wiley B. Rutledge	"	Iowa	1943-49
Sherman Minton	Truman	Ind.	1949-56
William Brennan, Jr.	Eisenhower	N.J.	1956-90
David H. Souter	Bush	N.H.	1990-
SEAT #5:			
John Blair	Washington	Va.	1789-96
Samuel Chase	"	Md.	1796-1811
Gabriel Duval	Madison	"	1811-35
Philip P. Barbour	Jackson	Va.	1836-41
Peter V. Daniel	Van Buren	"	1841-60
Samuel F. Miller	Lincoln	Iowa	1862-90
Henry B. Brown	Harrison	Mich.	1890-1906
William H. Moody	T. Roosevelt	Mass.	1906-10
Joseph R. Lamar	Taft	Ga.	1910-16
Louis D. Brandeis	Wilson	Mass.	1916-39
William O. Douglas	F. Roosevelt	Conn.	1939-75
John Paul Stevens	Ford	Ill.	1975-
SEAT #6:			
James Iredell	Washington	N.C.	1790-99

Appendix 1 (continued)

NAME OF JUSTICE AND SEAT OCCUPIED	APPOINTING PRESIDENT	STATE FROM WHICH APPOINTED	COURT TENURE
SEAT #6 (cont.):			
Alfred Moore	Adams	N.C.	1799-1804
William Johnson	Jefferson	S.C.	1804-34
James M. Wayne	Jackson	Ga.	1835-67
Joseph Bradley	Grant	N.J.	1870-92
George Shiras, Jr.	Harrison	Penn.	1892-1903
William R. Day	T. Roosevelt	Ohio	1903-22
Pierce Butler	Harding	Minn.	1922-39
Frank Murphy	F. Roosevelt	Mich.	1940-49
Tom C. Clark	Truman	Tex.	1949-67
Thurgood Marshall	L. Johnson	N.Y.	1967-
SEAT #7:			
Thomas Todd	Jefferson	Ky.	1807-26
Robert Trimble	J. Q. Adams	"	1826-28
John McLean	Jackson	Ohio	1829-61
Noah H. Swayne	Lincoln	"	1862-81
Stanley Matthews	Garfield	"	1881-89
David J. Brewer	Harrison	Kan.	1889-1910
Charles E. Hughes	Taft	N.Y.	1910-16
John H. Clarke	Wilson	Ohio	1916-22
George Sutherland	Harding	Utah	1922-38
Stanley F. Reed	F. Roosevelt	Ky.	1938-57
Charles E. Whittaker	Eisenhower	Mo.	1957-62
Byron R. White	Kennedy	Colo.	1962-
SEAT #8:			
John Catron	Jackson	Tenn.	1837-65
Harlan F. Stone	Coolidge	N.Y.	1925-41
Robert H. Jackson	F. Roosevelt	"	1941-54
John M. Harlan II	Eisenhower	"	1955-71
William H. Rehnquist	Nixon	Ariz.	1972-86
Antonin Scalia	Reagan	Va.	1986-
SEAT #9:			
John McKinley	Van Buren	Ala.	1837-52
John Campbell	Pierce	"	1853-61
David Davis	Lincoln	Ill.	1862-77
John M. Harlan I	Hayes	Ky.	1877-1911
Mahlon Pitney	Taft	N.J.	1912-22
Edward T. Sanford	Harding	Tenn.	1923-30
Owen Roberts	Hoover	Penn.	1930-45
Harold H. Burton	Truman	Ohio	1945-58

Appendix 1 (continued)

NAME OF JUSTICE AND SEAT OCCUPIED	APPOINTING PRESIDENT	STATE FROM WHICH APPOINTED	COURT TENURE
SEAT #9 (cont.):			
Potter Stewart	Eisenhower	Ohio	1958-81
Sandra Day O'Connor	Reagan	Ariz.	1981-
SEAT #10:			
Stephen J. Field	Lincoln	Cal.	1863-97
Joseph McKenna	McKinley	"	1898-25

Sources: Henry J. Abraham, <u>Justices and Presidents: A Political History of Appointments to the Supreme Court</u>, 2d ed. (New York: Oxford University Press, 1985), and Alfred H. Kelly and Winfred A. Harbison, <u>The American Constitution: Its Origins and Development</u>, 4th ed. (New York: W. W. Norton & Co., 1970).

*The Supreme Court began with six seats in 1789 (one chief justice and five associate justices). Its size increased to seven in 1807 with the addition of the Seventh Circuit. The creation of two new circuits in 1837, increased the Court's size to nine. In 1863 a tenth seat was added with the establishment of the Tenth Circuit in the West. Congress reduced the number of circuits to nine in 1866 and sought to limit the size of the Court to its original six seats by prohibiting appointments. In 1869 Congress restored the Court to nine justices.

Appendix 2
Catholic, Jewish, Black, and Female Justices of the United States Supreme Court

NAME OF JUSTICE	APPOINTING PRESIDENT	COURT TENURE
CATHOLIC:		
Roger B. Taney*	Jackson	1836-1864
Edward D. White, Jr.	Cleveland	1894-1910
Joseph McKenna	McKinley	1898-1925
Edward D. White, Jr.*	Taft	1910-1921
Pierce Butler	Harding	1922-1939
Frank Murphy	F. Roosevelt	1940-1949
Wm. J. Brennan, Jr.	Eisenhower	1956-1990
Antonin Scalia	Reagan	1986-
Anthony M. Kennedy	Reagan	1988-
JEWISH:		
Louis D. Brandeis	Wilson	1916-1939
Benjamin N. Cardozo	Hoover	1932-1938
Felix Frankfurter	F. Roosevelt	1939-1962
Arthur J. Goldberg	Kennedy	1962-1965
Abe Fortas	L. Johnson	1965-1969
BLACK:		
Thurgood Marshall	L. Johnson	1967-
FEMALE:		
Sandra Day O'Connor	Reagan	1981-

*Chief Justice

Bibliography

ARTICLES AND PERIODICALS

Abraham, Henry J. " 'A Bench Happily Filled:' Some Historical Reflections on the Supreme Court Appointment Process." 66 *Judicature* 7 (February 1983): 282–95.

———. " 'Merit' or 'Seniority'?: Reflections on the Politics of Recent Appointments to the Chief Justiceship of India." *Journal of Commonwealth and Comparative Politics*, November 1978: 303–08.

———, and Edward M. Goldberg. "A Note on the Appointment of Justices of the Supreme Court of the United States." *American Bar Association Journal*, February 1960: 147–50, 219–22.

Abzug, Bella S. and Cynthinia Edgar. "Women and Politics: The Struggle for Representation." *The Massachusetts Review*, Winter–Spring 1972: 17–24.

Antell, Joan B. "The Suffrage Movement." *Current History*, May 1976: 203–05, 231–32.

Bergold, Laurel R. "The Changing Legal Status of American Women." *Current History*, May 1976: 206–10, 230–31.

"The Black Judge in America: A Statistical Profile." A Special Society Report. 57 *Judicature* (1973): 18, 20.

Carbon, Susan B. "Women on the Judiciary: An Introduction." 65 *Judicature* 6 (December–January 1982): 285.

Carmen, Ira H. "The President, Politics and the Power of Appointment: Hoover's Nomination of Mr. Justice Cardozo." 55 *Virginia Law Review* 4 (May 1969): 616–65.

Chase, Harold, Margaret Green, and Robert Mollan. "Catholics on the Court." *The New Republic*, September 26, 1960, pp. 13–15.

Cook, Beverly Blair. "Black Representation in the Third Branch." 1 *Black Law Journal* 2 and 3 (1971): 260–79.

Crockett, George W., Jr. "Judicial Selection and the Black Experience." 58 *Judicature* 9 (1975): 438–42.

Evans, Evan A. "Political Influences in the Selection of Federal Judges." *Wisconsin Law Review* (1948): 330–51.

Ewing, Cortez. "Geography and the Supreme Court." 9 *Southwestern Political and Social Quarterly* (June 1930): 26–46.

Frank, John P. "The Appointment of Supreme Court Justices: Prestige, Principles, and Politics." 16 *Wisconsin Law Review* (1941): 172–210, 343, 461.

Frankfurter, Felix. "The Supreme Court in the Mirror of Justices." 105 *University of Pennsylvania Law Review* (1957): 781–96.

Gelhorn, Ernest. "The Law Schools and the Negro." *Duke Law Review*, 1968: 1069–97.

Goff, John S. "The Rejection of Supreme Court Appointments." 5 *The American Journal of Legal History* (1961): 357–68.

Goldman, Sheldon. "Judicial Selection and the Qualities That Make a 'Good' Judge." 462 *Annals of the American Academy of Social and Political Science* (July 1982): 113–17.

———. "Reaganizing the Judiciary: The First Term Appointments." 68 *Judicature* 9–10 (April–May 1985): 312–29.

———. "Reagan's Judicial Legacy: Completing the Puzzle and Summing Up." 72 *Judicature* 6 (April–May 1989): 318–30.

———. "Should There Be Affirmative Action for the Judiciary?" 62 *Judicature* 10 (May 1979): 488–94.

Gottschall, Jon. "Carter's Judicial Appointments: The Influence of Affirmative Action and Merit Selection on Voting on the U.S. Court of Appeals." 67 *Judicature* 4 (October 1983): 164–73.

Grossman, Joel. "Social Backgrounds and Judicial Decision-Making." 79 *Harvard Law Review* (1966): 1551–64.

Haupt, Donna. "Justice William J. Brennan, Jr." *Constitution*, Winter 1989: 50–57.

Knebel, Fletcher. "A Visit With Justice Brennan." *Look*, December 18, 1962, pp. 127–37.

Leeds, Jeffrey. "A Life on the Court." *New York Times Magazine*, October 5, 1986, p. 25.

Lipshutz, Robert J. and Douglas B. Huron. "Achieving a More Representative Federal Judiciary." 62 *Judicature* 10 (May 1979): 483–85.

Luney, Percy R., Jr. "Minorities in the Legal Profession." *American Bar Association Journal*, April 1984: 58–60.

Perry, Barbara A. "The Life and Death of the 'Catholic Seat' on the United States Supreme Court." VI *Journal of Law and Politics* 1 (Fall 1989): 55–92.

Reinhardt, Stephen. "Jewishness and Judging: A Judge's Thoughts on *Two Jewish Justices*," 10 *Cardozo Law Review* (1989): 2345–57.

Schmidhauser, John R. "The Justices of the Supreme Court: A Collective Portrait." 3 *Midwest Journal of Political Science* (February 1959): 1–57.

Silas, Faye A. "Business Reasons to Hire Minority Lawyers." *American Bar Association Journal*, April 1984: 52–57.

Slotnik, Elliot E. "Reforms in Judicial Selection: Will They Affect the Senate's Role?" Parts I and II, 64 *Judicature* 2 and 3 (August and September 1980): 62 and 114–31.

Stucker, John J. "Women's Political Role." *Current History*, May 1976: 211–14, 232–33.

Tollet, Kenneth S. "Black Lawyers, Their Education, and the Black Community." 17 *Howard Law Journal* (1972): 326–57.

Winters, Glenn R. "Selection of Judges: An Historical Introduction." 44 *Texas Law Review* (1966): 1081–87.

"Women and Social Reform: The Nineteenth Century." Editors of *Current History*, May 1976: 197–98.

BOOKS

Abraham, Henry J. *Freedom and the Court: Civil Rights and Liberties in the United States.* 5th ed. New York: Oxford University Press, 1988.

——. *The Judicial Process: An Introductory Analysis of the Courts of the United States, England, and France.* 5th ed. New York: Oxford University Press, 1986.

——. *Justices and Presidents: A Political History of Appointments to the Supreme Court.* 2d ed. New York: Oxford University Press, 1985.

Abzug, Bella, with Mim Kelber. *Gender Gap.* Boston: Houghton Mifflin, 1984.

Ahlstrom, Sydney E. *A Religious History of the American People.* New Haven, Conn.: Yale University Press, 1972.

Aiken, Charles, ed. *The Negro Votes.* San Francisco: Chandler, 1962.

Allen, Florence. *To Do Justly.* Cleveland: Western Reserve University Press, 1965.

Anderson, Judith Icke. *William Howard Taft: An Intimate History.* New York: W. W. Norton, 1981.

Ashman, A. and J. J. Alfini. *The Key to Judicial Merit Selection: The Nominating Process.* Chicago: American Judicature Society, 1974.

Bailey, Harry A., Jr., ed. *Negro Politics in America.* Columbus, Ohio: Charles E. Merrill, 1967.

Baker, Leonard. *Brandeis and Frankfurter: A Dual Biography.* New York: Harper & Row, 1984.

Baker, Liva. *Felix Frankfurter.* New York: Coward-McCann, 1969.

Baker, Ray Stannard. *Woodrow Wilson: Life and Letters, Facing War, 1915–1917.* New York: Greenwood Press, 1968.

Baum, Lawrence. *The Supreme Court.* 3d ed. Washington: CQ Press, 1989.

Benson, Peter L. and Dorothy L. Williams. *Religion on Capitol Hill: Myths and Realities.* New York: Harper & Row, 1982.

Berkson, Larry C. and Susan B. Carbon. *Federal Judicial Selection During the Carter Administration, The United States Circuit Judge Nominating Commission: Its Members, Procedures, and Candidates.* Chicago: American Judicature Society, 1980.

Berkson, Larry C. and Donna Vandenberg. *National Roster of Women Judges, 1980.* Chicago: American Judicature Society, 1980.

Berlin, William S. *On the Edge of Politics: The Roots of Jewish Political Thought in America.* Westport, Conn.: Greenwood Press, 1978.

Billington, Ray Allen. *The Protestant Crusade, 1800–1860: A Study of the Origins of American Nativism.* New York: Rinehart, 1938.

Bland, Randall W. *Private Pressure on Public Law: The Legal Career of Justice Thurgood Marshall.* Port Washington, N.Y.: Kennikat Press, 1973.

Bradlee, Benjamin C. *Conversations with Kennedy*. New York: W. W. Norton, 1975.

Brigham, John. *The Cult of the Court*. Philadelphia: Temple University Press, 1987.

Burt, Robert A. *Two Jewish Justices: Outcasts in the Promised Land*. Berkeley: University of California Press, 1988.

Butt, Archie. *Taft and Roosevelt: The Intimate Letters of Archie Butt, Military Aide*. 2 vols. Garden City, N.Y.: Doubleday, Doran, 1930.

Carroll, Susan J. *Women as Candidates in American Politics*. Bloomington: Indiana University Press, 1985.

Chafe, William H. *Women and Equality: Changing Patterns in American Culture*. New York: Oxford University Press, 1977.

Chase, Harold W. *Federal Judges: The Appointing Process*. Minneapolis: University of Minnesota Press, 1972.

Christopher, Maurine. *America's Black Congressmen*. New York: Thomas Y. Crowell, 1971.

Cleary, Daniel F. *Catholicism in America*. New York: Harcourt, Brace, 1953.

Cogley, John. *Catholic America*. New York: Dial Press, 1973.

Cox, Archibald. *The Court and the Constitution*. Boston: Houghton Mifflin, 1987.

Crites, Laura L. and Winifred L. Hepperle, eds. *Women, the Courts, and Equality*. Beverly Hills, Calif.: Sage Publications, 1987.

Cross, Robert D. *The Emergence of Liberal Catholicism in America*. Cambridge, Mass.: Harvard University Press, 1958.

Daly, John Charles, moderator. "Whom Do Judges Represent?" Washington: American Enterprise Institute, 1981.

Danelski, David J. *A Supreme Court Justice Is Appointed*. New York: Random House, 1964.

Daniels, Josephus. *The Wilson Era: Years of Peace—1910–1917*. Chapel Hill: The University of North Carolina Press, 1944.

Douglas, William O. *The Court Years, 1939–1975, The Autobiography of William O. Douglas*. New York: Vintage Books, 1981.

Elazar, Daniel J. *Community and Polity: The Organizational Dynamics of American Jewry*. Philadelphia: The Jewish Publication Society of America, 1976.

Ellis, John Tracy. *American Catholicism*. 2d ed. Chicago: The University of Chicago Press, 1969.

Epstein, Cynthia Fuchs. *Women in Law*. New York: Basic Books, 1981.

Ernst, Robert T. and Lawrence Hugg, eds. *Black America: Geographic Perspectives*. Garden City, N.Y.: Doubleday, 1976.

Evans, Eli N. *Judah P. Benjamin: The Jewish Confederate*. New York: The Free Press, 1988.

Ewing, Cortez. *The Judges of the Supreme Court*. Minneapolis: University of Minnesota, 1938.

Farley, James A. *Jim Farley's Story: The Roosevelt Years*. New York: McGraw-Hill, 1948.

Farrand, Max. *Records of the Federal Convention of 1787*. 3 vols. New Haven, Conn.: Yale University Press, 1937.

Fine, Sidney. *Frank Murphy: The Detroit Years*. Ann Arbor: The University of Michigan Press, 1975.

———. *Frank Murphy: The New Deal Years.* Chicago: The University of Chicago Press, 1979.

———. *Frank Murphy: The Washington Years.* Ann Arbor: The University of Michigan Press, 1984.

Ford, Gerald R. *A Time to Heal.* New York: Harper & Row and Readers Digest Association, 1979.

Frank, John. *The Marble Palace: The Supreme Court in American Life.* New York: Alfred A. Knopf, 1958.

Freedman, Max, ed. *Roosevelt and Frankfurter: Their Correspondence 1928–1945.* Boston: Little, Brown, 1968.

Friedman, Leon and Fred Israel, eds. *The Justices of the United States Supreme Court, 1789–1969,* 5 vols. New York: Chelsea House, 1969.

Fuchs, Lawrence. *John F. Kennedy and American Catholicism.* New York: Meredith Press, 1967.

Gallup, George, Jr. and Jim Castelli. *The American Catholic People: Their Beliefs, Practices, and Values.* Garden City, N.Y.: Doubleday, 1987.

Gerber, David A., ed. *Anti-Semitism in American History.* Urbana: University of Illinois Press, 1986.

Gleason, Philip. *Keeping the Faith: American Catholicism Past and Present.* Notre Dame, Ind.: University of Notre Dame Press, 1987.

Goldberg, Dorothy. *A Private View of a Public Life.* New York: Charterhouse, 1975.

Greeley, Andrew M. *The American Catholic: A Social Portrait.* New York: Basic Books, 1977.

———. *The Catholic Experience.* Garden City, N.Y.: Doubleday, 1969.

Grossman, Joel B. *Lawyers and Judges: The ABA and the Politics of Judicial Selection.* New York: John Wiley, 1965.

Harris, J. P. *The Advice and Consent of the Senate: A Study of the Confirmation of Appointments by the U.S. Senate.* Berkeley: University of California Press, 1953.

Hellman, George S. *Benjamin N. Cardozo.* New York: McGraw Hill, 1940.

Hennesey, James, S.J. *American Catholics: A History of the Roman Catholic Community in the United States.* New York: Oxford University Press, 1981.

Higham, John. *Strangers in the Land: Patterns of American Nativism 1860–1925.* Westport, Conn.: Greenwood Press, 1981.

Highsaw, Robert B. *Edward Douglass White: Defender of the Conservative Faith.* Baton Rouge: Louisiana State University Press, 1981.

Howard, J. Woodford, Jr. *Mr. Justice Murphy: A Political Biography.* Princeton, N.J.: Princeton University Press, 1968.

Ickes, Harold L. *The Secret Diary of Harold L. Ickes.* 3 vols. New York: Simon and Schuster, 1954.

The Intimate Papers of Colonel House. 4 vols. Arranged as a narrative by Charles Seymour. Boston: Houghton Mifflin, 1926.

Isaacs, Stephen D. *Jews and American Politics.* Garden City, N.Y.: Doubleday, 1974.

Jacquette, Jane S., ed. *Women in Politics.* New York: John Wiley, 1974.

Jaynes, Gerald D. and Robin M. Williams, Jr., eds. *A Common Destiny: Blacks and American Society.* Washington, D.C.: National Academy Press, 1989.

Johnson, Lyndon. *The Vantage Point: Perspectives on the Presidency*. New York: Holt, Rinehart and Winston, 1971.

Kanawada, Leo V., Jr. *Franklin D. Roosevelt's Diplomacy and American Catholics, Italians, and Jews*. Ann Arbor, Mich.: UMI Research Press, 1982.

Karfunkel, Thomas and Thomas W. Ryley. *The Jewish Seat: Anti-Semitism and the Appointment of Jews to the Supreme Court*. Hicksville, N.Y.: Exposition Press, 1978.

Karp, Abraham J. *Haven and Home: A History of the Jews in America*. New York: Schocken Books, 1985.

Keech, William R. *The Impact of Negro Voting*. Chicago: Rand McNally, 1968.

Kinzer, Donald L. *An Episode in Anti-Catholicism: The American Protective Association*. Seattle: University of Washington Press, 1964.

Klinkhamer, Marie Carolyn, O. P. *Edward Douglas White, Chief Justice of the U.S.* Washington, D.C.: The Catholic University of America Press, 1943.

Krislov, Samuel. *Representative Bureaucracy*. Englewood Cliffs, N.J.: Prentice-Hall, 1974.

———. *The Supreme Court in the Political Process*. New York: Macmillan, 1965.

——— and David H. Rosenbloom. *Representative Bureaucracy and the American Political System*. New York: Praeger, 1981.

Lash, Joseph P. *From the Diaries of Felix Frankfurter*. New York: W. W. Norton, 1975.

Lasky, Victor. *Arthur J. Goldberg: The Old and the New*. New Rochelle, N.Y.: Arlington House, 1970.

Learsi, Rufus. *The Jews in America: A History*. Cleveland: World, 1954.

Leech, Margaret. *In the Days of McKinley*. New York: Harper & Brothers, 1959.

Lewis, Walker. *Without Fear or Favor: A Biography of Chief Justice Roger Brooke Taney*. Boston: Houghton Mifflin, 1965.

Lief, Alfred. *Brandeis: The Personal History of an American Ideal*. New York: Stackpole Sons, 1936.

Link, Arthur, ed. *The Papers of Woodrow Wilson*. Princeton, N.J.: Princeton University Press, 1981.

Lovenduski, Joni and Jill Hills, eds. *The Politics of the Second Electorate: Women and Public Participation*. London: Routledge & Kegan Paul, 1981.

Lunt, Richard D. *The High Ministry of Government: The Political Career of Frank Murphy*. Detroit: Wayne State University Press, 1965.

McAvoy, Thomas T. *History of the Catholic Church in America*. Notre Dame, Ind.: University of Notre Dame Press, 1969.

McCune, Wesley. *The Nine Young Men*. New York: Harper, 1947.

McDevitt, Matthew. *Joseph McKenna: Associate Justice of the United States*. Washington, D.C.: The Catholic University of America Press, 1946.

Mason, Alpheus Thomas. *Brandeis: A Free Man's Life*. New York: Viking, 1946.

———. *William Howard Taft: Chief Justice*. New York: Simon and Schuster, 1965.

Matthews, Donald R. *The Social Background of Political Decision-Makers*. Garden City, N.Y.: Doubleday, 1954.

Maynard, Theodore. *The Story of American Catholicism*. New York: Macmillan, 1942.

Meier, August and Elliott M. Rudwick. *From Plantation to Ghetto: An Interpretive History of American Negroes*. New York: Hill and Wang, 1966.

Mersky, Roy M. and J. Myron Jacobstein, eds. *The Supreme Court of the United States: Hearings and Reports on Successful and Unsuccessful Nominations of Supreme Court Justices by the Senate Judiciary Committee 1916–1972.* 11 vols. Buffalo: W. S. Hein, 1975.

Mosher, Frederick. *Democracy and the Public Service.* 2d ed. New York: Oxford University Press, 1982.

Murphy, Bruce Allen. *The Brandeis/Frankfurter Connection: The Secret Political Activities of Two Supreme Court Justices.* New York: Oxford University Press, 1982.

———. *Fortas: The Rise and Ruin of a Supreme Court Justice.* New York: William Morrow, 1988.

Navasky, Victor S. *Kennedy Justice.* New York: Atheneum, 1977.

Nevins, Allan. *Grover Cleveland: A Study in Courage.* New York: Dodd, Mead, 1933.

O'Brien, David M. *Storm Center: The Supreme Court in American Politics.* 2d ed. New York: W. W. Norton, 1990.

Paper, Lewis J. *Brandeis.* Englewood Cliffs, N.J.: Prentice-Hall, 1983.

Pennock, J. Roland and John Chapman. *Representation.* Nomos Vol. X. New York: Atherton, 1968.

Pitkin, Hanna. *The Concept of Representation.* Berkeley: University of California Press, 1967.

Pollard, Joseph P. *Mr. Justice Cardozo: A Liberal Mind in Action.* New York: The Yorktown Press, 1935.

Poole, Keith T. and L. Harmon Zeigler. *Women, Public Opinion, and Politics: The Changing Political Attitudes of American Women.* New York: Longman, 1985.

Posner, Richard A. *Cardozo: A Study in Reputation.* Chicago: University of Chicago Press, 1990.

Pringle, Henry F. *The Life and Times of William Howard Taft.* 2 vols. New York: Farrar & Rinehart, 1939.

Rehnquist, William H. *The Supreme Court: How It Was, How It Is.* New York: Quill/William Morrow, 1987.

Schlesinger, Arthur M., Jr. *Robert Kennedy and His Times.* New York: Ballantine Books, 1978.

———. *A Thousand Days: John F. Kennedy in the White House.* Boston: Houghton Mifflin, 1965.

Schmidhauser, John R. *Judges and Justices: The Federal Appellate Judiciary.* Boston: Little, Brown, 1979.

———. *The Supreme Court: Its Politics, Personalities, and Procedures.* New York: Holt, Rinehart and Winston, 1960.

Segal, Geraldine R. *Blacks in the Law: Philadelphia and the Nation.* Philadelphia: University of Pennsylvania Press, 1983.

Shaughnessy, Gerald, S.M. *Has the Immigrant Kept the Faith?* New York: Macmillan, 1925.

Shogun, Robert. *A Question of Judgment: The Fortas Case and the Struggle for the Supreme Court.* Indianapolis: Bobbs-Merrill, 1972.

Smith, Charles William. *Roger B. Taney: Jacksonian Jurist.* Chapel Hill: The University of North Carolina Press, 1936.

Sorensen, Theodore C. *Kennedy*. New York: Harper & Row, 1965.

Steiner, Gilbert Y. *Constitutional Inequality: The Political Fortunes of the Equal Rights Amendment*. Washington, D.C.: The Brookings Institution, 1985.

Stineman, Esther. *American Political Women: Contemporary and Historical Profiles*. Littleton, Colo.: Libraries Unlimited, 1980.

The Success of Women and Minorities in Achieving Judicial Office: The Selection Process. New York: Fund for Modern Courts, 1985.

Swisher, Carl B. *Roger B. Taney*. New York: Macmillan, 1935.

Tocqueville, Alexis de. *Democracy in America*. Trans. George Lawrence, ed. J. P. Mayer. Garden City, N.Y.: Doubleday, 1969.

Todd, A. L. *Justice on Trial: The Case of Louis D. Brandeis*. Chicago: The University of Chicago Press, 1964; Phoenix Edition, 1968.

Tribe, Laurence H. *God Save This Honorable Court: How the Choice of Supreme Court Justices Shapes Our History*. New York: Random House, 1985.

Tuve, Jeannette E. *First Lady of the Law: Florence Ellinwood Allen*. Lanham, Md.: University Press of America, 1984.

Tyler, Samuel. *Memoir of Roger Brooke Taney: Chief Justice of the Supreme Court of the United States*. Baltimore: John Murphy, 1872.

Urofsky, Melvin I. and David W. Levy, eds. *Letters of Louis D. Brandeis*. Vol. IV. Albany: State University of New York Press, 1975.

Vanderbilt, Arthur T. *Judges and Jurors: Their Functions, Qualifications and Selection*. Boston: Boston University Press, 1956.

Walworth, Arthur. *Woodrow Wilson*. 3d ed. New York: W. W. Norton, 1978.

Ware, Gilbert. *William Hastie: Grace Under Pressure*. New York: Oxford University Press, 1984.

Weyl, Nathaniel. *The Jew in American Politics*. New Rochelle, N.Y.: Arlington House, 1968.

———. *The Negro in American Civilization*. Washington, D.C.: Public Affairs Press, 1960.

Williams, James D., ed. *The State of Black America, 1983*. National Urban League, 1983.

———. *The State of Black America, 1984*. National Urban League, 1984.

Wilson, William J. *The Declining Significance of Race in America*. Chicago: University of Chicago Press, 1978.

Witt, Elder. *A Different Justice: Reagan and the Supreme Court*. Washington, D.C.: Congressional Quarterly, 1986.

MANUSCRIPTS

Louis Dembitz Brandeis Papers. University of Louisville Library, Louisville, Kentucky.

NEWSPAPERS

Boston Globe
Boston Traveler
Charlottesville *Daily Progress*
Christian Science Monitor

Florida Catholic
Louisville *Courier-Journal*
Louisville *Record*
Miami Herald
New York Herald
New York Times
Orlando Sentinel
Philadelphia *Sunday Bulletin*
Washington Post

PERSONAL INTERVIEWS

Justice William J. Brennan, Jr. United States Supreme Court. Washington, D.C.
    April 1, 1985.
Justice Sandra Day O'Connor. United States Supreme Court. Washington, D.C.
    May 14, 1985.
Justice Lewis F. Powell, Jr. United States Supreme Court. Washington, D.C.
    February 20, 1986.
Justice William H. Rehnquist. United States Supreme Court. Washington, D.C.
    September 24, 1985.
Justice Antonin Scalia. United States Supreme Court. Washington, D.C. March
    18, 1987.
Justice John Paul Stevens. United States Supreme Court. Washington, D.C.
    September 12, 1985.
Justice Byron R. White. United States Supreme Court. Washington, D.C. October
    31, 1985.

PUBLIC DOCUMENTS

U.S. Congress. Senate. Action on Thurgood Marshall nomination for solicitor
    general. 89th Cong., 1st sess., 11 August 1965. *Congressional Record*, vol.
    111.
U.S. Congress. Senate. Vote on Thurgood Marshall nomination to U.S. Court of
    Appeals for Second Circuit, 87th Cong., 2nd sess., 11 September 1962.
    Congressional Record, vol. 108.
U.S. Department of Education. *Digest of Education Statistics 1989*. Washington,
    D.C.: Government Printing Office, 1989.

UNPUBLISHED MATERIALS

Brubaker, Stanley C. "Benjamin Nathan Cardozo: An Intellectual Biography."
    Unpublished Ph.D. dissertation, University of Virginia, 1979.
McHargue, Daniel S. "Appointments to the Supreme Court of the United States:
    The Factors That Have Affected Appointments, 1789–1932." Unpublished
    Ph.D. dissertation, University of California, Los Angeles, 1949.
Rusch, Jonathan J. "William M. Hastie and the Vindication of Civil Rights."
    Unpublished M.A. thesis, University of Virginia, 1978.

Index

About the Author

BARBARA A. PERRY is an assistant professor and chairman of the Department of Government at Sweet Briar College, Virginia. She wrote with Paul J. Weber *Unfounded Fears: Myths and Realities of a Constitutional Convention* (Greenwood Press, 1989) and has contributed articles to the *Journal of Church and State* and the *Journal of Law and Politics*. Currently, she is at work on a civil rights and liberties casebook.